MW01487036

The Boys' And Girls' Herodotus: Being Parts Of The History Of Herodotus

Herodotus

In the interest of creating a more extensive selection of rare historical book reprints, we have chosen to reproduce this title even though it may possibly have occasional imperfections such as missing and blurred pages, missing text, poor pictures, markings, dark backgrounds and other reproduction issues beyond our control. Because this work is culturally important, we have made it available as a part of our commitment to protecting, preserving and promoting the world's literature. Thank you for your understanding.

THE

BOYS' AND GIRLS'

HERODOTUS

BEING

PARTS OF THE HISTORY OF HERODOTUS

EDITED FOR BOYS AND GIRLS, WITH AN INTRODUCTION

BY

JOHN S. WHITE, LL.D.

HEAD-MASTER, BERKELEY SCHOOL; EDITOR OF THE BOYS' AND GIRLS' PLUTARCH

WITH FIFTY ILLUSTRATIONS

NEW YORK & LONDON

G. P. PUTNAM'S SONS

The Knickerbocker Press

1908

THE NEW YORK
PUBLIC LIBRARY

5911

ASTOR, LENOX AND
TILDEN FOUNDATIONS.

COPYRIGHT BY
G. P. PUTNAM'S SONS
1884

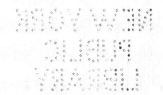

THE PYRAMIDS AND SPHINX

THE NEW YORK
PUBLIC LIBRARY

ASTOR, LENOX AND
TILDEN FOUNDATIONS

C 888
H

INTRODUCTION.

IMAGINE yourself in the city of Athens near the close of the year 446 B.C. The proud city, after many years of supremacy over the whole of Central Greece, has passed her zenith, and is surely on the decline. She has never recovered from the blow received at Coronea. The year has been one of gloom and foreboding. The coming spring will bring the end of the five years' truce ; and an invasion from the Peloponnesus is imminent. But, as the centre of learning, refinement, and the arts, the lustre of her fame is yet undimmed, and men of education throughout the world deem their lives incomplete until they have sought and reached this intellectual Mecca. During this year a stranger from Halicarnassus, in Asia Minor, after many years of travel in Asia, Scythia, Libya, Egypt, and Magna Græcia, has taken up his abode at Athens. He is still a young man, hardly thirty-seven, yet his fame is that of the first and greatest of historians. Dramatists and poets immortal there have been, but never man has written such exquisite prose. Twenty centuries and more shall wear away, and his history will be read in a hundred different tongues, as well as in the beautiful and simple Greek that he wrote. His name will grow into a household word ; the school-boy will revel in his delightful tales, and wise men will call him the Father of History ! For weeks the people of Athens have listened entranced to the public reading of his great work, and now the Assembly has passed a decree tendering to him the city's thanks, together with a most substantial gift in recognition of his talents—a purse of money equal to twelve thousand American dollars.

Such is the account which Eusebius gives, and others to whom
we may fairly accord belief; and it adds no slight tinge of romance
to the picture to discover among the listening throng the figure of
the boy Thucydides, moved to tears by the recital, who then and
there received the impulse that made of him also a great student
and writer of history. Herodotus, noticing how intensely his
reading had affected the youth, turned to Olorus, the father of
Thucydides, who was standing near, and said: " Olorus, thy son's
soul yearns after knowledge."

Herodotus was born at Halicarnassus, 484 B.C., and died
at Thurium in Italy, about the year 425. As in the case of
Plutarch, our knowledge of his personal history is very meagre,
aside from the little we glean from his own writings. His parents,
Lyxes and Rhœo, appear to have been of high rank and consideration in Halicarnassus, and possessed of ample means; and his
acquaintance both at home and in Athens was of the best. A
lover of poetry and a poet by nature, the whole plan of his work,
the tone and character of his thoughts, and a multitude of words
and expressions, show him to have been perfectly familiar with the
Homeric writings. There is scarcely an author previous to his time
with whose works he does not appear to have been thoroughly
acquainted. Hecatæus, to be sure, was almost the only writer of
prose who had attained any distinction, for prose composition was
practically in its infancy; but from him and from several others, too
obscure even to be named, he freely quotes, while the poets,
Hesiod, Olen, Musæus, Archilochus, the authors of the " Cypria " and
the " Epigoni," Alcæus, Sappho, Solon, Æsop, Aristeas, Simonides
of Ceos, Phrynichus, Æschylus, and Pindar, are referred to, or
quoted, in such a way as to show an intimate acquaintance with
their works.

The design of Herodotus was to record the struggles between
the Greeks and barbarians, but, in carrying it out, as Wheeler, the
English analyst of the writings of Herodotus, has happily expressed
it, he is perpetually led to trace the causes of the great events of
his history; to recount the origin of that mighty contest between

liberty and despotism which marked the whole period ; to describe the wondrous manners and mysterious religions of nations, and the marvellous geography and fabulous productions of the various countries, as each appeared on the great arena ; to tell to an inquisitive and credulous people of cities vast as provinces and splendid as empires ; of stupendous walls, temples and pyramids ; of dreams, omens, and warnings from the dead ; of obscure traditions and their exact accomplishment ;—and thus to prepare their minds for the most wonderful story in the annals of men, when all Asia united in one endless array to crush the states of Greece ; when armies bridged the seas and navies sailed through mountains ; when proud, stubborn-hearted men arose amid anxiety, terror, confusion, and despair, and staked their lives and homes against the overwhelming power of a foreign despot, till Heaven itself sympathized with their struggles, and the winds and waves delivered their country, and opened the way to victory and revenge.

The personal character of Herodotus, reflected from every page that he wrote, renders his vivid story all the more happily suited to the reading and study of boys and girls. He is as honest as the sun ; equally impartial to friends and foes ; candid in the statement of both sides of a question ; and an artist withal in the gift of delineating a character or a people with a few rapid strokes, so bold and masterly that the sketch is placed before you with stereoscopic distinctness. For so early a writer he presents a surprising unity of plan, combined with a variety of detail that is amazing. What if he does crowd and enrich his story with a world of anecdote ? What if he feels bound always to paint for you the customs, manners, dress, and peculiarities of a people before he begins their history ? This very biographical style is the charm of his pen. Like the flowers of the magnolia-tree, his bright stories and vivid descriptions at times almost overwhelm the root and branch of his narrative ; yet, after all, we remember the magnolia more because of its cloud of snowy bloom in the few fleeting days of May than for all its green and shade in the other months.

Herodotus, to be sure, lacks that far-seeing faculty of discerning accurately the real causes of great movements, wars, and migrations of men—a faculty possessed pre-eminently by Thucydides and largely by Xenophon, but he is equally far removed from the coldness of the one and the ostentatious display of the other. He is above all things natural, simple, and direct. " He writes," says Aristotle, " sentences which have a continuous flow, and which end only when the sense is complete."

I have allowed Herodotus, as I did Plutarch, to tell you his story in his own words, as closely as the English idiom can reproduce the spirit and flow of the Greek, calling gratefully to my aid the labors of such students, analysts, and translators of Herodotus as Rawlinson, Dahlmann, Cary, and Wheeler; and I have discarded from the text only what is indelicate to the modern ear, or what the young reader might find tedious, redundant, or irrelevant to the main story. But so small a part comes under this head, that I am sure I can fairly say to you : " This is Herodotus himself." If you read him through and do not like him, who will be the disappointed one ? Not you, but I !

NEW YORK, *June* 15, 1884.

CONTENTS.

LIST OF ILLUSTRATIONS.

HERODOTUS.

BOOK I. CLIO.

CHAPTER I.

ORIGIN OF THE WAR BETWEEN THE GREEKS AND BARBARIANS.

THIS is a publication of the researches of Herodotus of Halicarnassus, made in order that the actions of men may not be effaced by time, and that the great and wondrous deeds displayed both by Greeks and barbarians [1] may not be deprived of renown ; and, furthermore, that the cause for which they waged war upon each other may be known.

The learned among the Persians assert that the Phœnicians were the original authors of the quarrel; that they migrated from that which is called the Red Sea to the Mediterranean and, having settled in the country which they now inhabit, forthwith applied themselves to distant voyages ; and that they exported Egyptian and Assyrian merchandise, touching at other places, and also at Argos. Argos, at that period, surpassed in every respect all those states which are now comprehended under the general appellation of Greece. They say, that on their arrival at Argos, the Phœnicians exposed their merchandise for sale, and that on the fifth or sixth day after their arrival, when they had almost disposed of their cargo, a great number of women came down to the sea-shore, and among them Io the daughter of the king Inachus. While these women

---

[1] Under the name " barbarians " the Greeks included all who were not sprung from themselves—all who did not speak the Greek language.

were standing near the stern of the vessel, and were bargaining for such things as most pleased them, the Phœnicians made an attack upon them. Most of the women escaped, but Io with some others was seized. Then the traders hurried on board and set sail for Egypt. Thus the Persians say that Io went to Egypt, and that this was the beginning of wrongs. After this certain Greeks (for they are unable to tell their name), having touched at Tyre in Phœnicia, carried off the king's daughter Europa. These must have been Cretans. Thus far they say that they had only returned like for like, but that after this the Greeks were guilty of the second provocation; for having sailed down in a vessel of war to Æa, a city of Colchis on the river Phasis, when they had accomplished the more immediate object of their expedition, they carried off the king's daughter Medea; and the king of Colchis, having despatched a herald to Greece, demanded satisfaction and the restitution of the princess; but the Greeks replied, that as they of Asia had not given satisfaction for the stealing of Io, they would not give any to them. In the second generation after this, Alexander, the son of Priam, having heard of these events, was desirous of obtaining a wife from Greece by means of violence, being fully persuaded that he should not have to give satisfaction, since the Greeks had not done so. When, therefore, he had carried off Helen, the Greeks immediately sent messengers to demand her back again and require satisfaction; but when they brought forward these demands they were met with this reply: "You who have not yourselves given satisfaction, nor made it when demanded, now wish others to give it to you." After this the Greeks were greatly to blame, for they levied war against Asia before the Asiatics did upon Europe. Now, to carry off women by violence the Persians think is the act of wicked men; to trouble one's self about avenging them when so carried off is the act of foolish ones; and to pay no regard to them when carried off, of wise men: for it is clear, that if they had not been willing, they could not have been carried off. Accordingly the Persians say, that they of Asia made no account of women that were carried off; but that the

Greeks for the sake of a Lacedæmonian woman assembled a mighty fleet, sailed to Asia, and overthrew the empire of Priam. From this event they had always considered the Greeks as their enemies : for the Persians claim Asia, and the barbarous nations that inhabit it, as their own, and consider Europe and the people of Greece as totally distinct.

Such is the Persian account ; and to the capture of Troy they ascribe the commencement of their enmity to the Greeks. As relates to Io, the Phœnicians do not agree with this account of the Persians but affirm that she voluntarily sailed away with the traders. I, however, am not going to inquire further as to facts ; but having pointed out the person whom I myself know to have been the first guilty of injustice toward the Greeks, I will then proceed with my history, touching as well on the small as the great estates of men : for of those that were formerly powerful many have become weak, and some that were formerly weak became powerful in my time. Knowing, therefore, the precarious nature of human prosperity, I shall commemorate both alike.

Crœsus was a Lydian by birth, son of Alyattes, and sovereign of the nations on this side the river Halys. This river flowing from the south between the Syrians[1] and Paphlagonians, empties itself northward into the Euxine Sea. This Crœsus was the first of the barbarians whom we know of that subjected some of the Greeks to the payment of tribute, and formed alliances with others. He subdued the Ionians and Æolians, and those of the Dorians who had settled in Asia, and formed an alliance with the Lacedæmonians ; but before his reign all the Greeks were free.

---

[1] Syria was at that time the name of Cappadocia, as Herodotus himself elsewhere states.

CHAPTER II.

HISTORY OF LYDIA.

THE government, which formerly belonged to the Heraclidæ, passed to the family of Crœsus, who were called Mermnadæ. Candaules, whom the Greeks call Myrsilus, was tyrant of Sardis, and a descendant of Alcæus, son of Hercules. For Agron, son of Ninus, grandson of Belus, great-grandson of Alcæus, was the first of the Heraclidæ who became king of Sardis ; and Candaules, son of Myrsus, was the last. They who ruled over this country before Agron, were descendants of Lydus, son of Atys, from whom this whole people, anciently called Mæonians, derived the name of Lydians. The Heraclidæ, descended from a female slave of Jardanus and Hercules, having been intrusted with the government by these princes, retained the supreme power in obedience to the declaration of an oracle : they reigned for twenty-two generations, a space of five hundred and five years, the son succeeding to the father to the time of Candaules, son of Myrsus. Candaules was murdered by his favorite, Gyges, who thus obtained the kingdom, and was confirmed in it by the oracle at Delphi. For when the Lydians resented the murder of Candaules, and were up in arms, the partisans of Gyges and the other Lydians came to the following agreement, that if the oracle should pronounce him king of the Lydians, he should reign ; if not, he should restore the power to the Heraclidæ. The oracle answered that Gyges should become king. But the Pythian added this, "that the Heraclidæ should be avenged on the fifth descendant of Gyges." Of this prediction neither the Lydians nor their kings took any notice until it was actually accomplished.

Thus the Mermnadæ deprived the Heraclidæ of the supreme

power. Gyges sent many offerings to Delphi ; indeed most of the silver offerings at Delphi are his ; and besides the silver, he gave a vast quantity of gold ; among the rest six bowls of gold, which now stand in the treasury of the Corinthians, and are thirty talents in weight ; though, to tell the truth, this treasury does not belong to the people of Corinth, but Cypselus son of Eetion. Gyges was the first of the barbarians of whom we know who made offerings at Delphi, except Midas, son of Gordius, the king of Phrygia, who dedicated the royal throne, on which he used to sit and administer justice, a piece of workmanship deserving of admiration. The throne stands in the same place as the bowls of Gyges.

Periander the son of Cypselus was king of Corinth, and the Corinthians say (and the Lesbians confirm their account) that a wonderful prodigy occurred in his life-time. Arion of Methymna, second to none of his time in accompanying the harp, and the first who composed, named, and represented the dithyrambus at Corinth, was carried to Tænarus on the back of a dolphin. Arion, having continued a long time with Periander, made a voyage to Italy and Sicily, acquired great wealth there, and determined to return to Corinth. He set out from Tarentum, and hired a ship of some Corinthians, because he put more confidence in them than in any other nation ; but these men, when they were in the open sea, conspired together to throw him overboard and seize his money. Learning of this he offered them his money, and entreated them to spare his life. But he could not prevail on them ; the sailors ordered him either to kill himself, that he might be buried ashore, or to leap immediately into the sea. Arion, reduced to this strait, entreated them, since such was their determination, to permit him to stand on the stern of the vessel in his full dress and sing, and he promised when he had sung to make way with himself. The seamen, pleased that they should hear the best singer in the world, retired from the stern to the middle of the vessel. Arion put on all his robes, took his harp in his hands, stood on the rowing benches and went through the Orthian strain ;

the strain ended, he leaped into the sea as he was, in full dress; the sailors continuing their voyage to Corinth: but a dolphin caught him upon his back, and carried him to Tænarus; so that, having landed, he proceeded to Corinth in his full dress, and upon his arrival there, related all that happened. Periander gave no credit to his relation, put Arion under close confinement, and watched anxiously for the arrival of the seamen. When they appeared, he summoned them and inquired if they could give any account of Arion. They answered that he was safe in Italy, and that they had left him flourishing at Tarentum. At that instant Arion appeared before them just as he was when he leaped into the sea; at which they were so astonished that, being fully convicted, they could no longer deny the fact. These things are reported by the Corinthians and Lesbians; and there is a little bronze statue of Arion at Tænarus, representing a man sitting on a dolphin.

Alyattes the Lydian and father of Crœsus, having waged a long war against the Milesians, died after a reign of fifty-seven years. Once upon recovery from an illness he dedicated at Delphi a large silver bowl, with a saucer of iron inlaid; an object that deserves attention above all the offerings at Delphi. It was made by Glaucus the Chian, who first invented the art of inlaying iron.

At the death of Alyattes, Crœsus, then thirty-five years of age, succeeded to the kingdom. He attacked the Ephesians before any other Greek people. The Ephesians being besieged by him, consecrated their city to Diana, by fastening a rope from the temple to the wall. The distance between the old town, which was then besieged, and the temple, is seven stadia. Crœsus afterward attacked the several cities of the Ionians and Æolians in succession, alleging different pretences against the various states. After he had reduced the Greeks in Asia to the payment of tribute, he formed a design to build ships and attack the Islanders. But when all things were ready for the building of ships, Bias of Priene (or, as others say, Pittacus of Mitylene) arriving at Sardis, put a stop to his ship-building by making this reply, when Crœsus inquired if he had any news from Greece : "O king, the Islanders are enlisting a large body of cavalry, with the intention of making war upon you and Sardis." Crœsus, thinking he had spoken the truth, said : "May the gods put such a thought into the Islanders, as to attack the sons of the Lydians with horse." The other answering said : "Sire, you appear to wish above all things to see the Islanders on horseback upon the continent ; and not without reason. But what can you imagine the Islanders more earnestly desire, after having heard of your resolution to build a fleet to attack them, than to catch the Lydians at sea, that they may revenge on you the cause of those Greeks who dwell on the continent, whom you hold in subjection ? " Crœsus, much pleased with the conclusion, and convinced, (for he appeared to speak to the purpose,) put a stop to the ship-building, and made an alliance with the Ionians that inhabit the islands.

In course of time, when nearly all the nations that dwell within the river Halys, except the Cilicians and Lycians, were subdued, and Crœsus had added them to the Lydians, all the wise men of that time, as each had opportunity, came from Greece to Sardis, which had then attained to the highest degree of prosperity ; and amongst them Solon, an Athenian, who made laws for the Athenians at their request, and absented himself for ten years, sailing away under pretence of seeing the world, that he might not be compelled to abrogate any of the laws he had established : for the Athenians could not do it themselves, since they were bound by solemn oaths to observe for ten years whatever laws Solon should enact for them. On his arrival Solon was hospitably entertained by Crœsus, and on the third or fourth day, by order of the king, the attendants conducted him round the treasury, and showed him all their grand and costly contents. After he had seen and examined every thing sufficiently, Crœsus asked him this question : "My Athenian guest, the great fame as well of your wisdom as of your travels has reached even to us ; I am therefore desirous of asking you who is the most happy man you have seen ? " He asked this question because he thought himself the most happy

HERODOTUS.

of men. But Solon, speaking the truth freely, without any flattery, answered, " Tellus, the Athenian." Crœsus, astonished at his answer, eagerly asked him : " On what account do you deem Tellus the happiest? " He replied: " Tellus, in the first place, lived in a well-governed commonwealth ; had sons who were virtuous and good; and he saw children born to them all, and all surviving. In the next place, when he had lived as happily as the condition of human affairs will permit, he ended his life in a most glorious manner. For coming to the assistance of the Athenians in a battle with their neighbors of Eleusis, he put the enemy to flight and died nobly. The Athenians buried him at the public charge in the place where he fell, and honored him greatly."

When Solon had roused the attention of Crœsus by relating many happy circumstances concerning Tellus, Crœsus, expecting at least to obtain the second place, asked, whom he had seen next to him. " Cleobis," said he, " and Biton, natives of Argos, for they possessed a sufficient fortune, and had withal such strength of body, that they were both alike victorious in the public games ; and moreover the following story is related of them :—When the Argives were celebrating a festival of Juno, it was necessary that their mother should be drawn to the temple in a chariot; but the oxen did not come from the field in time, the young men therefore put themselves beneath the yoke, and drew the car in which their mother sat ; and having conveyed it forty-five stades, they reached the temple. After they had done this in sight of the assembled people, a most happy termination was put to their lives ; and in them the Deity clearly showed that it is better for a man to die than to live. For the men of Argos, who stood round, commended the strength of the youths, and the women blessed her as the mother of such sons ; but the mother herself, transported with joy both on account of the action and its renown, stood before the image and prayed that the goddess would grant to Cleobis and Biton, her own sons, who had so highly honored her, the greatest blessing man could receive. After this prayer, when they had sacrificed and partaken of the feast, the youths fell asleep in the

temple itself, and never woke more, but met with such a termination of life. Upon this the Argives, in commemoration of their
filial affection, caused their statues to be made and dedicated at
Delphi."

Thus Solon adjudged the second place of felicity to these
youths. Then Crœsus was enraged, and said : " My Athenian
friend, is my happiness then so slighted by you as worth nothing,
that you do not think me of so much value as private men ? " He
answered : " Crœsus, do you inquire of me concerning human affairs—of me, who know that the divinity is always jealous, and delights in confusion. For in lapse of time men are constrained to
see many things they would not willingly see, and to suffer
many things they would not willingly suffer. Now I put the
term of man's life at seventy years ; these seventy years then give
twenty-five thousand two hundred days, without including the intercalary months of the leap years, and if we add that month
to every other year, in order that the seasons arriving at the
proper time may agree, the intercalary months will be thirty-five
more in the seventy years, and the days of these months will be
one thousand and fifty. Yet in all this number of twenty-six
thousand two hundred and fifty days, that compose these seventy
years, one day produces nothing exactly the same as another.
Thus, then, O Crœsus, man is altogether the sport of fortune. You
appear to me to be master of immense treasures, and king of many
nations ; but as relates to what you inquire of me, I cannot say,
till I hear that you have ended your life happily. For the richest
of men is not more happy than he that has a sufficiency for a day,
unless good fortune attend him to the grave, so that he ends his
life in happiness. Many men who abound in wealth are unhappy ;
and many who have only a moderate competency are fortunate.
He that abounds in wealth and is yet unhappy, surpasses the other
only in two things ; but the other surpasses the wealthy and the
miserable in many things. The former indeed is better able to
gratify desire and to bear the blow of adversity. But the latter
surpasses him in this ; he is not indeed equally able to bear mis-

fortune or satisfy desire, but his good fortune wards off these things from him; and he enjoys the full use of his limbs, he is free from disease and misfortune, he is blessed with good children and a fine form, and if, in addition to all these things, he shall end his life well, he is the man you seek and may justly be called happy; but before he die we ought to suspend our judgment, and not pronounce him happy, but fortunate."

When Solon had spoken thus to Crœsus, Crœsus did not confer any favor on him, but holding him in no account, dismissed him as a very ignorant man, because he overlooked present prosperity, and bade men look to the end of every thing.

After the departure of Solon, the indignation of the gods fell heavily upon Crœsus, probably because he thought himself the most happy of all men. A dream soon after visited him while sleeping, which pointed out to him the truth of the misfortunes that were about to befall him in the person of one of his sons. For Crœsus had two sons, of whom one was grievously afflicted, for he was dumb; but the other, whose name was Atys, far surpassed all the young men of his age. Now the dream intimated to Crœsus that he would lose this Atys by a wound inflicted with the point of an iron weapon. When he awoke, and had considered the matter with himself, he relieved Atys from the command of the Lydian troops, and never after sent him out on that business; and causing all spears, lances, and such other weapons as men use in war, to be removed from the men's apartments, he had them laid up in private chambers, that none of them being suspended might fall upon his son. While Crœsus was engaged with the nuptials of his son, a man oppressed by misfortune, and whose hands were polluted, a Phrygian by birth, and of royal family, arrived at Sardis. This man, having come to the palace of Crœsus, sought permission to obtain purification according to the custom of the country. Crœsus purified him, performing the usual ceremony, and then inquired: "Stranger, who art thou, and from what part of Phrygia hast thou come as a suppliant to my hearth? and what man or woman hast thou slain?" The stranger answered: "I am the son of Gordius, and grandson of Midas, and am called Adrastus. I unwittingly slew my own brother, and being banished by my father and deprived of every thing, I have come hither." Then said Crœsus : "You were born of parents who are our friends, and you have come to friends, among whom, if you will stay, you shall want nothing ; and by bearing your misfortune as lightly as possible you will be the greatest gainer." So Adrastus took up his abode in the palace of Crœsus.

At this time a boar of enormous size appeared in Mysian Olympus, and rushing down from that mountain, ravaged the fields of the Mysians. The Mysians, though they often went out against him, could not hurt him, but suffered much from him. At last deputies from the Mysians came to Crœsus and said : "O king, a boar of enormous size has appeared in our country, and ravages our fields : though we have often endeavored to take him, we cannot. We therefore earnestly beg, that you will send with us your son and some chosen youths with dogs, that we may drive him from the country." But Crœsus, remembering the warning of his dream, answered : "Make no further mention of my son ; I shall not send him with you, because he is lately married, but I will give you chosen Lydians, and the whole hunting train, and will order them to assist you with their best endeavors in driving the monster from your country." The Mysians were content with this, but Atys, who had heard of their request, came in, and earnestly protested : "Father, you used to permit me to signalize myself in the two most noble and becoming exercises of war and hunting ; but now you keep me excluded from both, without having observed in me either cowardice or want of spirit. How will men look on me when I go or return from the forum? What kind of a man shall I appear to my fellow-citizens? What to my newly married wife? Either let me then go to this hunt, or convince me that it is better for me to do as you would have me." "My son," said Crœsus, "I act thus, not because I have seen any cowardice, or any thing else unbecoming in you ; but a vision in a dream warned me that you would be short-lived, and would die by the point of an iron weapon. It was on account of this that I hastened your marriage, and now refuse to send you on this expedition ; taking care to preserve you, if by any means I can, as long as I live ; for you are my only son ; the other, who is deprived of his hearing, I consider as lost." The youth answered : " You are not to blame, my father, if after such a dream you take so much care of me ; but you say the dream signified that I should die by the point of an iron weapon. What hand, or what pointed iron weapon has a boar, to occasion such fears in you ? Had it said I should lose my life by a tusk, you might do as you have, but it said by the point of a weapon ; then since we have not to contend against men, let me go." " You have outdone me," replied Crœsus, " in explaining the import of the dream, you shall go to the chase."

Then turning to the Phrygian Adrastus, he exclaimed : " Adrastus, I beg you to be my son's guardian, when he goes to the chase, and take care that no skulking villains show themselves in the way to do him harm. Besides, you ought to go for your own sake, where you may signalize yourself by your exploits ; this was the glory of your ancestors, and you are besides in full vigor." Adrastus answered : " On no other account, my lord, would I take part in this enterprise ; it is not fitting that one in my unfortunate circumstances should join with his prosperous compeers. But since you urge me, I ought to oblige you. Rest assured, that your son, whom you bid me take care of, shall, as far as his guardian is concerned, return to you uninjured."

Then all went away, well provided with chosen youths and dogs, and, having arrived at Mount Olympus, they sought the wild beast, found him and encircled him around. Among the rest, the stranger, Adrastus, throwing his javelin at the boar, missed him, and struck the son of Crœsus ; thus fulfilling the warning of the dream. Upon this, some one ran off to tell Crœsus what had happened, and having arrived at Sardis, gave him an account of the action, and of his son's fate. Crœsus, exceedingly distressed by the death of his son, lamented it the more bitterly, because he fell by the hand of one, whom he himself had purified from blood ; and vehemently deploring his misfortune, he invoked Jove the Expiator, attesting what he had suffered by this stranger. He invoked also the same deity, by the name of the god of hospitality and private friendship : as the god of hospitality, because by receiving a stranger into his house, he had unawares fostered the murderer of his son ; as the god of private friendship, because, having sent him as a guardian, he found him his greatest enemy. Soon the Lydians approached, bearing the corpse, and behind it followed the murderer. He, having advanced in front of the body, delivered himself up to Crœsus, stretching out his hands and begging him to kill him upon it; for he ought to live no longer. When Crœsus heard this, though his own affliction was so great, he pitied Adrastus, and said to him : " You have made me full satisfaction by condemning yourself to die. You are not the author of this misfortune, except as far as you were the involuntary agent; but that god, whoever he was, that long since foreshowed what was about to happen." Crœsus buried his son as the dignity of his birth required ; but the son of Gordius, when all was silent around, judging himself the most heavily afflicted of all men, killed himself on the tomb.

Some time after, the overthrow of the kingdom of Astyages, son of Cyaxares, by Cyrus, son of Cambyses, and the growing power of the Persians, put an end to the grief of Crœsus ; and it entered into his thoughts whether he could by any means check the growing power of the Persians before they became formidable. After he had formed this purpose, he determined to make trial as well of the oracles in Greece as of that in Lydia; and sent different persons to different places, some to Delphi, some to Abæ of Phocis, and some to Dodona.

He endeavored to propitiate the god at Delphi by magnificent sacrifices ; for he offered three thousand head of cattle of every kind fit for sacrifice, and having heaped up a great pile, he burned on it beds of gold and silver, vials of gold, and robes of purple and garments ; hoping by that means more completely to conciliate the god. When the sacrifice was ended, having melted down a vast quantity of gold, he cast half-bricks from it ; of which the longest were six palms in length, the shortest three, and in thickness one palm : their number was one hundred and seventeen : four of these, of pure gold, weighed each two talents and a half ; the other half-bricks of pale gold, weighed two talents each. He made also the figure of a lion of fine gold, weighing ten talents. This lion, when the temple of Delphi was burned down, fell from the half-bricks, for it had been placed on them ; and it now lies in the treasury of the Corinthians, weighing six talents and a half ;

OFFERING AT THE TEMPLE OF DELPHI.

for three talents and a half were melted from it. Crœsus, having finished these things sent them to Delphi, and with them these following : two large bowls, one of gold, the other of silver ; that of gold was placed on the right hand as you enter the temple, and that of silver on the left ; but these also were removed when the temple was burnt down ; and the golden one weighing eight talents and a half and twelve minæ, is placed in the treasury of Clazomenæ ; the silver one, containing six hundred amphoræ, lies in a corner of the vestibule, and is used by the Delphians for mixing the wine on the Theophanian festival. The Delphians say it was the workmanship of Theodorus the Samian ; and I think so too, for it appears to be no common work. He also sent four casks of silver, which stand in the treasury of the Corinthians ; and he dedicated two lustral vases, one of gold, the other of silver : on the golden one is an inscription, OF THE LACEDÆMONIANS, who say that it was their offering, but wrongfully, for it was given by Crœsus : a certain Delphian made the inscription, in order to please the Lacedæmonians ; I know his name, but forbear to mention it. The boy, indeed, through whose hand the water flows, is their gift ; but neither of the lustral vases. At the same time Crœsus sent many other offerings without an inscription : amongst them some round silver covers ; and a statue of a woman in gold three cubits high, which the Delphians say is the image of Crœsus's baking woman ; and to all these things he added the necklaces and girdles of his wife.

These were the offerings he sent to Delphi ; and to Amphiaraus, having ascertained his virtue and sufferings, he dedicated a shield all of gold, and a lance of solid gold, the shaft as well as the points being of gold. These are now at Thebes in the temple of Ismenian Apollo.

To the Lydians appointed to convey these presents to the temples, Crœsus gave it in charge to inquire of the oracles, whether he should make war on the Persians, and if he should invite any other nation as an ally. Accordingly, when the Lydians arrived at the places to which they were sent, and had dedicated the offerings, they consulted the oracles, saying : " Crœsus, king of the Lydians and of other Nations, esteeming these to be the only oracles among men, sends these presents in acknowledgment of your discoveries ; and now asks whether he should lead an army against the Persians, and whether he should join any auxiliary forces with his own ? " Such were their questions ; and the opinions of both oracles concurred, foretelling : " That if Crœsus should make war on the Persians, he would destroy a mighty empire ;" and they advised him to engage the most powerful of the Greeks in his alliance. When Crœsus heard the answers that were brought back, he was beyond measure delighted with the oracles ; and fully expecting that he should destroy the kingdom of Cyrus, he again sent to Delphi, and having ascertained the number of the inhabitants, presented each of them with two staters of gold.   In return for this, the Delphians gave Crœsus and the Lydians the right to consult the oracle before any others, and ex-emption from tribute, and the first seats in the temple, and the privilege of being made citizens of Delphi, to as many as should desire it in all future time.   Crœsus, having made these presents to the Delphians, sent a third time to consult the oracle.   For after he had ascertained the veracity of the oracle, he had frequent recourse to it.   His demand now was whether he should long en-joy the kingdom ? to which the Pythian gave this answer : " When a mule shall become king of the Medes, then, tender-footed Lydian, flee over pebbly Hermus, nor tarry, nor blush to be a coward." With this answer, when reported to him, Crœsus was more than ever delighted, thinking that a mule should never be king of the Medes instead of a man, and consequently that neither he nor his posterity should ever be deprived of the kingdom.   In the next place he began to enquire carefully who were the most powerful of the Greeks whom he might gain over as allies ; and on inquiry found that the Lacedæmonians and Athenians excelled the rest, the former being of Dorian, the latter of Ionic descent : for these were in ancient time the most distinguished, the latter being a Pelasgian, the other an Hellenic nation.

CHAPTER III.

What language the Pelasgians used I cannot with certainty affirm ; but if I may form a conjecture from those Pelasgians who now exist, and inhabit the town of Crestona above the Tyrrhenians, and from those Pelasgians settled at Placia and Scylace on the Hellespont, they spoke a barbarous language. And if the whole Pelasgian body did so, the Attic race, being Pelasgic, must at the time they changed into Hellenes have altered their language. The Hellenic race, however, appears to have used the same language from the time they became a people. At first insignificant, yet from a small beginning they have increased to a multitude of nations, chiefly by a union with many other barbarous nations. But the Pelasgic race, being barbarous, never increased to any great extent.

Of these nations Crœsus learnt that the Attic was oppressed and distracted by Pisistratus, then reigning in Athens. When a quarrel happened between those who dwelt on the sea-coast and the Athenians, the formed header by Megacles, the latter by Lycurgus, Pisistratus aiming at the sovereign power, formed a third party; and having assembled his partisans under color of protecting those of the mountains, he contrived this stratagem. He wounded himself and his mules, drove his chariot into the public square, as if he had escaped from enemies that designed to murder him in his way to the country, and besought the people to grant him a guard, having before acquired renown in the expedition against Megara, by taking its port, Nisæa, and displaying other illustrious deeds. The people of Athens, deceived by this, gave him such of the citizens as he selected, who were not to be

his javelin men, but club-bearers, for they attended him with clubs
of wood. These men, joining in revolt with Pisistratus seized the
Acropolis, and Pisistratus assumed the government of the Athenians, neither disturbing the existing magistracies, nor altering the
laws ; but he administered the government according to the established institutions, liberally and well. Not long after, the partisans
of Megacles and Lycurgus became reconciled and drove him out.
In this manner Pisistratus first made himself master of Athens,
and, his power not being firmly rooted, lost it. But those who
expelle' Pisistratus quarrelled anew with one another; and
Megacles, harassed by the sedition, sent a herald to Pisistratus to
ask if he was willing to marry his daughter, on condition of having
the sovereignty. Pisistratus having accepted the proposal and
agreed to his terms, in order to his restitution, they contrive the
most ridiculous project that, I think, was ever imagined; especially
if we consider, that the Greeks have from old been distinguished
from the barbarians as being more acute and free from all foolish
simplicity, and more particularly as they played this trick upon the
Athenians, who are esteemed among the wisest of the Greeks. In
the Pæanean tribe was a woman named Phya, four cubits high,
wanting three fingers, and in other respects handsome ; this woman
they dressed in a complete suit of armor, placed her on a chariot,
and having shown her beforehand how to assume the most becoming demeanor, they drove her to the city, with heralds before, who,
on their arrival in the city, proclaimed what was ordered in these
terms: "O Athenians, receive with kind wishes Pisistratus whom
Minerva herself honoring above all men now conducts back to
her own citadel." The report was presently spread among the
people that Minerva was bringing back Pisistratus ; and the people
in the city believing this woman to be the goddess, both adored a
human being, and received Pisistratus.

Pisistratus having recovered the sovereignty in the manner
above described, married the daughter of Megacles in accordance
with his agreement, but Pisistratus soon hearing of designs that
were being formed against him, withdrew entirely out of the

ATHENS FROM MOUNT HYMETTUS.

country, and arriving in Eretria, consulted with his sons. The opinion of Hippias prevailing, to recover the kingdom, they immediately began to collect contributions from those cities which felt any gratitude to them for benefits received; and though many gave large sums, the Thebans surpassed the rest in liberality. At length (not to give a detailed account) time passed, and every thing was ready for their return, for Argive mercenaries arrived from Peloponnesus; and a man of Naxos, named Lygdamis, who had come as a volunteer, and brought both men and money, showed great zeal in the cause. Setting out from Eretria, they they came back in the eleventh year of their exile, and first of all possessed themselves of Marathon. While they lay encamped in this place, their partisans from the city joined them, and others from the various districts, to whom a tyranny was more welcome than liberty, crowded to them. The Athenians of the city, on the other hand, had shown very little concern all the time Pisistratus was collecting money, or even when he took possession of Marathon. But when they heard that he was marching from Marathon against the city, they at length went out to resist him; and marched with their whole force against the invaders. In the mean time Pisistratus's party, advanced towards the city, and arrived in a body at the temple of the Pallenian Minerva, and there took up their position. Here Amphilytus, a prophet of Acarnania, moved by divine impulse, approached Pisistratus, and pronounced this oracle in hexameter verse:

"The cast is thrown—the net expanded wide—
At night the tunnies in the snare will glide."

He, inspired by the god, uttered this prophecy; and Pisistratus, comprehending the oracle, and saying he accepted the omen, led on his army. The Athenians of the city were then engaged at their breakfast, and some of them after breakfast had betaken themselves to dice, others to sleep; so that the army of Pisistratus, falling upon them by surprise, soon put them to flight. As they were flying, Pisistratus contrived a clever stratagem to prevent their rallying again, and forced them thoroughly to disperse.

He mounted his sons on horseback and sent them forward. They, overtaking the fugitives, spoke as they were ordered by Pisistratus, bidding them be of good cheer, and to depart every man to his own home. The Athenians yielded a ready obedience, and thus Pisistratus, having a third time possessed himself of Athens, secured his power, more firmly, both by the aid of auxiliary forces, and by revenues partly collected at home and partly drawn from the mines along the river Strymon. He seized as hostages the sons of the Athenians who had held out against him, and had not immediately fled, and settled them at Naxos. He moreover purified the island of Delos, in obedience to an oracle, and having dug up the dead bodies, as far as the prospect from the temple reached, he removed them to another part of Delos.

Crœsus was informed that such was, at that time, the condition of the Athenians; and that the Lacedæmonians, having extricated themselves out of great difficulties, had gained the mastery over the Tegeans in war. They had formerly been governed by the worst laws of all the people in Greece, both as regarded their dealings with one another, and in holding no intercourse with strangers. But they changed to a good government in the following manner: Lycurgus, a man much esteemed by the Spartans, having arrived at Delphi to consult the oracle, no sooner entered the temple, than the Pythian spoke as follows :

> " Lycurgus, thou art come to my rich fane,
> Beloved by Zeus and all the heavenly train,
> But whether god or man I fear to say,
> Yet god thou must be more than mortal clay."

Some men say that, besides this, the Pythian also communicated to him that form of government now established among the Spartans. But, as the Lacedæmonians themselves affirm, Lycurgus being appointed guardian to his nephew Leobotis,[1] king of Sparta, brought those institutions from Crete. For as soon as he had taken the guardianship, he altered all their customs, and took

---

[1] It is generally agreed that the name of Lycurgus's nephew was not Leobotas, but Charilaus. See the life of Lycurgus in the " Boys' and Girls' Plutarch."

care that no one should transgress them. Afterwards he established military regulations, and instituted the ephori and senators.
Thus, having changed their laws, they established good institutions in their stead. They erected a temple to Lycurgus after his
death, and held him in the highest reverence. As they had a
good soil and abundant population, they quickly sprang up and
flourished. And now they were no longer content to live in
peace ; but proudly considering themselves superior to the Arcadians, they sent to consult the oracle at Delphi, touching the con-
quest of the whole country of the Arcadians ; and the Pythian
gave them this answer : " Dost thou ask of me Arcadia? thou
askest a great deal ; I cannot grant it thee. There are many
acorn-eating men in Arcadia, who will hinder thee. But I do not
grudge thee all; I will give thee Tegea to dance on with beating
of the feet, and a fair plain to measure out by the rod." When
the Lacedæmonians heard this answer reported, they laid aside
their design against all Arcadia ; and relying on an equivocal
oracle, led an army against Tegea only, carrying fetters with them,
as if they would surely reduce the Tegeans to slavery. But being
defeated in an engagement, as many of them as were taken alive,
were compelled to work, wearing the fetters they had brought, and
measuring the lands of the Tegeans with a rod. Those fetters in
which they were bound, were, even in my time, preserved in
Tegea, suspended around the temple of Alean Minerva.

In the first war, therefore, they had constantly fought against
the Tegeans with ill success, but in the time of Crœsus, and during
the reign of Anaxandrides and Ariston at Lacedæmon, they at
length became superior in the following manner : When they had
always been worsted in battle by the Tegeans, they sent to enquire of the oracle at Delphi, what god they should propitiate, in
order to become victorious over the Tegeans. The Pythian
answered, they should become so, when they had brought back the
bones of Orestes the son of Agamemnon. But as they were unable to find the sepulchre of Orestes, they sent again to inquire
of the god in what spot Orestes lay interred, and the Pythian gave
this answer to the inquiries of those who came to consult her :

" Down in Arcadia's level plain I know,
 Tegea lies :—and where woe lies on woe—
 Where two bound winds impatient of the yoke,
 Are forced to blow—where stroke replies to stroke :
 Beneath the earth lies Agamemnon's son,
 Bear him to Sparta and Tegea 's won."

When the Lacedæmonians heard this, they were as far off the discovery as ever, though they searched every where, till Lichas, one
of the Spartans who are called Agathoergi, found it. These Agathoergi consist of citizens who are discharged from serving in the
cavalry, such as are senior, five in every year. It is their duty
during the year in which they are discharged from the cavalry,
not to remain inactive, but go to different places where they are
sent by the Spartan commonwealth. Lichas, who was one of these
persons, discovered it in Tegea, both meeting with good fortune
and employing sagacity. For as the Lacedæmonians had at that
time intercourse with the Tegeans, he, coming to a smithy, looked
attentively at the iron being forged, and was struck with wonder
when he saw what was done. The smith perceiving his astonishment desisted from his work, and said : " O Laconian stranger, you
would certainly have been astonished had you seen what I saw,
since you are so surprised at the working of iron. For as I was
endeavoring to sink a well in this enclosure, in digging, I came to
a coffin seven cubits long ; and because I did not believe that men
were ever taller than they now are, I opened it and saw that the
body was equal to the coffin in length, and after I had measured
it I covered it up again. The man told him what he had seen, and
Lichas, reflecting on what was said, conjectured from the words of
the oracle, that this must be the body of Orestes, forming his conjecture on the following reasons : seeing the smith's two bellows
he discerned in them the two winds, and in the anvil and ham-
mer the stroke answering to stroke, and in the iron that was being
forged the woe that lay on woe ; representing it in this way, that
iron had been invented to the injury of man. He then returned
to Sparta, and gave the Lacedæmonians an account of the whole
matter ; but they brought a feigned charge against him and sent

him into banishment. He, going back to Tegea, related his misfortune to the smith, and wished to hire the enclosure from him,
but he would not let it. But in time, when he had persuaded him,
he took up his abode there ; and having opened the sepulchre and
collected the bones, he carried them away with him to Sparta.
From that time, whenever they made trial of each other's strength,
the Lacedæmonians were by far superior in war ; and the greater
part of Peloponnesus had been already subdued by them.

CHAPTER IV.

CONQUEST OF LYDIA BY CYRUS.

CRŒSUS being informed of all these things, sent ambassadors to Sparta, with presents, and to request their alliance, having given them orders what to say ; and when they were arrived they spoke as follows : " Crœsus, king of the Lydians and of other nations, has sent us with this message : ' O Lacedæmonians, since the deity has directed me by an oracle to unite myself to a Grecian friend, therefore (for I am informed that you are pre-eminent in Greece), I invite you in obedience to the oracle, being desirous of becoming your friend and ally, without treachery or guile.' " But the Lacedæmonians, who had before heard of the answer given by the oracle to Crœsus, were gratified at the coming of the Lydians, and exchanged pledges of friendship and alliance ; and indeed certain favors had been formerly conferred on them by Crœsus ; for when the Lacedæmonians sent to Sardis to purchase gold, wishing to use it in erecting the statue of Apollo that now stands at Thornax in Laconia, Crœsus gave it as a present to them. For this reason, and because he had selected them from all the Greeks, and desired their friendship, the Lacedæmonians accepted his offer of alliance ; and in the first place they promised to be ready at his summons ; and in the next, having made a great bronze bowl, capable of containing three hundred amphoræ, and covered it outside to the rim with various figures, they sent it to him, being desirous of making Crœsus a present in return. But this bowl never reached Sardis, for one of the two following reasons : the Lacedæmonians say, that when the bowl, on its way to Sardis, was off Samos, the Samains having heard of it, sailed out in long ships, and took it away by force. On the other hand the Samains affirm, that when the Lace-

dæmonians who were conveying the bowl found they were too
late, and heard that Sardis was taken and Crœsus a prisoner, they
sold the bowl in Samos, and that some private persons, who bought
it dedicated it in the temple of Juno.

Crœsus, mistaking the oracle, prepared to invade Cappadocia,
hoping to overthrow Cyrus and the power of the Persians. Whilst
Crœsus was preparing for his expedition against the Persians, a
Lydian named Sandanis, who before that time was esteemed a
wise man, and on this occasion acquired a very great name in
Lydia, gave him advice in these words : " O king, you are preparing to make war against a people who wear leather trousers,
and the rest of their garments of leather ; who inhabit a barren
country, and feed not on such things as they choose, but such as
they can get. Besides they do not habitually use wine, but drink
water ; nor have they figs to eat, nor any thing that is good. In
the first place, then, if you should conquer, what will you take
from them, since they have nothing ? On the other hand, if you
should be conquered, consider what good things you will lose.
For when they have tasted of our good things, they will become
fond of them, nor will they be driven from them. As for me, I
thank the gods, that they have not put it into the thoughts of the
Persians to make war on the Lydians." Sandanis did not, however, persuade Crœsus, for he proceeded to invade Cappadocia, as
well from a desire of adding it to his own dominions, as a wish to
punish Cyrus on account of Astyages. For Cyrus, son of Cambyses, had subjugated Astyages, son of Cyaxares, who was brother-
in law of Crœsus, and king of Medes.

Crœsus, alleging this against him, sent to ask the oracle, if he
should make war on the Persians ; and when an ambiguous answer came back, he, interpreting it to his own advantage, led his
army against the territory of the Persians. When he arrived at
the river Halys, Crœsus transported his forces, as I believe, by the
bridges which are now there. But the common opinion of the
Greeks is, that Thales the Milesian procured him a passage in the
following way : Whilst Crœsus was in doubt how his army should

pass over the river, for they say that these bridges were not at that time in existence, Thales, who was in the camp, caused the stream, which flowed along the left of the army, to flow on the right instead. He contrived it thus : having begun above the camp, he dug a deep trench, in the shape of a half-moon, so that the river, being turned into this from its old channel, might pass in the rear of the camp pitched where it then was, and afterward, having passed by the camp, might fall into its former course; so that as soon as the river was divided into two streams it became fordable in both. Some say, that the ancient channel of the river was entirely dried up ; but this I cannot assent to ; for how then could they have crossed it on their return ?

However, Crœsus, having passed the river with his army, came to a place called Pteria, in Cappadocia. (Now Pteria is the strongest position of the whole of this country, and is situated over against Sinope, a city on the Euxine Sea.) Here he encamped and ravaged the lands of the Syrians ; and took the city of the Pterians, and enslaved the inhabitants ; he also took all the adjacent places, and expelled the inhabitants, who had given him no cause for blame. But Cyrus, assembling his own army, and taking with him all who inhabited the intermediate country, went to meet Crœsus. But before he began to advance, he sent heralds to the Ionians, to persuade them to revolt from Crœsus, which the Ionians, refused to do. When Cyrus had come up and encamped opposite Crœsus, they made trial of each other's strength on the plains of Pteria ; but when an obstinate battle took place, and many fell on both sides, they at last parted, on the approach of night, neither having been victorious.

Crœsus laying the blame on his own army on account of the smallness of its numbers, for his forces that engaged were far fewer than those of Cyrus,—marched back to Sardis, designing to summon the Egyptians according to treaty, and to require the presence of the Lacedæmonians at a fixed time : having collected these together, and assembled his own army, he purposed, when winter was over, to attack the Persians in the beginning of the spring.

With this design, when he reached Sardis, he despatched ambassadors to his different allies, requiring them to meet at Sardis before the end of five months ; but the army that was with him, and that had fought with the Persians, which was composed of mercenary troops, he entirely disbanded, not imagining that Cyrus, who had come off on such equal terms, would venture to advance upon Sardis. While Crœsus was forming these plans the whole suburbs were filled with serpents, and when they appeared, the horses, forsaking their pastures, came and devoured them. When Crœsus beheld this, he considered it to be, as it really was, a prodigy, and sent immediately to consult the interpreters at Telmessus ; but the messengers having arrived there, and learnt from the Telmessians what the prodigy portended, were unable to report it to Crœsus, for before they sailed back to Sardis, Crœsus had been taken prisoner. The Telmessians had pronounced as follows : " that Crœsus must expect a foreign army to invade his country, which, on its arrival, would subdue the natives, because, they said, the serpent is a son of the earth, but the horse is an enemy and a stranger."

Cyrus, as soon as Crœsus had retreated after the battle at Pteria, having discovered that it was the intention of Crœsus to disband his army, saw that it would be to his advantage to march with all possible expedition on Sardis, before the forces of the Lydians could be a second time assembled. Whereupon Crœsus, thrown into great perplexity, seeing that matters had turned out contrary to his expectations, drew out the Lydians to battle. At that time no nation in Asia was more valiant and warlike than the Lydians. Their mode of fighting was from on horseback ; they were armed with long lances, and managed their horses with admirable address.

The place where they met was the plain that lies before the city of Sardis, which is extensive and bare ; the Hyllus and several other rivers flowing through it force a passage into the greatest, called the Hermus, which, flowing from the sacred mountain of mother Cybele, falls into the sea near the city of Phocæa. Here Cyrus, when he saw the Lydians drawn up in order of battle, alarmed at the cavalry, had recourse to the following stratagem, on the suggestion of Harpagus, a Mede. Collecting together all the camels that followed his army with provisions and baggage, and causing their burdens to be taken off, he mounted men upon them equipped in cavalry accoutrements, and ordered them to go in advance of the rest of his army against the Lydian horse ; his infantry he bade follow the camels, and placed the whole of his cavalry behind the infantry. When all were drawn up in order, he charged them not to spare any of the Lydians, but to kill every one they met ; but on no account to kill Crœsus, even if he should offer resistance when taken. He drew up the camels in the front of the cavalry for this reason : a horse is afraid of a camel, and cannot endure either to see its form or to scent its smell ; this then would render the cavalry useless to Crœsus, by which the Lydian expected to signalize himself. Accordingly, when they joined battle, the horses no sooner smelt the camels and saw them, than they wheeled round, and the hopes of Crœsus were destroyed. Nevertheless, the Lydians were not discouraged, but leaped from their horses and engaged with the Persians on foot; but at last, when many had fallen on both sides, the Lydians were put to flight, and being shut up within the walls, were besieged by the Persians.

Sardis was taken in the following manner. On the fourteenth day after Crœsus had been besieged, Cyrus sent horsemen throughout his army, and proclaimed that he would liberally reward the man who should first mount the wall ; upon this several attempts were made, and as often failed ; till, after the rest had desisted, a Mardian, whose name was Hyrœades, endeavored to climb up on that part of the citadel where no guard was stationed, for on that side the citadel was precipitous and impracticable. Hyrœades had seen a Lydian the day before come down this precipice for a helmet that had rolled down, and carry it up again. He thereupon ascended the same way, followed by divers Persians ; and when great numbers had gone up, Sardis was thus taken, and the whole town plundered.

The following incidents befel Crœsus himself.   He had a son of whom I have before made mention, who was dumb.   Now, in the time of his former prosperity, Crœsus had done every thing he could for him, and among other expedients had sent to consult the oracle of Delphi concerning him ; but the Pythian gave him this answer :

> " O foolish king of Lydia, do not seek
> To hear thy son within thy palace speak !
> Better for thee that pleasure to forego—
> The day he speaks will be a day of woe."

When the city was taken, one of the Persians, not knowing Crœsus, was about to kill him ; Crœsus, though he saw him approach, took no heed of him, caring not if he should die by the blow ; but this speechless son of his, when he saw the Persian advancing against him, through dread and anguish, burst into speech, and said : " Man, kill not Crœsus." These were the first words he ever uttered ; but from that time he continued to speak during the remainder of his life.   So the Persians got possession of Sardis, and made Crœsus prisoner, after he had reigned fourteen years, been besieged fourteen days, and lost his great empire, as the oracle had predicted.   The Persians, having taken him, conducted him to Cyrus ; and he, having heaped up a great pile, placed Crœsus upon it, bound with fetters, and with him fourteen young Lydians ; designing either to offer this sacrifice to some god, as the first fruits of his victory, or wishing to perform a vow ; or perhaps, having heard that Crœsus was a religious person, he placed him on the pile for the purpose of discovering whether any deity would save him from being burned alive.   When Crœsus stood upon the pile, notwithstanding the weight of his misfortunes, the words of Solon recurred to him, as spoken by inspiration of the deity, that " No living man could be justly called happy." When this occurred to him, it is said, that after a long silence he recovered himself, and uttering a groan, thrice pronounced the name of Solon ; when Cyrus heard him, he commanded his interpreters to ask Crœsus whom it was he called upon ; Crœsus for some time kept silence ; but at last, being constrained to speak, said : "I named a man, whose discourses I more desire all tyrants might hear, than to be possessor of the greatest riches." When he gave them this obscure answer, they again inquired what he said, and were very importunate ; he at length told them that Solon, an Athenian, formerly visited him, and having viewed all his treasures, made no account of them ; telling, in a word, how every thing had befallen him as Solon had warned him, though his discourse related to all mankind as much as to himself, and especially to those who imagine themselves happy. The pile now was kindled, and the outer parts began to burn ; when Cyrus, informed by the interpreters of what Crœsus had said, relented, considering that being but a man, he was yet going to burn another man alive, who had been no way inferior to himself in prosperity ; and moreover, fearing retribution, and reflecting that nothing human is constant, commanded the fire to be instantly extinguished, and Crœsus, with those who were about him, to be taken down. But they with all their endeavors were unable to master the fire. Crœsus, perceiving that Cyrus had altered his resolution, when he saw every man endeavoring to put out the fire, but unable to get the better of it, shouted aloud, invoking Apollo, and besought him, if ever any of his offerings had been agreeable to him, to protect and deliver him from the present danger. And the Lydians relate, as he with tears invoked the god, on a sudden clouds were seen gathering in the air, which before was serene, and that a violent storm burst forth and vehement rain fell and extinguished the flames ; by which Cyrus perceiving that Crœsus was beloved by the gods, and a good man, when he had had him taken down from the pile, asked him the following question : " Who persuaded you, Crœsus, to invade my territories, and to become my enemy instead of my friend ? " He answered : " O king, I have done this for your good but my own evil fortune, and the god of the Greeks who encouraged me to make war is the cause of all. For no man is so void of understanding as to prefer war before peace ; for in the latter children bury their fathers ; in the former, fathers bury their chil-

dren.   But, I suppose, it pleased the gods that these things should
be so."

Cyrus, having set him at liberty, placed him by his own side,
and showed him great respect.   But Crœsus, absorbed in thought
remained silent ; and presently turning round and beholding the
Persians sacking the city of the Lydians, he said, "Does it become
me, O king, to tell you what is passing through my mind, or to
keep silence?"   Cyrus bade him say with confidence whatever
he wished ; upon which Crœsus asked him,   "What is this vast
crowd so earnestly employed about?"   He answered, "They are
sacking your city, and plundering your riches."   "Not so," Crœsus
replied, "they are neither sacking my city, nor plundering my
riches, for they are no longer mine ; they are ravaging what
belongs to you."   The reply of Crœsus attracted the attention of
Cyrus ; he therefore ordered all the rest to withdraw, and asked
Crœsus what he thought should be done in the present conjunc-
ture.   He answered :   "Since the gods have made me your servant, I think it my duty to acquaint you, if I perceive anything
deserving of remark.   The Persians, who are by nature overbear-
ing, are poor.   If, therefore, you permit them to plunder and
possess great riches, you may expect the following results ; whoso
acquires the greatest riches, be assured, will be ready to rebel.
Therefore, if you approve what I say, adopt the following plan :
place some of your body-guard as sentinels at every gate, with
orders to take the booty from all those who would go out, and to
acquaint them that the tenth must of necessity be consecrated to
Jupiter : thus you will not incur the odium of taking away their
property ; and they, acknowledging your intention to be just,
will readily obey."   Cyrus was exceedingly delighted at this suggestion, and ordered his guards to carry it out, then turning to
Crœsus, he said :   "Since you are resolved to display the deeds and
words of a true king, ask whatever boon you desire on the instant."
"Sir," he answered, "the most acceptable favor you can bestow
upon me is, to let me send my fetters to the god of the Greeks,
whom I have honored more than any other deity, and to ask him,

if it be his custom to deceive those who deserve well of him." Certain Lydians were accordingly sent to Delphi, with orders to lay his fetters at the entrance of the temple, and to ask the god, if he were not ashamed to have encouraged Crœsus by his oracles to make war on the Persians assuring him that he would put an end to the power of Cyrus, of which war such were the first-fruits (commanding them at these words to show the fetters), and at the same time to ask if it were the custom of the Grecian gods to be ungrateful. When the Lydians arrived at Delphi, and had delivered their message, the Pythian is reported to have made this answer: "The god himself even cannot avoid the decrees of fate ; and Crœsus has atoned for the crime of Gyges his ancestor in the fifth generation, who,˙ being one of the body-guard of the Heraclidæ, murdered his master, Candaules, and usurped his dignity, to which he had no right. But although Apollo was desirous that the fall of Sardis might happen in the time of the sons of Crœsus, and not during his reign, yet it was not in his power to avert the fates ; but so far as they allowed he accomplished, and conferred the boon on him ; for he delayed the capture of Sardis for the space of three years. Let Crœsus know, therefore, that he was taken prisoner three years later than the fates had ordained ; and in the next place, he came to his relief, when he was upon the point of being burnt alive. Then, as to the prediction of the oracle, Crœsus has no right to complain ; for Apollo foretold him that if he made war on the Persians, he would subvert a great empire ; and had he desired to be truly informed, he ought to have sent again to inquire, whether his own or that of Cyrus was meant. But since he neither understood the oracle, nor inquired again, let him lay the blame on himself. And when he last consulted the oracle, he did not understand the answer concerning the mule ; for Cyrus was that mule ; inasmuch as he was born of parents of different nations, the mother superior, but the father inferior. For she was a Mede, and daughter of Astyages, king of Media ; but he was a Persian, subject to the Medes. When Crœsus heard this reply of the priestess of Apollo, he acknowledged the fault to be his and not the god's.

The customs of the Lydians differ little from those of the Greeks. They are the first of all nations we know of that introduced the art of coining gold and silver ; and they were the first retailers. The Lydians themselves say that the games which are now common to themselves and the Greeks, were invented by them during the reign of Atys, when a great scarcity of corn pervaded all Lydia. For when they saw famine staring them in the face they sought for remedies, and some devised one thing, some another ; and at that time the games of dice, knucklebones, ball, and all other kinds of games except draughts, were invented, (for the Lydians do not claim the invention of this ancient game,) and having made these inventions to alleviate the famine, they employed them as follows : they used to play one whole day that they might not be in want of food ; and on the next, they ate and abstained from play. Thus they passed eighteen years ; but when the evil did not abate, but on the contrary, became still more virulent, their king divided the whole people into two parts, and cast lots which should remain and which quit the country, and over that part whose lot it should be to stay he appointed himself king ; and over that part which was to emigrate he appointed his own son, whose name was Tyrrhenus. Those to whose lot it fell to leave their country went down to Smyrna, built ships, and having put all their movables which were of use on board, set sail in search of food and land, till having passed by many nations, they reached the Ombrici, where they built towns, and dwell to this day. From being called Lydians, they changed their name to one after the king's son, who led them out ; from him they gave themselves the appellation of Tyrrhenians.

CHAPTER V.

My history hence proceeds to inquire who Cyrus was that overthrew the power of Crœsus, and how the Persians became masters of Asia. In which narration I shall follow those Persians, who do not wish to magnify the actions of Cyrus, but to relate the plain truth ; though I am aware that there are three other ways of relating Cyrus's history. After the Assyrians had ruled over Upper Asia five hundred and twenty years, the Medes first began to revolt from them ; and they it seems, in their struggle with the Assyrians for liberty, proved themselves brave men ; and having shaken off the yoke, became free : afterward the other nations also did the same as the Medes. When all throughout the continent were independent, they were again reduced under a despotic government. There was among the Medes a man famous for wisdom, named Deioces, son of Phraortes. This Deioces, aiming at absolute power, had recourse to the following plan. The Medes were at that time distributed into villages, and Deioces, who was already highly esteemed in his own district, applied himself with great zeal to the exercise of justice ; and this he did, since great lawlessness prevailed throughout the whole of Media, and he knew that injustice and justice are ever at variance. The Medes of the same village, observing his conduct, chose him for their judge ; and he, constantly keeping the sovereign power in view, showed himself upright and just. By this conduct he acquired no slight praise from his fellow citizens, so much so that the inhabitants of other villages, hearing that Deioces was the only one who judged uprightly, having before met with unjust sentences, when they heard of him gladly came from all parts to Deioces, in order to submit their quarrels to his decision ; and at last they would commit the decision to no one else. In the end, when the number of those who had recourse to him continually increased as men heard of the justice of his decisions, Deioces, seeing the whole devolved upon himself, would no longer occupy the seat where he used to sit to determine differences, and refused to act as judge any more, for it was of no advantage to him to neglect his own affairs, and spend the day in deciding the quarrels of others. Upon this, rapine and lawlessness growing far more frequent throughout the villages than before, the Medes called an assembly and consulted together about the present state of things, but, as I suspect, the partisans of Deioces spoke to the following purpose : " Since it is impossible for us to inhabit the country if we continue in our present condition, let us constitute a king over us, and so the country will be governed by good laws, and we ourselves shall be able to attend to our business, nor be any longer driven from our homes by lawlessness." By some such words they persuaded them to submit to a kingly government. Upon their immediately putting the question, whom they should appoint king, Deioces was unanimously preferred and commended : so that at last they agreed that he should be their king. But he required them to build him a palace suitable to the dignity of a king, and give him guards for security of his person. The Medes accordingly did so : and built him a strong and spacious palace in the part of the country that he selected, and permitted him to choose guards for his person out of all the Medes. Being thus possessed of the power, he compelled the Medes to build one city, and having carefully adorned that, to pay less attention to the others. As the Medes obeyed him in this also, he built lofty and strong walls, which now go under the name of Ecbatana,[1] one placed in a circle within the other ; and this fortification was so contrived, that each circle was raised above the other by the height of the battlements only. The situation of the ground, rising by an easy ascent, was very favorable to the design. There were seven circles altogether, the king's palace and the treasury, situated within

---

[1] There is a Scriptual account of Ecbatana, in the Apocrypha. Judith i 1—4.

the innermost of them. The largest of these walls was about equal in circumference to the city of Athens ; the battlements of the first circle were white, of the second black, of the third purple, of the fourth blue, of the fifth bright red. Thus the battlements of all circles were painted with different colors ; but the two last had their battlements plated, the one with silver, the other with gold.[1]

Deioces then built these fortifications for himself, and round his own palace ; and he commanded the rest of the people to fix their habitations round the fortification ; and when all the buildings were completed he, for the first time, established the following regulations : that no man should be admitted to the king's presence, but every one should consult him by means of messengers, and, moreover, that it should be accounted indecency for any one to laugh or spit before him. He established such ceremony about his own person, in order that those who were brought up with him, and of no meaner family, nor inferior to him in manly qualities, might not, when they saw him, grieve and conspire against him ; but that he might appear to be of a different nature to those who did not see him. When he had established these regulations, and settled himself in the tyranny, he was very severe in the distribution of justice. And the parties contending were obliged to send him their case in writing. All other things were regulated by him : so that, if he received information that any man had injured another, he would send for him, and punish him in proportion to his offence. For this purpose he had spies and eaves-droppers in every part of his dominions.

Now Deioces collected the Medes into one nation, and ruled over it. The following are the tribes of the Medes, the Busæ, Parataceni, Struchates, Arizanti, Budii, and the Magi. Deioces had a son, Phraortes, who, when his father died, after a reign of fifty-three years, succeeded him in the kingdom; but having so succeeded, he was not content to rule over the Medes only, but, made war on the Persians, and reduced them under the dominion of the

---

[1] Major Robinson states that the seven colors described by Herodotus, are those employed by the Orientals, to denote the seven planetary bodies.

Medes. And afterward being master of these two nations, both of them powerful, he subdued Asia, attacking one nation after another; till at last he invaded the Assyrians, who inhabited the city of Nineveh, and having made war on them. perished with the greater part of his army, after he had reigned twenty-two years.

When Phraortes was dead, Cyaxares his son, grandson of Deioces, succeeded him. He is said to have been more warlike

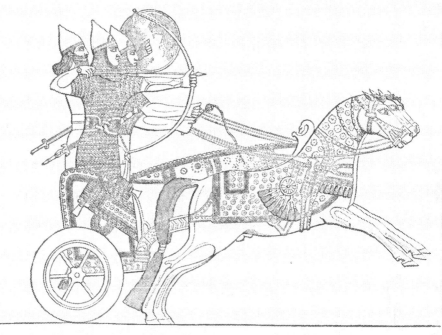

ASSYRIAN WARRIORS IN A CHARIOT.

than his ancestors. He was the first to divide the people of Asia into cohorts, and then into spearmen, archers, and cavalry; whereas before they had been confusedly mixed together. It was he that fought with the Lydians, when the day was turned into night. as they were fighting; and who subjected the whole of Asia above the river Halys. He assembled the forces of all his subjects, and marched against Nineveh to avenge his father, and destroy that city. He took Nineveh (how they took it, I will relate in another work),[1] and reduced the Assyrians into subjection, with the exception of the Babylonian district. Having accomplished these things, Cyaxares died, after a reign of forty years.

'Astyages the son of Cyaxares succeeded him in the kingdom. He had a daughter, to whom he gave the name of Mandane. When she arrived at a marriageable age he gave her to no one of the Medes who was worthy of her, but to a Persian, named Cambyses, whom he found descended of a good family, and of a peaceful disposition, deeming him far superior to a Mede of moderate rank. In the first year after Mandane was married to Cambyses, Astyages saw a vision : it appeared to him that a vine sprang

SPHINX FROM S. W. PALACE (NIMROUD).

from his daughter, and spread over all Asia. Having seen this and communicated it to the interpreters of dreams, he sent to Persia for his daughter, and her son the infant Cyrus, and upon her arrival he put her under a guard, resolving to destroy her child, for the Magian interpreters had signified to him from his vision, that the issue of his daughter would reign in his stead. Astyages therefore, sent for Harpagus, a kinsman of his, and the most faithful of all the Medes, and the manager of all his affairs, and said to

[1] Several passages of our author seem to prove that Herodotus wrote other histories than those which have come down to us. Elsewhere in this book he speaks of his Assyrian history ; and the second of the Libyan.

him : " Harpagus, on no account fail to perform the business I now charge you with ; nor expose me to danger by deceiving me ; nor, by preferring another, draw ruin upon thy own head. Take the child of Mandane carry him to your own house and kill him, and afterward bury him in whatever way you think fit." Harpagus answered : " O king, you have never yet observed any ingratitude in me, and I shall take care never to offend you for the future. If it is your pleasure that this thing should be done, it is fitting that I readily obey you." Harpagus, having given this answer, when the child had been put into his hands, adorned as if for death, returned home weeping ; and upon his arrival he told his wife all that Astyages had said. She asked him, " What then do you purpose to do ? " He answered : " Not as Astyages has commanded ; though he should be yet more outrageous and mad than he is, I will not comply with his wishes, nor will I submit to him by performing such a murder : and for many reasons I will not murder the child ; both because he is my own relation, and because Astyages is old, and has no male offspring ; besides, if, after his death, the sovereignty should devolve on his daughter, whose son he would now murder by my means, what else remains for me but the greatest danger ? It is necessary, however, for my safety that the child should die, but as necessary that one of Astyages' people should be the executioner, and not one of mine." He accordingly sent a messenger for one of Astyages' herdsmen, who he knew grazed his cattle on pastures most convenient for the purpose, and on mountains abounding with wild beasts. His name was Mitradates, and he had married his fellow-servant. The foot of the mountains at which this herdsman grazed his cattle, lies to the north of Ecbatana, toward the Euxine Sea. For the Medic territory on this side toward the Saspires, is very mountainous, lofty, and covered with forests ; while all the rest of Media is level. When the herdsman, summoned in great haste, arrived, Harpagus addressed him as follows : " Astyages bids thee take this infant, and expose him on the bleakest part of the mountains, that he may speedily perish ; and has charged me to add, that if thou by any means shouldst save the child, thou shalt die by the most cruel death ; and I am appointed to see the child exposed." The herdsman, having heard these words, took the infant, returned by the same way, and reached his cottage. It so happened that an infant of his own lay dead at home. When he returned and came up to his wife she asked him why Harpagus had sent for him in such haste. "Wife," said he, " when I reached the city, I saw and heard what I wish I had never seen, nor had ever befallen our masters. The whole house of Harpagus was filled with lamentations ; I, greatly alarmed, went in, and as soon as I entered, I saw an infant lying before me, panting and crying, dressed in gold and a robe of various colors. Harpagus bade me to take up the child directly, and carry him away, and expose him in the part of the mountain most frequented by wild beasts; telling me at the same time, that it was Astyages who imposed this task on me, and threatening the severest punishment if I should fail to do it. I took up the infant and carried him away, supposing him to belong to one of the servants ; for I had then no suspicion whence he came; though I was astonished at seeing him dressed in gold and fine apparel ; and also at the sorrow which evidently prevailed in the house of Harpagus. But soon after, on my way home, I learnt the whole truth, from a servant who accompanied me out of the city, and delivered the child into my hands ; that he was born of Mandane, Astyages' daughter, and of Cambyses son of Cyrus, and that Astyages had commanded him to be put to death."

As the herdsman uttered these last words, he uncovered the child, and showed it to his wife ; she seeing that the child was large and of a beautiful form, embraced the knees of her husband, and with tears besought him by no means to expose it. He said that it was impossible to do otherwise ; for spies would come from Harpagus to see the thing done, and he must himself die the most cruel death if he should fail to do it. "Since, then said she I cannot persuade you not to expose the child, do this : take our own dead child and expose it, and let us bring up the son of Astyages' daughter as our own. Thus you will neither be convicted of having wronged our masters, nor shall we have consulted ill for our own interests; for the child that is dead will have a royal burial, and the one that survives will not be deprived of life." The herdsman, happy at the suggestion of his wife, gave to her the child that he had brought for the purpose of putting to death, and his own, which was dead, he put into the basket in which he had brought the other, and having dressed it in all the finery of the other child, exposed it in the most desolate part of the mountains. On the third day after the infant had been exposed, the herdsman, having left one of his assistants as a guard, went to the city, and arriving at the house of Harpagus, told him he was ready to show the dead body of the infant. Harpagus accordingly sent some of the most trusty of his guards, and by that means saw the body, and buried the herdsman's child. The other, who afterwards had the name of Cyrus, was brought up by the herdsman's wife, who gave him some other name, and not that of Cyrus.

When the child attained the age of ten years, the following circumstance discovered him. He was playing in the village in which the ox-stalls were, with boys of his own age in the road. The boys had chosen this reputed son of the herdsman for their king. He in sport appointed some of them to build houses, and others to be his body-guards; one of them to be the king's eye, and to another he gave the office of bringing messages to him, assigning to each his proper duty. One of these boys who was playing with him, son of Artembares, a man of rank among the Medes, refused to obey the orders of Cyrus; he therefore commanded the others to seize him, and when they obeyed, Cyrus scourged the boy very severely. But the boy, as soon as he was let loose, considering that he had been treated with great indignity, took it very much to heart, and hastening to the city, complained to his father of the treatment he had met with from the son of Astyages' herdsman. Artembares, in a transport of anger, went immediately to Astyages, and taking his son with him, said that he suffered treatment that was not to be borne, adding, "Thus, O king, are we insulted by your slave, the son of a herdsman ;" showing the boy's shoulders. Astyages having heard and seen what was done, resolving, on account of the rank of Artembares, to avenge the indignity offered to the youth, sent for the herdsman and his son. When both came into his presence, Astyages, looking upon Cyrus, said : " Have you, who are the son of such a man as this, dared to treat the son of one of the principal persons in my kingdom with such indignity ?" But Cyrus answered : "Sir, I treated him as I did with justice. For the boys of our village, of whom he was one, in their play made me their king, because I appeared to them the most fitted for that office. All the other boys performed what they were ordered, but he refused to obey and paid no attention to my commands, so he was punished : if I deserve punishment for this here I am ready to submit to it." As the boy spoke Astyages recognised him ; the character of his face appeared like his own, and his answer more free than accorded with his condition ; the time also of the exposure seemed to agree with the age of the boy. Alarmed at this discovery, he was for some time speechless ; and at last, having with difficulty recovered himself (being desirous of sending Artembares away in order that he might examine the herdsman in private), he said : "Artembares, I will take care that neither you nor your son shall have any cause of complaint," and dismissed him ; but the servants, at the command of Astyages, conducted Cyrus into an inner room ; and when the herdsman remained alone, he asked him in the absence of witnesses, whence he had the boy, and from whose hands he received him ? He affirmed that the boy was his own son, and that the mother who bore him was still living with him. Astyages told him, that he did not consult his own safety in wishing to be put to the torture ; and as he said this he made a signal to his guards to seize him. The man, when brought to the torture, discovered the whole matter, speaking the truth throughout ; and concluded with prayers and entreaties for pardon. Astyages, when the herdsman had confessed the truth, did not concern himself much about him afterwards ; but attaching great blame to Harpagus, he ordered his guards to summon him : and when

Astyages asked, "Harpagus, by what kind of death did you dispose of the child which I delivered to you, born of my daughter?" Harpagus, seeing the herdsman present, had not recourse to falsehood, lest he should be detected and convicted, but said, "O king, when I had received the infant, I carefully considered how I could act according to your wish and command, and, without offending you, I might be free from the crime of murder both in your daughter's sight and in yours. I therefore sent for this herdsman and gave him the child, saying that you had commanded him to put it to death, and in saying this I did not speak falsely, for such indeed were your orders. In this manner I delivered the infant to him, charging him to place it in some desert mountain, and to stay and watch till the child was dead, threatening the severest punishment if he should not fully carry out these injunctions. When he had executed these orders, and the child was dead, I sent some of the most trusty of my servants, and by means of them beheld the body, and buried it. This is the whole truth, O king, and such was the fate of the child."

Thus Harpagus told the real truth; but Astyages, dissembling the anger which he felt on account of what had been done, again related to Harpagus the whole matter as he had heard it from the herdsman; and afterwards, when he had repeated it throughout, he ended by saying that the child was alive and all was well. "For," he added, "I suffered much on account of what had been done regarding this child, and could not easily bear the reproaches of my daughter; therefore, since fortune has taken a more favorable turn, do you, in the first place, send your own son to accompany the boy I have recovered; and, in the next place, (for I propose to offer a sacrifice for the preservation of the child to the gods, to whom that honor is due), do you be with me at supper."

Harpagus on hearing these words, when he had paid his homage, and had congratulated himself that his fault had turned to so good account, and that he was invited to the feast under such auspicious circumstances, went to his own home. And as soon as he entered he sent his only son, who was about thirteen years of age, and bade him go to Astyages, and do whatever he should command; and then, being full of joy, he told his wife what had happened. But when the son of Harpagus arrived, having slain him and cut him into joints, Astyages roasted some parts of his flesh and boiled others, and having had them well dressed, kept them in readiness. At the appointed hour, when the other guests and Harpagus were come, tables full of mutton were placed before the rest and Astyages himself, but before Harpagus all the body of his son, except the head, the hands and the feet; these were laid apart in a basket covered over. When Harpagus seemed to have eaten enough, Astyages asked him if he was pleased with the entertainment; and when Harpagus replied that he was highly delighted, the officers appointed for that purpose brought him the head of his son covered up with the hands and feet, and standing before Harpagus, the bade him uncover the basket and take what he chose. Harpagus doing as they desired, and uncovering the basket, saw the remains of his son's body, but he expressed no alarm at the sight, and retained his presence of mind; whereupon Astyages asked him if he knew of what animal he had been eating. He said he knew very well, and that whatever a king did was agreeable to him. After he had given this answer he gathered the remains of the flesh and went home, purposing, as I conjecture, to collect all that he could and bury it.

Astyages thus punished Harpagus; and then, considering what he should do with Cyrus, summoned the Magi, who had formerly interpreted his dream. When they were come, Astyages asked them in what way they had interpreted his vision. They gave the same answer as before; and said that if the boy was still alive, and had not already died, he must of necessity be king. He answered them as follows: "The boy still survives, and while living in the country, the boys of the village made him king, and he has already performed all such things as kings really do, for he has appointed guards, door-keepers, messengers, and all other things in like manner; and now I desire to know to what do these things appear to you to tend." The Magi answered, " If the boy be living and has already been a king by no settled plan, you may take courage on his account and make your mind easy, for he will not reign a second time. For some of our predictions terminate in trifling results; and dreams, and things like them, are fulfilled by slight events." To this Astyages replied : "I too, O Magi, am very much of the same opinion, that since the child has been named king, the dream is accomplished, and that the boy is no longer an object of alarm to me; yet consider well, and carefully weigh what will be the safest course for my family and yourselves." The Magi answered : " O king, it is of great importance to us that your empire should be firmly established, for otherwise it is alienated, passing over to this boy, who is a Persian, and we, who are Medes, shall be enslaved by Persians, and held in no account as being foreigners; whereas while you, who are of our own country, are king, we have a share in the government, and enjoy great honors at your hands. Thus, then, we must on every account provide for your safety and that of your government; and now if we saw any thing to occasion alarm we should tell you of it beforehand; but now, since the dream has issued in a trifling event, we ourselves take courage, and advise you to do the like, and to send the boy out of your sight to his parents in Persia." When Astyages heard this he was delighted, and, calling for Cyrus, said to him : " Child, I have been unjust to you, by reason of a vain dream; but you survive by your own destiny. Now go in happiness to Persia, and I will send an escort to attend you; when you arrive there you will find a father and mother very different from the herdsman Mitradates and his wife."

Astyages, thus sent Cyrus away, and, upon his arrival at the house of Cambyses, his parents received him with the greatest tenderness and joy, having been assured that he had died immediately after his birth; and they inquired of him by what means his life had been preserved. He told them, that till that time he believed he was the son of Astyages' herdsman. He related that he had been brought up by the herdsman's wife; and he went on constantly praising her.

When Cyrus had reached man's estate, and proved the most manly and beloved of his equals in age, Harpagus paid great court to him, sending him presents, from his desire to be avenged on Astyages; for he did not see that he himself, who was but a private man, could be able to take vengence on Astyages; perceiving, therefore, that Cyrus was growing up to be his avenger, he contracted a friendship with him, comparing the sufferings of Cyrus with his own. And before this he had made the following preparations. Seeing Astyages severe in his treatment of the Medes, Harpagus holding intercourse with the chief persons

EGYPTIAN HARE.

of the nation, one after another, persuaded them that they ought to place him at their head, and depose Astyages. When he had effected his purpose, and all was ready, Harpagus, wishing to discover his designs to Cyrus, who resided in Persia, and having no other way left, because the roads were all guarded, contrived the following artifice. Having cunningly contrived a hare, by opening its belly, and tearing off none of the hair, he put a letter, containing what he thought necessary to write, into the body; and having sewed up the belly of the hare, he gave it with some nets to the most trusty of his servants, dressed as a hunter, and sent him to

Persia; having by word of mouth commanded him to bid Cyrus, as he gave him the hare, to open it with his own hand, and not to suffer any one to be present when he did so. This was accordingly done, and Cyrus having received the hare, opened it; and found the letter which was in it, to the following purport: " Son of Cambyses, seeing the gods watch over you, (for otherwise you could never have arrived at your present fortune), do you now avenge yourself on your murderer Astyages; for as far as regards his purpose you are long since dead, but by the care of the gods and of me you survive. I suppose you have been long since informed both what was done regarding yourself, and what I suffered at the hands of Astyages, because I did not put you to death, but gave you to the herdsman. Then, if you will follow my counsel, you shall rule over the whole territory that Astyages now governs. Persuade the Persians to revolt, and invade Media; and whether I or any other illustrious Mede be appointed to command the army opposed to you, every thing will turn out as you wish; for they, on the first onset, having revolted from him, and siding with you, will endeavor to depose him. Since, then, every thing is ready here, do as I advise, and do it quickly."

Cyrus, upon receiving this intelligence, began to consider by what measures he could best persuade the Persians to revolt. Having written such a letter as he thought fit, he called an assembly of the Persians, read the letter and said that Astyages had appointed him general of the Persians: " Now," he continued, " I require you to attend me, every man with a sickle." When all had come with their sickles, as had been ordered, Cyrus selected a tract of land in Persia, about eighteen or twenty stadia square (nearly two and one half miles), which was overgrown with briers, and directed them to clear it during the day: when the Persians had finished the appointed task, he bade them come again on the next day, washed and well attired. In the meantime Cyrus collected all his father's flocks and herds, had them killed and dressed, to entertain the Persian forces, and provided wine and bread in abundance. The next day, when the Persians had assembled, he made them lie down on the turf, and feasted them; and, after the repast was over, asked them whether the treatment they had received the day before, or the present, was preferable. They answered, that the difference was great; for on the preceding day they had every hardship, but on the present everything that was good. Then Cyrus discovered his intentions, and said: "Men of Persia, the case stands thus; if you will hearken to me, you may enjoy these, and numberless other advantages, without any kind of servile labor; but if you will not hearken to me, innumerable hardships, like those of yesterday, await you. Now, therefore, obey me, and be free; for I am persuaded I am born by divine providence to undertake this work; and I deem you to be men in no way inferior to the Medes, either in other respects or in war; then revolt with all speed from Astyages."

The Persians under such a leader, gladly asserted their freedom, having for a long time felt indignant at being governed by the Medes. Astyages, informed of what Cyrus was doing, sent a messenger and summoned him; but Cyrus bade the messenger take back word, "that he would come to him sooner than Astyages desired." When Astyages heard this, he armed all the Medes; and, as if the gods had deprived him of understanding, made Harpagus their general, utterly forgetting the outrage he had done him. And when the Medes came to an engagement with the Persians, such of them as knew nothing of the plot, fought; but others went over to the Persians; and the far greater part purposely behaved as cowards and fled. As soon as the news was brought to Astyages that the Medes were thus shamefully dispersed, he exclaimed: "Not even so shall Cyrus have occasion to rejoice." His first act was to impale the Magi, who had interpreted his dream, and advised him to let Cyrus go; then he armed all the Medes that were left in the city, old and young; and leading them out, engaged the Persians, and was defeated. Astyages himself was made prisoner, and lost all the Medes whom he had led out. Harpagus, standing by Astyages after he was taken, exulted over him and jeered at him; and among other galling words, he asked him about the supper, at which he had feasted him with his son's flesh, and inquired, " how he liked slavery in exchange for a kingdom." Astyages, looking steadfastly on Harpagus, asked in return, whether he thought himself the author of Cyrus's success. Harpagus said, he did, for, as he had written, the achievement was justly due to himself. Astyages thereupon proved him to be " the weakest and most unjust of all men ; the weakest, in giving the kingdom to another, which he might have assumed to himself, if indeed he had effected this change ; and the most unjust, because he had enslaved the whole nation of the Medes on account of the supper.

So Astyages, after he had reigned thirty-five years, was deposed. But Cyrus kept him with him till he died, without doing him any further injury. Thus did Cyrus come to the throne, conquer Crœsus, and become master of all Asia.

The Persians, according to my own knowledge, observe the following customs :—It is not their practice to erect statues, or temples, or altars, but they charge those with folly who do so ; because, as I conjecture, they do not think the gods have human forms, as the Greeks do. They are accustomed to ascend the highest parts of the mountains, and offer sacrifice to Jupiter, and they call the whole circle of the heavens by the name of Jupiter. They sacrifice to the sun and moon, to the earth, fire, water, and the winds. To these alone they sacrificed in the earliest times : but they have since learnt from the Arabians and Assyrians to sacrifice to Venus Urania, whom the Assyrians call Venus Mylitta, the Arabians, Alitta, and the Persians Mitra. They do not erect altars nor kindle fires when about to sacrifice ; they do not use libations, or flutes, or fillets, or cakes ; but, when any one wishes to offer sacrifice to any one of these deities, he leads the victim to a clean spot, and invokes the god, usually having his tiara decked with myrtle. He that sacrifices is not permitted to pray for blessings for himself alone ; but he is obliged to offer prayers for the prosperity of all the Persians, and the king, for he is himself included in the Persians. When he has cut the victim into small pieces, and boiled the flesh, he strews under it a bed of tender grass, generally trefoil, and then lays all the flesh upon it ; when he has put every thing in order, one of the Magi standing by sings an ode concerning the original of the gods, which they say is the incantation ; and without one of the Magi it is not lawful for them to sacrifice. After having waited a short time, he that has sacrificed carries away the flesh and disposes of it as he thinks fit. It is their custom to honor their birthday above all other days ; and on this day they furnish their table in a more plentiful manner than at other times. The rich then produce an ox, a horse, a camel, and an ass, roasted whole in an oven ; but the poor produce smaller cattle. They are moderate at their meals, but eat of many after-dishes, and those not served up together. On this account the Persians say, " that the Greeks rise hungry from the table, because nothing worth mentioning is brought in after dinner, and that if any thing were brought in, they would not leave off eating." The Persians are much addicted to wine. They are accustomed to debate the most important affairs when intoxicated ; but whatever they have determined on in such deliberation, is on the following day, when they are sober, proposed to them by the master of the house where they have met to consult ; and if they approve of it when sober also, then they adopt it ; if not, they reject it. And whatever they have first resolved on when sober, they reconsider when intoxicated. When they meet one another in the streets, one may discover by the following custom, whether those who meet are equals. For instead of accosting one another, they kiss on the mouth ; if one be a little inferior to the other, they kiss the cheek ; but if he be of a much lower rank, he prostrates himself before the other.

The Persians are of all nations the most ready to adopt foreign customs ; for they wear the Medic costume, thinking it handsomer than their own ; and in war they use the Egyptian cuirass. From the age of five years to twenty, they instruct their sons in three things only : to ride, to use the bow, and to speak the truth. Before he is five years of age, a son is not admitted to the presence of his father, but lives entirely with the women : the reason of this custom is, that if he should die in childhood, he may occasion no grief to his father.

Now I much approve of the above custom, as also of the following, that not even the king is allowed to put any one to death for a single crime, nor any private Persian exercise extreme severity against any of his domestics for one fault, but if on examination he should find that his misdeeds are more numerous and greater than his services, he may in that case give vent to his anger. They say that no one ever yet killed his own father or mother. To tell a lie is considered by them the greatest disgrace ; next to that, to be in debt ; for the reason that one who is in debt must of necessity tell lies. Whosoever of the citizens has the leprosy or scrofula, is not permitted to stay within a town, nor to have communication with other Persians ; and they say that a man is afflicted with these diseases from having committed some offence against the sun. Every stranger that is seized with these distempers they drive out of the country ; and they do the same to white pigeons, making the same charge against them. They neither spit, nor wash their hands in a river, but pay extreme veneration to all rivers. Another circumstance is also peculiar to them which has escaped the notice of the Persians themselves, but not of us. Their names, which correspond with their personal forms and their rank, all terminate in the same letter (s) which the Dorians call *San*, and the Ionians *Sigma*. If you inquire into this you will find, that all Persian names, without exception, end in the same letter. These things I can with certainty affirm to be true, since I myself know them. But what follows, relating to the dead, is only secretly mentioned, viz. : that the dead body of a Persian is never buried until it has been torn by some bird or dog ; but I know for a certainty that the Magi do this, for they do it openly. The Persians then, having covered the body with wax, conceal it in the ground. The Magi differ very much from all other men, and particularly from the Egyptian priests, for the latter hold it matter of religion not to kill any thing that has life, except such things as they offer in sacrifice ; whereas the Magi kill every thing with their own hands, except a dog or a man ; and they think they do a meritorious thing, when they kill ants, serpents, and other reptiles and birds.

CHAPTER VI.

THE ASIATIC GREEKS AND THE LYDIAN REVOLT.

THE Ionians and Æolians, as soon as the Lydians were subdued by the Persians, sent ambassadors to Cyrus at Sardis, wishing to become subject to him, on the same terms as they had been to Crœsus. But, when he heard their proposal, he told them this story: "A piper seeing some fishes in the sea, began to pipe, expecting that they would come to shore; but finding his hopes disappointed, he took a casting-net, with which he caught a great number of fishes, and drew them out. When he saw them leaping about, he said to the fishes: 'Cease your dancing, since when I piped you would not come out and dance.'" Cyrus told this story to the Ionians and Æolians, because the Ionians, when Cyrus pressed them by his ambassador to revolt from Crœsus, refused to consent, and now, when the business was done, were ready to listen to him. When the Ionians heard this message, they severally fortified themselves with walls, and met together at the Panionium, with the exception of the Milesians; for Cyrus made an alliance with them on the same terms as the Lydians had done. The rest of the Ionians resolved unanimously to send ambassadors to Sparta, to implore them to succor the Ionians. These Ionians, to whom the Panionium belongs, have built their cities under the finest sky and climate of the world that we know of; for neither the regions that are above it, nor those that are below, nor the parts to the east or west, are at all equal to Ionia; for some of them are oppressed by cold and rain, others by heat and drought. These Ionians do not all use the same language, but have four varieties of dialect. Miletus, the first of them, lies toward the south.

The Milesians were sheltered from danger, as they had made an alliance. The islanders also had nothing to fear ; for the Phœnicians were not yet subject to the Persians, nor were the Persians themselves at all acquainted with maritime affairs. Now the Milesians had seceded from the rest of the Ionians only for this reason, that weak as the Grecian race then was, the Ionian was weakest of all, and of least account ; for except Athens, there was no other city of note. The other Ionians, therefore, and the Athenians shunned the name, and would not be called Ionians ; and even now many of them appear to me to be ashamed of the name. But these twelve cities gloried in the name, and built a temple for their own use, to which they gave the name of Panionium.

When the ambassadors of the Ionians and Æolians arrived at Sparta, they made choice of a Phocæan, whose name was Pythermus, to speak in behalf of all. Putting on a purple robe, in order that as many as possible of the Spartans might hear of it and assemble, he addressed them at length, imploring their assistance. But the Lacedæmonians would not listen to him, and determined not to assist the Ionians : they therefore returned home. Yet the Lacedæmonians, though they had rejected the Ionian ambassadors, despatched men in a penteconter, to keep an eye upon the affairs of Cyrus and Ionia. These men arriving in Phocæa, sent the most eminent person among them, whose name was Lacrines, to Sardis, to warn Cyrus in the name of the Lacedæmonians, "not to injure any city on the Grecian territory, for in that case they would not pass it by unnoticed." When the herald gave this message, it is related that Cyrus inquired of the Greeks who were present, who the Lacedæmonians were, and how many in number, that they sent him such a warning. And when informed, he said to the Spartan herald, " I was never yet afraid of those, who in the midst of their city have a place set apart, in which they collect and cheat one another by false oaths ; and if I continue in health, not the calamities of the Ionians shall be talked about, but their own." This taunt of Cyrus was levelled at the Greeks in general, who have markets for the purposes of buying and selling ; for the Persians have no such a thing as a market. After this, Cyrus intrusted Tabalus a Persian with the government of Sardis, and appointed Pactyas a Lydian to bring away the gold, both that belonging to Crœsus and to the other Lydians, and departed with Cyrus for Ecbatana, for from the first he took no account of the Ionians. But Babylon was an obstacle to him, as were also the Bactrians, the Sacæ, and the Egyptians ; against whom he resolved to lead an army in person, and to send some other general against the Ionians. But as soon as Cyrus had marched from Sardis, Pactyas prevailed on the Lydians to revolt from Tabalus and Cyrus ; and going down to the sea-coast, with all the gold taken from Sardis in his possession, he hired mercenaries and persuaded the inhabitants of the coast to join him ; and then having marched against Sardis, he besieged Tabalus, who was shut up in the citadel.

When Cyrus heard this news on his march, he said to Crœsus ; "Crœsus, what will be the end of these things ? the Lydians, it seems, will never cease to give trouble to me, and to themselves. I am in doubt whether it will not be better to reduce them to slavery ; for I appear to have acted like one who, having killed the father, has spared the children ; so I am carrying away you, who have been something more than a father to the Lydians, and have intrusted their city to the Lydians themselves : and then I wonder at their rebellion ! " Crœsus, fearing lest he should utterly destroy Sardis, answered : " Sir, you have but too much reason for what you say ; yet do not give full vent to your anger, nor utterly destroy an ancient city, which is innocent as well of the former as of the present offence : for of the former I myself was guilty, and now bear the punishment on my own head ; but in the present instance Pactyas, to whom you intrusted Sardis, is the culprit ; let him therefore pay the penalty. But pardon the Lydians, and enjoin them to observe the following regulations, to the end that they may never more revolt, nor be troublesome to you : send to them and order them to keep no weapons of war in their possession ; and enjoin them to wear tunics under their cloaks, and buskins on their feet ; and require them to teach their sons to play on the cithara, to strike the guitar, and to sell by retail; and then you will soon see them becoming women instead of men, so that they will never give you any apprehensions about their revolting." Crœsus suggested this plan, thinking it would be more desirable for the Lydians, than that they should be sold for slaves ; and being persuaded, that unless he could suggest some feasible proposal, he should not prevail with him to alter his resolution : and he dreaded also, that the Lydians, if they should escape the present danger, might hereafter revolt from the Persians, and bring utter ruin on themselves. Cyrus, pleased with the expedient, laid aside his anger, and said that he would follow his advice : then having sent for Mazares, a Mede, he commanded him to order the Lydians to conform themselves to the regulations proposed by Crœsus, and moreover to enslave all the rest who had joined the Lydians in the attack on Sardis ; but by all means to bring Pactyas to him alive. Cyrus having given these orders on his way, proceeded to the settlements of the Persians. But Pactyas heard that the army which was coming against him was close at hand, and fled in great consternation to Cyme. Mazares marched against Sardis with an inconsiderable division of Cyrus's army, but found that Pactyas and his party were no longer there. He, however, compelled the Lydians to conform to the injunctions of Cyrus ; who, by his order, completely changed their mode of life: after this Mazares despatched messengers to Cyme, requiring them to deliver up Pactyas. But the Cymæans, in order to come to a decision, resolved to refer the matter to the deity at Branchidæ, for an oracular shrine was there erected in former times, which all the Ionians and Æolians were in the practice of consulting. The Cymæans asked the oracle " what course they should pursue respecting Pactyas, that would be most pleasing to the gods : " the answer to their question was, that they should deliver up Pactyas to the Persians. When this answer was reported, they determined to give him up; but, Aristodicus the son of Heraclides, a man of high repute among the citizens, distrusting the oracle, and suspecting the sincerity of the consulters, prevented them from doing so ; till at last other messengers, among whom was Aristodicus, went to inquire a second time concerning Pactyas. When they arrived at Branchidæ, Aristodicus consulted the oracle in the name of all, inquiring in these words: "O king, Pactyas, a Lydian, has come to us as a suppliant, to avoid a violent death at the hands of the Persians. They now demand him, and require the Cymæans to give him up. We, however, though we dread the Persian power, have not yet dared to surrender the suppliant, till it be plainly declared by thee what we ought to do." The oracle gave the same answer as before. Upon this Aristodicus deliberately acted as follows ; walking round the temple, he took away all the sparrows and all other kinds of birds that had built nests in the temple ; whereupon a voice issued from the sanctuary ; addressing Aristodicus, it spoke as follows : "O most impious of men, how darest thou do this ? Dost thou tear my suppliants from my temple ?" Aristodicus without hesitation answered, "O king, art thou then so careful to succor thy suppliants, but biddest the Cymæans to deliver up theirs ?" The oracle again rejoined: "Yes, I bid you do so ; that having acted impiously, ye may the sooner perish, and never more come and consult the oracle about the delivering up of suppliants." When the Cymæans heard this latter answer, not wishing to bring destruction on themselves by surrendering Pactyas, or to subject themselves to a siege by protecting him, they sent him away to Mitylene. But the Mitylenæans, when Mazares sent a message to them requiring them to deliver up Pactyas, were preparing to do so for some remuneration ; what, I am unable to say precisely, for the proposal was never completed. For the Cymæans, being informed of what was being done by the Mitylenæans, despatched a vessel to Lesbos, and transported Pactyas, to Chios, whence he was torn by violence from the temple of Minerva Poliuchus by the Chians, and delivered up. The Chians delivered him up in exchange for Atarneus, a place situate in Mysia, opposite Lesbos. In this manner Pactyas fell into the hands of the Persians ; who kept him under guard in order that they might deliver him to Cyrus. For a long time after this, none of the Chians would offer barley-meal from Atarneus to any of the gods, or make any cakes of the fruit that came from them ; but all the productions of that country were excluded from the temples. Mazares, after this, marched against those who had assisted in besieging Tabalus ; and in the first place reduced the Prienians to slavery, and in the next overran the whole plain of the Mæander, and gave it to his army to pillage ; and he treated Magnesia in the same manner : but shortly afterward fell sick and died.

On his death Harpagus came down as his successor in the command ; he also was by birth a Mede, the same whom Astyages king of the Medes entertained at the impious feast, and who assisted Cyrus in ascending the throne. This man being appointed general by Cyrus, on his arrival in Ionia, took several cities by means of earth-works ; for he forced the people to retire within their fortifications, and then, having heaped up mounds against the walls, he carried the cities by storm. Phocæa was the first place in Ionia that he attacked.

These Phocæans were the first of all the Greeks who undertook long voyages, and they are the people who discovered the Adriatic and Tyrrhenian seas, Iberia, and Tartessus.[1] They made their voyages in fifty-oared galleys, and not in merchant-ships. When they arrived at Tartessus they were kindly received by the king of the Tartessians, whose name was Arganthonius ; he reigned eighty years over Tartessus, and lived to the age of one hundred and twenty. The Phocæans became such great favorites with him, that he at first solicited them to abandon Ionia, and to settle in any part of his territory they should choose ; but afterward, finding he could not prevail with them to accept his offer, and hearing from them the increasing power of the Mede, he gave them money for the purpose of building a wall around their city : he must have given it unsparingly, for the wall is not a few stades in circumference, and is entirely built of large and well-compacted stones. When Harpagus had marched his army against the

---

[1] Tartessus was situated between the two branches of the Bœtis, now the Guadalquiver.

Phocæans, he besieged them, but offered these terms : " that he would be content if the Phocæans would throw down only one of their battlements, and consecrate one house *to the king's use.*" The Phocæans, detesting slavery, said, " that they wished for one day to deliberate, and would then give their answer "; but while they were deliberating they required him to draw off his forces from the wall. Harpagus said, that " though he well knew their design, yet he would permit them to consult together." In the interval, then, during which Harpagus withdrew his army from the wall, the Phocæans launched their fifty-oared galleys, and having put their wives, children, and goods on board, together with the images from the temples and other offerings, except works of bronze or stone, or pictures, they embarked themselves, and set sail for Chios : and the Persians took possession of Phocæa, abandoned by all its inhabitants. The Phocæans, when the Chians refused to sell them the Œnyssæ Islands, for fear they should become the seat of trade, and their own island be thereby excluded, directed their course to Cyrnus ; where, by the admonition of an oracle, they had twenty years before built a city, named Alalia. But Arganthonius was at that time dead. On their passage to Cyrnus, having first sailed down to Phocæa, they put to death the Persian garrison which had been left by Harpagus to guard the city. Afterward, when this was accomplished, they pronounced terrible imprecations on any who should desert the fleet ; besides this, they sunk a mass of red-hot iron, and swore " that they would never return to Phocæa, till this burning mass should appear again." Nevertheless, as they were on their way toward Cyrnus, more than one half of the citizens were seized with regret and yearning for their city and dwellings in the country, and violating their oaths, sailed back to Phocæa ; but such of them as kept to their oath weighed anchor and sailed from the Œnyssæ Islands. On their arrival at Cyrnus they lived for five years in common with the former settlers : but as they ravaged the territories of all their neighbors, the Tyrrhenians and Carthaginians combined together to make war against them, each with sixty ships : and the

Phocæans, on their part, having manned their ships, consisting of sixty in number, met them in the Sardinian Sea ; and having engaged, the Phocæans obtained a kind of Cadmean victory ;[1] for forty of their own ships were destroyed, and the twenty that survived were disabled, for their prows were blunted. They therefore sailed back to Alalia, took on board their wives and children, with what property their ships were able to carry, and leaving Cyrnus, sailed to Rhegium. As to the men belonging to the ships destroyed, most of them fell into the hands of the Carthaginians and Tyrrhenians, who took them on shore and stoned them to death. But afterward all animals belonging to the Argyllæans that passed by the spot where the Phocæans who had been stoned lay, became distorted, maimed, and crippled, as well sheep, as beasts of burden and men. The Argyllæans, therefore, being anxious to expiate the guilt, sent to Delphi ; and the Pythian enjoined them to use those rites which they still observe ; for they commemorate their death with great magnificence, and have established gymnastic and equestrian contests. This was the fate of these Phocæans ; but the others, who fled to Rhegium, left that place, and got possession of the town in the territory of Œnotria, which is now called Hyela, which they colonized by the advice of a certain Posidonian, who told them the Pythia had directed them to establish sacrèd rites to Cyrnus as being a hero, but not to colonize the island of that name.

The Teians also acted nearly in the same manner as the Phocæans. For when Harpagus by means of his earth-works had made himself master of their walls, they all went on board their ships, and sailed away to Thrace, and there settled in the city of Abdera ; which Timesius of Clazomenæ having formerly founded, did not enjoy, but was driven out by the Thracians, and is now honored as a hero by the Teians of Abdera.

These were the only Ionians who abandoned their country rather than submit to servitude. The rest, except the Milesians, gave battle to Harpagus, and as well as those who abandoned

---

[1] A proverbial expression signifying "that the victors suffered more than the vanquished."

their country, proved themselves brave men, each fighting for his own; but defeated and subdued, they remained in their own countries, and submitted to the commands imposed on them. The Milesians, as I have before mentioned, having made a league with Cyrus, remained quiet. So was Ionia a second time enslaved, and the islanders, dreading the same fate, made their submission to Cyrus. When the Ionians were brought into this wretched condition, and nevertheless still held assemblies at Panionium, I am informed that Bias of Priene gave them most salutary advice, which, had they harkened to him, would have made them the most flourishing of all the Greeks. He advised, "that the Ionians, should sail in one common fleet to Sardinia, and there build one city for all the Ionians; thus being freed from servitude, they would flourish, inhabiting the most considerable of the islands, and governing the rest; whereas if they remained in Ionia, he saw no hope of recovering their liberty." But before Ionia was ruined, the suggestion of Thales, the Milesian, who was of Phœnician extraction, was also good, who advised that the Ionians should constitute one general council in Teos, which stands in the centre of Ionia; and that the rest of the inhabited cities should be governed as independent states.

Harpagus having subdued Ionia, marched against the Carians, Cannians, Lycians, Ionians, and Æolians; of whom the Carians were by far the most famous of all nations in those times. They introduced three inventions which the Greeks have adopted. For the Carians set the example of fastening crests upon helmets and of putting devices on shields; they are also the first who attach handles to shields; until their time all who used shields carried them without handles, guiding them with leathern thongs, having them slung round their necks and left shoulders.

The Lycians were originally sprung from Crete, for in ancient time Crete was entirely in the possession of barbarians. But a dispute having arisen between Sarpedon and Minos, sons of Europa, respecting the sovereign power, when Minos got the upper hand in the struggle, he drove out Sarpedon with his partisans;

and they being expelled came to the land of Milyas in Asia, and were afterwards joined by Lycus son of Pandion of Athens, who was likewise driven out by his brother Ægeus, and came to be called Lycians after him. Their customs are partly Cretan and partly Carian ; but they have one peculiar to themselves, in which they differ from all other nations : they take their name from their mothers and not from their fathers ; so that if any one asks another who he is, he will describe himself by his mother's side, and reckon his ancestry in the female line. And if a free-born woman marry a slave, the children are accounted of pure birth ; but if a man though a citizen, and of high rank, marry a foreigner, the children are considered low born.

All Cnidia, except a small space, is surrounded by water ; for the Ceramic gulf bounds it on the north, and on the south the sea by Syme and Rhodes : now this small space, which is about five stades in breadth, the Cnidians, wishing to make their territory insular, designed to dig through, while Harpagus was subduing Ionia. For the whole of their dominions were within the isthmus ; and where the Cnidian territory terminates toward the continent, there is the isthmus that they designed to dig through. But, as they were carrying on the work with great diligence, the workmen appeared to be wounded to a greater extent and in a more strange manner than usual, both in other parts of the body, and particularly in the eyes, by the chipping of the rock ; they therefore sent deputies to Delphi to inquire what was the cause of the obstruction ; and, as the Cnidians say, the Pythia answered as follows in trimeter verse : " Build not a tower on the isthmus, nor dig it through, for Jove would have made it an island had he so willed." So the Cnidians desisted from their work, and surrendered without resistence to Harpagus, as soon as he approached with his army. The Pedasians were situated inland above Halicarnassus. When any mischief is about to befall them or their neighbors, the priestess of Minerva has a long beard : this has three times occurred. These were the only people about Caria who opposed Harpagus for any time and gave him much trouble, by fortifying a mountain called Lyda. After some time, however, they were subdued. The Lycians, when Harpagus marched his army toward the Xanthian plain, went out to meet him, and engaging with very inferior numbers, displayed great feats of valor. But being defeated and shut up within their city, they collected their wives, children, property, and servants within the citadel, and then set fire to it and burnt it to the ground. When they had done this, and engaged themselves by the strongest oaths, all the Xanthians went out and died fighting. Of the modern Lycians, who are said to be Xanthians, all, except eighty families, are strangers ; but these eighty families happened at the time to be away from home and so survived. Thus Harpagus got possession of Xanthus and Caunia almost in the same manner ; for the Caunians generally followed the example of the Lycians.

CHAPTER VII.

WHILE Harpagus was reducing the lower parts of Asia, Cyrus had conquered the upper parts, subduing every nation without exception. The greatest parts of these I shall pass by without notice ; but I will make mention of those which gave him most trouble, and are most worthy of being recorded.

Assyria contains many large cities, the most renowned and the strongest of which, where the seat of government was established after the destruction of Nineveh, was Babylon, which is of the following description. The city stands in a spacious plain, and is quadrangular, and shows a front on every side of one hundred and twenty stades [15 miles] ; these stades make up the sum of four hundred and eighty in the whole circumference. It was adorned in a manner surpassing any city we are acquainted with. In the first place, a moat deep, wide, and full of water, runs entirely round it ; next, there is a wall fifty royal cubits in breadth [about 84 feet], and in height two hundred [270 feet], but the royal cubit is larger than the common one by three fingers' breadth. And here I think I ought to explain how the earth, taken out of the moat, was consumed, and in what manner the wall was built. As they dug the moat they made bricks of the earth that was taken out ; and when they had moulded a sufficient number they baked them in kilns. Then making use of hot asphalt for cement, and laying wattled reeds between the thirty bottom courses of bricks, they first built up the sides of the moat, and afterward the wall itself in the same manner ; and on the top of the wall, at the edges, they built dwellings of one story, fronting each other, having spaces between these dwellings wide enough to turn a chariot with four horses. In the circumference of the wall there were a hundred gates, all of bronze, as also were the posts and lintels. Eight days' journey from Babylon [200 miles] stands another city, called Is, on a small river of the same name, which discharges its stream into the Euphrates; this river brings down with its water many lumps of bitumen, from which the bitumen used in the wall of Babylon was taken. The city consists of two divisions, for the Euphrates, separates it in the middle : this river, which is broad, deep, and rapid, flows from Armenia, and falls into the Red Sea. The wall on either bank has an elbow carried down to the river ; and thence along the curvatures of each bank runs a wall of baked bricks. The city itself, which is full of houses three and four stories high, is cut up into straight streets running at right angles to each other. At the end of each street a little gate is formed in the wall along the river side, in number equal to the streets ; and they are all made of bronze, and lead down to the edge of the river. This outer wall is the chief defence, but another wall runs round within, not much inferior to the other in strength, though narrower. In the middle of each division of the city fortified buildings were erected ; in one, the royal palace, with a spacious and strong enclosure, bronze-gated ; and in the other, the precinct of Jupiter Belus, which in my time was still in existence, a square building of two stades [$\frac{1}{4}$ of a mile] on every side. In the midst of this precinct is built a solid tower of one stade both in length and breadth, and on this tower rose another, and another upon that, to the number of eight. And there is an ascent to these outside, running spirally round all the towers. About the middle of the ascent there is a landing-place and seats on which those who go up may rest themselves ; and in the uppermost tower stands a spacious temple, handsomely furnished, and in it a large couch, with a table of gold by its side. No statue has been erected within it, but as the Chaldæans, who are priests of this deity, assert, though I cannot credit what they say, the god himself comes to the temple and reclines on the bed, in the same manner as the Egyptians say happens at Thebes in Egypt.

There is also another temple below, within the precinct at Babylon ; in it is a large golden statue of Jupiter seated, and near it a great table of gold ; the throne also and the step are of gold, which together weigh eight hundred talents [twenty-two tons], as the Chaldæans affirm. Outside the temple is a golden altar ; and another large altar, where full-grown sheep are sacrificed ; for on the golden altar only sucklings may be offered. On the great altar the Chaldæans consume yearly a thousand talents [twenty-seven tons] of frankincense when they celebrate the festival of this god. There was also at that time within the precincts of this temple a statue of solid gold, twelve cubits high [eighteen feet] ; I, indeed, did not see it, but only relate what is said by the Chaldæans. Darius, son of Hystaspes, formed a design to take away this statue, but dared not do so ; but Xerxes, son of Darius, took it, and killed the priest who forbade him to remove it.

There were many others who reigned over Babylon, whom I shall mention in my Assyrian history, who beautified the walls and temples, and amongst them were two women: The first of these, named Semiramis, lived five generations before the other ; she raised mounds along the plain, which are worthy of admiration ; for before, the river used to overflow the whole plain like a sea. But the other, who was queen next after her, and whose name was Nitocris, (and she was much more sagacious than the other queen,) in the first place left monuments of herself, which I shall presently describe ; and in the next place, when she saw the power of the Medes growing formidable and restless, and that, among other cities, Nineveh was captured by them, she took every possible precaution for her own defence. First of all, the River Euphrates, which before ran in a straight line, and which flows through the middle of the city, by having channels dug above, she made so winding, that in its course it touched three times at one and the same village in Assyria, called Arderica : and to this day, those who go from our sea to Babylon, if they travel by the Euphrates, come three times to this village on three successive days. She also raised on either bank of the river a mound, astonishing for its magnitude and height. At a considerable distance above Babylon, she had a reservoir for a lake dug, carrying it out some distance from the river, and in the depth digging down to water, and in width making its circumference of four hundred and twenty stades [about fifty-two and a half miles]: she consumed the soil from this excavacation by heaping it up on the banks of the river, and when it was completely dug, she had stones brought and built a casing to it all round. She had both these works done, the river made winding, and the whole excavation a lake, in order that the current, being broken by frequent turnings, might be more slow, and the navigation to Babylon tedious, and that after the voyage, a long march round the lake might follow. All this was done in that part of the country where the approach to Babylon is nearest, and where is the shortest way for the Medes ; in order that the Medes might not, by holding intercourse with her people, become acquainted with her affairs. She enclosed herself, therefore, with these defences by digging, and immediately afterwards made the following addition. As the city consisted of two divisions, which were separated by the river, during the reign of former kings, when any one had occasion to cross from one division to the other, he was obliged to cross in a boat : and this, in my opinion, was very troublesome : she therefore provided for this, for after she had dug the reservoir for the lake, she left this other monument built by similar toil. She had large blocks of stone cut, and when they were ready and the place was completely dug out, she turned the whole stream of the river into the place she had dug : while this was filling, and the ancient channel had become dry, in the first place, she lined with burnt bricks the banks of the river throughout the city, and the decents that lead from the gates to the river, in the same manner as the walls. In the next place, about the middle of the city, she built a bridge with the stones she had prepared, and bound them together with plates of lead and iron. Upon these stones she laid, during the day, square planks of timber, on which the Babylonians might pass over ; but at night these planks were removed, to prevent people from crossing by night and robbing one another.

When the hollow that was dug had become a lake filled by the
river, and the bridge was finished, she brought back the river to
its ancient channel from the lake.

The same queen also contrived the following deception. Over
the most frequented gate of the city she prepared a sepulchre for

WINGED HUMAN-HEADED LION.

herself, high up above the gate itself; and on the sepulchre she
had engraved, SHOULD ANY ONE OF MY SUCCESSORS, KINGS OF BABY-
LON, FIND HIMSELF IN WANT OF MONEY, LET HIM OPEN THIS SEPUL-
CHRE, AND TAKE AS MUCH AS HE CHOOSES; BUT IF HE BE NOT IN
WANT, LET HIM NOT OPEN IT; FOR THAT WERE NOT WELL. This

monument remained undisturbed, until the kingdom fell to Darius ;
but it seemed hard to Darius that this gate should be of no use,
and that when money was lying there, and this money inviting
him to take it, he should not do so ; but no use was made of this
gate for this reason, that a dead body was over the head of any
one who passed through it.   He therefore opened the sepulchre,
and instead of money, found only the body, and these words written : HADST THOU NOT BEEN INSATIABLY COVETOUS, AND GREEDY OF
THE MOST SORDID GAIN, THOU WOULDEST NOT HAVE OPENED THE
CHAMBERS OF THE DEAD.

Cyrus made war against the son of this queen, who bore the
name of his father Labynetus, and had the empire of Assyria.
Now when the great king leads his army in person, he carries with
him from home well prepared provisions and cattle ; and he takes
with him water from the river Choaspes, which flows past Susa, of
which alone, the king drinks.   A great number of four-wheeled
carriages drawn by mules carry the water of this river, after it has
been boiled in silver vessels, and follow him from place to place
wherever he marches.   Cyrus, in his march against Babylon, arrived at the river Gyndes, whose fountains are in the Matianian
mountains, and which flows through the land of the Dardanians,
and falls into another river, the Tigris ; the latter, flowing by the
city of Opis, discharges itself into the Red Sea.   When Cyrus
was endeavoring to cross this river Gyndes, which can be passed
only in boats, one of the sacred white horses through wantonness
plunged into the stream, and attempted to swim over, but the
stream having carried him away and drowned him, Cyrus was
much enraged with the river for this affront, and threatened to
make his stream so weak, that henceforth women should easily
cross it without wetting their knees.   After this menace, deferring
his expedition against Babylon, he divided his army into two parts ;
and marked out by lines one hundred and eighty channels, on
each side of the river, diverging every way ; then having distributed his army, he commanded them to dig.   His design was
indeed executed by the great numbers he employed ; but they

spent the whole summer in the work. When Cyrus had avenged himself on the river Gyndes, by distributing it into three hundred and sixty channels, and the second spring began to shine, he then advanced against Babylon. But the Babylonians, having taken the field, awaited his coming; and when he had advanced near the city, the Babylonians gave battle, and, being defeated, were shut up in the city. But as they had been long aware of the restless spirit of Cyrus, and saw that he attacked all nations alike, they had laid up provisions for many years; and therefore were under no apprehensions about a siege. On the other hand, Cyrus found himself in difficulty, since much time had elapsed, and his affairs were not at all advanced. Whether therefore some one else made the suggestion to him in his perplexity, or whether he himself devised the plan, he had recourse to the following stratagem. Having stationed the bulk of his army near the passage of the river where it enters Babylon, and again having stationed another division beyond the city, where the river makes its exit, he gave orders to his forces to enter the city as soon as they should see the stream fordable. Having thus stationed his forces, and given these directions, he himself marched away with the ineffective part of his army; and coming to the lake, Cyrus did the same with respect to the river and the lake as the queen of the Babylonians had done. For having diverted the river, by means of a canal, into the lake, which was before a swamp, he made the ancient channel fordable by the sinking of the river. When this took place, the Persians who were appointed to that purpose close to the stream of the river, which had now subsided to about the middle of a man's thigh, entered Babylon by this passage. If, however, the Babylonians had been aware of it beforehand, or had known what Cyrus was about, they would not have suffered the Persians to enter the city, but would have utterly destroyed them; for having shut all the little gates that lead down to the river, and mounting the walls that extend along the banks of the river, they would have caught them as in a net; whereas the Persians came upon them by surprise. It is related by the people who inhabited this city, that on account of its great extent, when they who were at the extremities were taken, those of the Babylonians who inhabited the centre knew nothing of the capture (for it happened to be a festival) but they were dancing at the time, and enjoying themselves, till they received certain information of the truth. Thus was Babylon taken for the first time.[1]

How great was the power of the Babylonians, I can prove by many other circumstances, and especially by the following. The whole territory over which the great king reigns, is divided into districts for the purpose of furnishing subsistence for him and his army, in addition to the usual tribute ; of the twelve months in the year, the Babylonian territory provides him with subsistence for four, and all the rest of Asia for the remaining eight ; so that the territory of Assyria amounts to a third part of the power of all Asia, and the government of this region, which the Persians call a satrapy, is remunerative ; since it yielded a full artabe of silver every day to Tritæchmes son of Artabazus, who held this district from the king : the artabe is a Persian measure, containing three Attic chœnices more than the Attic medimnus [or about twelve and a half gallons]. And he had a private stud of horses, in addition to those used in war, of eight hundred stallions, and sixteen thousand mares. He kept, too, such a number of Indian dogs, that four considerable towns in the plain were exempted from all other taxes and appointed to find food for the dogs. Such were the advantages accruing to the governor of Babylon. The land of Assyria is but little watered by rain, only enough in fact to nourish the root of the corn ; the stalk grows up, and the grain comes to maturity only by being irrigated from the river, not, as in Egypt, by the river overflowing the fields, but by the hand and by engines. The Babylonian territory, like Egypt, is intersected by canals ; and the largest of these is navigable, stretching in the direction of the winter sunrise[2] ; and it extends from the Euphrates to another river, the Tigris, on which the city of Nineveh stood. This

[1] It was again taken by Darius ; see end of Book III.
[2] That is, southeast.

is, of all lands with which we are acquainted, by far the best for the growth of corn : but it does not carry produce trees of any kind, either the fig, or the vine, or the olive ; yet it is so fruitful in the produce of corn, that it yields continually two hundred-fold, and when it produces its best, it yields even three hundred-fold. The blades of wheat and barley grow there to fully four fingers (three inches) in breadth ; and though I well know to what a height millet and sesama grow, I shall not mention it ; for I am well assured, that to those who have never been in the Babylonian country, what has been said concerning its productions will appear to many incredible. They use no other oil than such as is drawn from sesama. They have palm-trees growing all over the plain ; most of these bear fruit from which they make bread, wine, and honey. They also tie the fruit of that which the Greeks call the male palm, about those trees that bear dates, in order that the fly entering the date may ripen it, lest otherwise the fruit may fall before maturity ; for the male palms have flies in the fruit, just like wild fig-trees.

The most wonderful thing of all, next to the city itself, is what I am now going to describe : their vessels that sail down the river to Babylon are circular, and made of leather. For when they have cut the ribs out of willows that grow in Armenia above Babylon, they cover them with hides extended on the outside, by way of a bottom ; not making any distinction in the stern, nor contracting the prow, but making them circular like a buckler ; then having lined this vessel throughout with reeds, they suffer it to be carried down by the river freighted with merchandise, chiefly casks of palm-wine. The vessel is steered by two spars, held by two men standing upright, one of whom draws his spar in and the other thrusts his out. Some of these vessels are made very large, and others of a smaller size ; but the largest of them carry a cargo of five thousand talents [about one hundred and thirty-five tons]. Every vessel has a live ass on board, and the larger ones more. For after they arrive at Babylon, and have disposed of their freight, they sell the ribs of the boat and all the reeds by public auction ;

then having piled the skins on the asses, they return by land to
Armenia, for it is not possible by any means to sail up the river
because of the rapidity of the current : and for this reason they
make their vessels of skins and not of wood, and upon their return
to Armenia with their asses, they construct other vessels in the
same manner.   For their dress, they wear a linen tunic that reaches
down to the feet ; over this they put another garment of wool, and
over all a short white cloak ; they have sandals peculiar to the
country, very much like the Bœotian clogs.   They wear long hair,
binding their heads with turbans, and anoint the whole body with
perfumes.   Every man has a seal, and a staff curiously wrought ;
and on every staff is carved either an apple, a rose, a lily, an eagle,
or something of the kind ; for it is not allowable to wear a stick
without a device.

Many curious customs prevail amongst them.   This, in my
opinion, is the wisest, which I hear the Venetians, of Illyria, also
practise.   Once a year, in every village, whatever maidens are of
a marriageable age, they collect together and bring in a body to
one place ; around them gathers a crowd of men.   Then a crier
having made them stand up one by one, offers them for sale, beginning with the most beautiful ; and when she has been sold for
a large sum, he puts up another who is next in beauty.   They are
sold on condition that they shall be married.   Such men among
the Babylonians as are rich and desirous of marrying, bid against
one another, and purchase the handsomest.   But such of the lower
classes as are desirous of marrying, do not require a beautiful form,
but are willing to take the plainer damsels with a sum of money.
So when the crier has finished selling the handsomest of the maidens, he makes the ugliest stand up, or one that is a cripple, and
puts her up to auction, for the person who will marry her with the
smallest sum, until she is knocked down to the man who offers to
take the least.   This money is that obtained from the sale of the
handsome maidens ; so that the beautiful ones portion out the ugly
and the crippled.   A father is not allowed to give his daughter in
marriage to whom he pleases, nor can a purchaser carry off a

maiden without security ; but he is first obliged to give security that he will certainly marry her, and then he may take her away. If they do not agree, a law has been enacted that the money shall be repaid.   It is also lawful for any one who pleases to come from another village and purchase.   They have also this other custom, second only to the former in wisdom.   They bring their sick to the market-place, for they have no physicians ; then those who pass by the sick person confer with him about the disease, to discover whether they have themselves been afflicted with the same disease, or have seen others so afflicted.   They then advise him to have recourse to the same treatment as that by which they escaped a similar disease, or have known to cure others.   And no one passes by a sick person in silence, without inquiring into the nature of his distemper.   They embalm their dead in honey, and their funeral lamentations are like those of the Egyptians.

There are three tribes among them that eat nothing but fish ; these, when they have taken and dried them in the sun, they treat in the following manner : they put them into a mortar, and having pounded them with a pestle, sift them through a fine cloth ; then, whoever pleases, kneads them into a cake, or bakes them like bread.

When Cyrus had conquered this nation, he was anxious to reduce the Massagetæ to subjection.   This nation is said to be both powerful and valiant, dwelling toward the east and the rising sun beyond the river Araxes, over against the Issedonians ; there are some who say that this nation is Scythian.   The Araxes is reported by some persons to be greater, by others less, than the Ister ; they say that there are many islands in it, some nearly equal in size to Lesbos ; and that in them are men, who during the summer feed upon all manner of roots, which they dig out of the ground ; and that they store up for food ripe fruits which they find on the trees, and feed upon these during the winter.   They add, that they have discovered other trees that produce fruit of a peculiar kind, which the inhabitants, when they meet together in companies, and have lighted a fire, throw on it, as they sit around in a circle ; and that, inhaling the fumes of the burning fruit that has been thrown on, they become intoxicated by the odor, just as the Greeks do by wine; and that the more fruit is thrown on, the more intoxicated they become, until they rise up to dance and betake themselves to singing. The river Araxes flows from the Matienian mountains, whence also springs the river Gyndes, which Cyrus distributed into the three hundred and sixty trenches; and it gushes out from forty springs, all of which, except one, discharge themselves into fens and swamps, in which it is said men live who feed on raw fish, and clothe themselves in the skins of sea-calves; but the one stream of the Araxes flows through an unobstructed channel into the Caspian Sea. The Caspian is a sea by itself, having no communication with any other sea; for the whole of that which the Greeks navigate, and that beyond the Pillars, called the Atlantic, and the Red Sea, are all one. But the Caspian is a separate sea of itself; being in length a fifteen-days' voyage for a rowing boat; and in breadth, where it is widest, an eight-days' voyage. On the western shore of this sea stretches the Caucasus, which is in extent the largest, and in height the loftiest, of all mountains; it contains within itself many various nations of men, who for the most part live upon the produce of wild fruit-trees. In this country, it is said, there are trees which produce leaves of such a nature, that by rubbing them and mixing them with water the people paint figures on their garments; these figures do not wash out, but grow old with the wool, as if they had been woven in from the first. East of the Caspian is a plain in extent unbounded in the prospect. A great portion of this extensive plain is inhabited by the Massagetæ, against whom Cyrus resolved to make war; for the motives that urged and incited him to this enterprise were many and powerful: first of all his birth, which he thought was something more than human; and secondly, the good fortune which had attended him in his wars; for wherever Cyrus directed his arms, it was impossible for that nation to escape.

A woman whose husband was dead, was queen of the Massagetæ; her name was Tomyris; and Cyrus sent ambassadors under pretence of wooing her, and made her an offer of marriage.

But Tomyris, being aware that he was not wooing her, but the kingdom of the Massagetæ, forbade their approach. Upon this Cyrus, perceiving his artifice ineffectual, marched to the Araxes, and openly prepared to make war on the Massagetæ, by throwing bridges over the river, and building turrets on the boats which carried over his army. While he was employed in this work Tomyris sent a herald to him with this message : " King of the Medes, desist from your great exertions ; for you cannot know if they will terminate to your advantage ; and having desisted, reign over your own dominions, and bear to see me governing what is mine. But if you will not attend to my advice, and prefer every thing before peace ; in a word, if you are very anxious to make trial of the Massagetæ, toil no longer in throwing a bridge over the river ; but do you cross over to our side, while we retire three days' march from the river ; or if you had rather receive us on your side, do you the like." When Cyrus heard this proposal, he called a council of the principal Persians, laid the matter before them, and demanded their opinion as to what he should do : they unanimously advised him to let Tomyris pass with her army into his territory. But Crœsus the Lydian, who was present and disapproved this advice, delivered a contrary opinion to that which was put forward, and said : " O king, I assured you long ago, that since Jupiter delivered me into your hands, I would to the utmost of my power avert whatever misfortune I should see impending over your house ; and my own calamities,[1] sad as they are, have been lessons to me. If you think yourself immortal, and that you command an army that is so too, it is needless for me to make known to you my opinion. But if you know that you too are a man, and that you command such as are men, learn this first of all, that there is a wheel in human affairs, which, continually revolving, does not suffer the same persons to be always successful. My opinion touching the matter before us is wholly at variance with that already given. For if we shall receive the enemy into this country, there is danger that if you are defeated, you will lose, be-

---

[1] These words " pathemata mathemata " seem to have been a proverb in the Greek.

sides, your whole empire ; for it is plain that if the Massagetæ are victorious, they will not flee home again, but will march upon your territories : and if you are victorious, your victory is not so complete as if, having crossed over into their territory, you should conquer the Massagetæ and put them to flight ; for then you can march directly into the dominions of Tomyris. It is a disgrace too that Cyrus the son of Cambyses should give way and retreat before a woman. My opinion, therefore, is, that you should pass over and advance as far as they retire ; and then, by the following stratagem, endeavor to get the better of them. I hear the Massagetæ are unacquainted with the Persian luxuries, and are unused to the comforts of life. Suppose then that you cut up and dress an abundance of cattle, and lay out a feast in our camp for these men ; and besides, bowls of unmixed wine without stint; then leave the weakest part of your army behind, while the rest return again toward the river; for the Massagetæ, if I mistake not, when they see so much excellent fare, will turn to immediately, and after that there remains for us the display of mighty achievements."

Cyrus approved the suggestions of Crœsus and bade Tomyris retire, as he would cross over to her. She accordingly retired, as she had promised. Cyrus placed Crœsus in the hands of his son Cambyses, to whom he also intrusted the kingdom, and having strictly charged him to honor Crœsus, and treat him well in case his inroad on the Massagetæ should fail, sent them back to Persia and crossed the river with his army. When he had passed the Araxes, and night came on, he saw a vision, as he was sleeping in the country of the Massagetæ. He fancied that he saw the eldest son of Hystaspes with wings on his shoulders ; and that with one of these he overshadowed Asia, and with the other Europe. Now Darius, who was then about twenty years of age, was the eldest son of Hystaspes, son of Arsames, one of the Achæmenides ; and he had been left in Persia, for he had not yet attained the age of military service. When Cyrus awoke he considered his dream with attention ; and as it seemed to him of great moment, he summoned Hystaspes, and taking him aside, said :

" Hystaspes, your son has been detected plotting against me and my empire ; and I will show you how I know it for a certainty. The gods watch over me and forewarn me of every thing that is about to befall me.   Now, last night, as I was sleeping, I saw the eldest of your sons with wings on his shoulders, and with one of these he overshadowed Asia, and Europe with the other ; from this vision, it cannot be otherwise than that your son is forming designs against me ; do you therefore go back to Persia with all speed, and take care, that when I have conquered these people and return home, you bring your son before me to be examined." Cyrus spoke thus under a persuasion that Darius was plotting against him ; but the deity forewarned him that he himself would die in that very expedition, and that his kingdom would devolve on Darius. Hystaspes, however, answered in these words : " God forbid, O king, that a Persian should be born who would plot against you !   But if any such there be, may sudden destruction overtake him, for you have made the Persians free instead of being slaves, and instead of being ruled over by others to rule over all ; but if any vision informs you that my son is forming any plot against you, I freely surrender him to you to deal with as you please."   And Hystaspes repassed the Araxes and went to Persia, for the purpose of keeping his son Darius in custody for Cyrus.

Cyrus having advanced one day's march from the Araxes, proceeded to act according to the suggestion of Crœsus.   After this, when Cyrus and the effective part of the Persian army had marched back to the Araxes, leaving the ineffective part behind, a third division of the army of the Massagetæ attacked those of Cyrus' forces that had been left behind, and, after some resistance, put them to death.   Then, seeing the feast laid out, as soon as they had overcome their enemies they lay down and feasted ; and being filled with food and wine, fell asleep.   Then the Persians attacked them, and put many of them to death, and took a still greater number prisoners, among them the son of Queen Tomyris, who commanded the Massagetæ, and whose name was Spargapises. When she heard what had befallen her army and her son, she sent a herald to Cyrus with the following message : " Cyrus, insatiate with blood, be not elated with what has now happened, that by the fruit of the vine, with which ye yourselves, when filled with it, so rave, that when it descends into your bodies, evil words float on your lips ; be not elated, that by such a poison you have deceived and conquered my son, instead of by prowess in battle. But take the good advice that I offer you. Restore my son ; depart out of this country unpunished for having insolently disgraced a third division of the army of the Massagetæ. But if you will not do this, I swear by the sun, the Lord of the Massagetæ, that, insatiable as you are, I will glut you with blood." Cyrus, however, paid no attention to this message ; but Spargapises, the son of Queen

SEPULCHRAL VASES.

Tomyris, as soon as he recovered from the effects of the wine, and perceived in what a plight he was, begged of Cyrus that he might be freed from his fetters ; and as soon as he was set free, and found his hands at liberty, he put himself to death. But Tomyris, finding Cyrus did not listen to her, assembled all her forces, and engaged with him. I think that this battle was the most obstinate that was ever fought between barbarians. First of all, they stood at a distance and used their bows; afterward, when they had emptied their quivers, they engaged in close fight with their swords and spears, and thus they continued fighting for a long time, and neither was willing to give way ; but at length the Massagetæ got the better, and the greater part of the Persian army was cut in pieces on the spot, and Cyrus himself was killed, after he had reigned twenty-nine years. Tomyris filled a skin with human blood, sought for the body of Cyrus among the slain of the Persians, and, thrust the head into the skin, and insulting the dead body, said : " Thou hast indeed ruined me though alive and victorious in battle, since thou hast taken my son by stratagem ; but I will now glut thee with blood, as I threatened." Of the many accounts given of the end of Cyrus, this appears to me most worthy of credit.

The Massagetæ resemble the Scythians in their dress and mode of living ; they have both horse and foot bow-men, and javelin-men, who are accustomed to carry battle-axes : they use gold and bronze for every thing ; for in whatever concerns spears, and arrow-points, and battle-axes, they use bronze ; but the head, and belts, and shoulder-pieces, are ornamented with gold. In like manner with regard to the chest of horses, they put on breastplates of bronze ; but the bridle-bit and cheek-pieces are ornamented with gold. They make no use of silver or iron, for neither of those metals are found in their country, but they have bronze and gold in abundance. Their manners are as follows : when a man has attained a great age, all his kinsmen meet, and sacrifice him, together with cattle of several kinds ; and when they have boiled the flesh, they feast on it. This death they account the most happy ; but they do not eat the bodies of those who die of disease ; but bury them in the earth, and think it a great misfortune that they did not reach the age to be sacrificed. They sow nothing, but live on cattle, and fish which the river Araxes yields in abundance, and they are drinkers of milk. They worship the sun only of all the gods, and sacrifice horses to him ; and they assign as the reason of this custom that they think it right to offer the swiftest of all animals to the swiftest of all the gods.

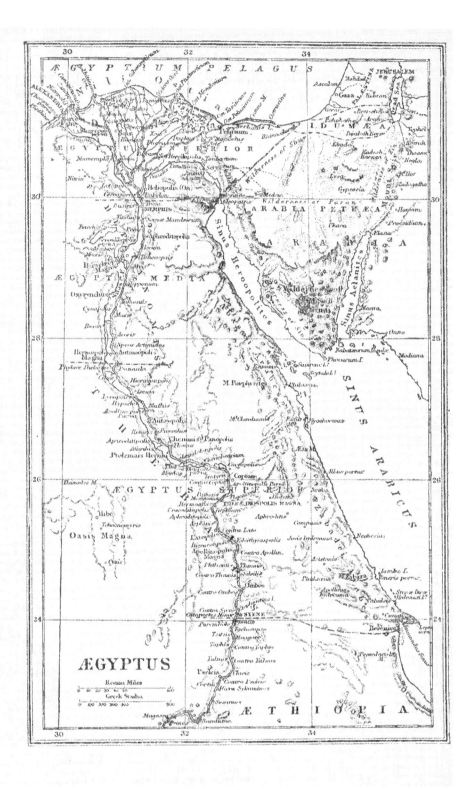

AEGYPTUS

Roman Miles

Greek Stadia

this same word was repeated to him whenever he went and tended the children, he at length acquainted his master, and by his command brought the children into his presence. When Psammitichus heard it he inquired what people call any thing by the name of "Becos"; and discovered that the Phrygians call bread by that name. So the Egyptians, convinced by the experiment, allowed that the Phrygians were more ancient than themselves. This relation I had from the priests of Vulcan at Memphis. But the Greeks tell many other foolish things, among them, that Psammitichus, having had the tongues of some women cut out, had the children brought up by them.

The Egyptians were the first to discover the year, which they divided into twelve parts, making this discovery from the stars; and so, I think, they act more wisely than the Greeks, who insert an intercalary month every third year, on account of the seasons; while the Egyptians, reckoning twelve months of thirty days each, add five days each year above that number, so that the circle of the seasons comes round to the same point. They say also, that the Egyptians were the first who introduced the names of the twelve gods, and that the Greeks borrowed those names from them; that they were the first to assign altars, images, and temples to the gods, and to carve the figures of animals on stone. They add that Menes was the first mortal who reigned over Egypt, and that in his time all Egypt, except the district of Thebes, was a morass, and that no part of the land that now exists below Lake Myris was then above water; to this place from the sea is a seven-days' passage up the river. It is evident to a man of common understanding, who sees it, that the part of Egypt which the Greeks frequent with their shipping, is land reclaimed by the Egyptians, and a gift from the river; for when you are at the distance of a day's sail from land, if you cast the lead you will bring up mud, yet find yourself in eleven fathoms of water; showing the immense alluvial deposit.

The length of Egypt along the sea-coast is sixty schœni (450 miles) from the Plinthinetic Bay to Lake Serbonis, near which

THE TWO GREAT PYRAMIDS AT THE TIME OF THE INUNDATION.

Mount Casius stretches. Men who are short of land measure their territory by fathoms; those who have some possessions, by stades; those who have much, by parasangs; and such as have a very great extent, by schœni. A parasang is equal to thirty stades, and each schœnus, which is an Egyptian measure, is equal to sixty stades. So the whole coast of Egypt is three thousand six hundred stades in length. As far as Heliopolis, inland, Egypt is wide, flat, without water, and a swamp. The distance to Heliopolis, as one goes up from the sea, is about equal in length to the road from Athens—that is to say, from the altar of the twelve gods,—to Pisa and the temple of Olympian Jupiter, or about fifteen hundred stades. From Heliopolis upward Egypt is narrow, for on one side the table-land of Arabia extends from north to south and southwest, stretching up continuously to that which is called the Red Sea. In this plateau are the stone quarries which were cut for the pyramids at Memphis. Where its length is the greatest, I have heard that it is a two-months' journey from east to west; and that eastward its confines produce frankincense. On that side of Egypt which borders upon Libya extends another rocky table-land covered with sand, on which the pyramids stand, stretching in the same direction as that part of the Arabian mountain that runs southward.

The greater part of all this country, as the priests informed me, has been reclaimed by the Egyptians from the sea and the marshes. For the space beyond the city of Memphis seems to me to have been formerly a bay of the sea; as is the case also with the parts about Ilium, Teuthrania, Ephesus, and the plain of the Mæander, if I may be permitted to compare small things with great. There are other rivers not equal in size to the Nile, which have wrought great works; amongst them one of the most remarkable is the Achelous, which, flowing through Acarnania, and falling into the sea, has already converted one half of the Echinades islands into a continent. There is in the Arabian territory, not far from Egypt, branching from the Red Sea, a bay of the sea of such a length that the voyage, from the innermost part of this bay to the broad sea, occupies forty days for a vessel with oars; but the width, where the bay is widest, only half a day's passage, and in it an ebb and flow takes place daily ; and I am of opinion that Egypt was formerly a similar bay ; this stretching from the Northern Sea toward Ethiopia ; and the Arabian Bay, which I am describing, from the south toward Syria ; and that they almost perforated their recesses so as to meet each other, overlapping to some small extent. Now, if the Nile were to turn its stream into this Arabian gulf, what could hinder it from being filled with soil by the river within twenty thousand years?—for my part, I think it would be filled within ten thousand. How, then, in the time that has elapsed before I was born, might not even a much greater bay than this have been filled up by such a great and powerful river ? I therefore give credit to those who relate these things concerning Egypt, when I see that Egypt projects beyond the adjoining land ; that shells are found on the mountains ; that a saline humor forms on the surface so as even to corrode the pyramids ; and that this mountain which is above Memphis is the only one in Egypt that abounds in sand : add to which, that Egypt, in its soil, is neither like Arabia or its confines, nor Libya, nor Syria, but is black and crumbling, as if it were mud and alluvial deposit, brought down by the river from Ethiopia ; whereas we know that the earth of Libya is reddish, and somewhat more sandy ; and that of Arabia and Syria is clayey and flinty.

The priests relate that in the reign of Mœris, when the river rose at least eight cubits, it irrigated all Egypt below Memphis ; and yet Mœris had not been nine hundred years dead when I received this information. But now, unless the river rises sixteen cubits, or fifteen at least, it does not overflow the country. It appears to me, therefore, that if the soil continues to grow in height, in the same proportion, those Egyptians below Lake Mœris, who inhabit other districts than that which is called Delta, must, by reason of the Nile not overflowing their land, for ever suffer the same calamity which they used to say the Greeks would suffer from. For hearing that all the lands of Greece were watered by rain, and not by rivers, as their own was, they said " that the Greeks at

some time or other would suffer miserably from famine." But
let me state how the matter stands with the Egyptians themselves :
if, as I said before, the land below Memphis should continue to increase in height in the same proportion as it has done in time past,
what else will happen but that the Egyptians who inhabit this part
will starve, if their land shall neither be watered by rain, nor the
river be able to inundate the fields ?   Now, indeed, they gather in
the fruits of the earth with less labor than any other people, for
they have not the toil of breaking up the furrows with the plough,
nor of hoeing, nor of any other work which all other men must
labor at to obtain a crop of corn ; but when the river has come of
its own accord and irrigated their fields, and again subsided, then
each man sows his own land and turns swine into it ; and when
the seed has been trodden in by the swine, he waits for harvest-
time ; then he treads out the corn with his swine, and gathers it in.

All Egypt, beginning from the cataracts and the city of Elephantine, is divided into two parts, and partakes of both names ;
one belongs to Libya, and the other to Asia.   The Nile, beginning
from the cataracts, flows to the sea, dividing Egypt in the middle.
Now, as far as the city of Cercasorus, the Nile flows in one stream ;
but from that point it is divided into three channels.   That which
runs eastward is called the Pelusiac mouth ; another of the channels
bends westward, and is called the Canopic mouth ; but the direct
channel of the Nile is the following : descending from above, it
comes to the point of the Delta, where it divides the Delta in the
middle, and discharges itself into the sea, supplying by this channel,
not by any means the least quantity of water, nor the least renowned ;
this is called the Sebennytic mouth.   There are also two other
mouths, that diverge from the Sebennytic and flow into the
sea,—the Saitic, and the Mendesian.   The Bolbitine and Bucolic
mouths are not natural, but artificial.   The Nile, when full, inundates not only Delta, but also part of the country said to belong to
Libya and Arabia, to the extent of about two days' journey on
each side.

At the summer solstice it fills and overflows for a hundred days ;

then falls short in its stream, and retires; so that it continues low all the winter, until the return of the summer solstice. In parts of Ethiopia, out of which the Nile flows, the inhabitants become black from the excessive heat; kites and swallows continue there all the year; and the cranes, to avoid the cold of Scythia, migrate to these parts as winter-quarters.

With respect to the sources of the Nile, no man of all the Egyptians, Libyans, or Greeks with whom I have conversed, ever pretended to know any thing; except the registrar of Minerva's treasury at Sais in Egypt. But even he seemed to be trifling with me, when he said he knew perfectly well. His account was: "That there are two mountains rising into a sharp peak, situated

NILE BOAT.

between the cities of Syene and Elephantine; the names of these mountains are Crophi and Mophi. The sources of the Nile, which are bottomless, flow from between these mountains, and half of the water flows north over Egypt, and the other half to the south-ward over Ethiopia. That the fountains of the Nile are bottom-less, he said, Psammitichus, king of Egypt, proved by experiment; for he twisted a line many thousand fathoms in length and let it down, but could not find a bottom." In my opinion, this simply proves that there are strong whirlpools and an eddy here; so that the water beating against the rocks, a sounding-line, when let down, cannot reach the bottom. As you ascend the river above the city of Elephantine, the country is so steep that it is necessary to attach a rope on both sides of a boat as you do with an ox in a plough, and so proceed; but if the rope should happen to break, the boat is carried away by the force of the stream. This kind of country lasts for a four-days' passage (or eighty miles), and the Nile here winds as much as the Mæander. After that you come to a level plain, where the Nile flows round an island named Tachompso. Ethiopians inhabit the country immediately above Elephantine, and one half of the island ; the other half is inhabited by Egyptians. Near to this island lies a vast lake, on the borders of which Ethiopian nomads dwell ; after sailing through this lake, you come to the channel of the Nile, which flows into it : then you have to land and travel forty days by the side of the river, for sharp rocks rise in the Nile, and there are many sunken ones, through which it is not possible to navigate a boat ; you then must go on board another boat, and sail for twelve days ; and will at last arrive at a large city called Meroe : this city is said to be the capital of all Ethiopia. The inhabitants worship no other gods than Jupiter and Bacchus ; but these they honor with great magnificence ; they have also an oracle of Jupiter ; and they make war, whenever that god bids them by an oracular warning, and against whatever country he bids them. Sailing from this city, you will arrive at the country of the Automoli, in a space of time equal to that which you took in coming from Elephantine to the capital of the Ethiopians. These Automoli are called by the name of Asmak, which in the language of Greece signifies, "those that stand at the left hand of the king." These, to the number of two hundred and forty thousand of the Egyptian war-tribe, once revolted to the Ethiopians, whose king made them the following recompense. There were certain Ethiopians disaffected toward him ; he bade them expel these, and take possession of their land ; by the settlement of these men among them, the Ethiopians became more civilized, and learned the manners of the Egyptians.

CHAPTER II.

EGYPT possesses more wonders than any other country, and exhibits works greater than can be described, in comparison with all
other regions ; therefore more must be said about it. The Egyptians besides having a peculiar climate and a river differing in
its nature from all other rivers, have adopted customs and usages
in almost every respect different from the rest of mankind.
Amongst them the women attend markets and traffic, but the men
stay at home and weave. Other nations, in weaving, throw
the wool upward ; the Egyptians, downward. The men carry
burdens on their heads ; the women, on their shoulders. No
woman can serve the office for any god or goddess ; but men are
employed for both offices. Sons are not compelled to support
their parents unless they choose, but daughters are compelled
to do so, whether they choose or not. In other countries the
priests of the gods wear long hair ; in Egypt they have it shaved.
With other men it is customary in mourning for the nearest relations to have their heads shorn ; the Egyptians, on occasions
of death, let the hair grow both on the head and face, though till
then shaven. Other men feed on wheat and barley, but it is
a very great disgrace for an Egyptian to make food of them ; but
they make bread from spelt, which some call zea. They knead the
dough with their feet ; but mix clay with their hands. Every
man wears two garments ; the women, but one. Other men
fasten the rings and sheets of their sails outside ; but the Egyptians, inside. The Greeks write and cipher, moving the hand from
left to right ; but the Egyptians, from right to left : and doing

so, they say they do it right-ways, and the Greeks left-ways. They have two sorts of letters, one of which is called sacred, the other common.

They are of all men the most excessively attentive to the worship of the gods, and observe the following ceremonies: They drink from cups of bronze, which they scour every day. They wear linen garments, constantly fresh-washed, thinking it better to be clean than handsome. The priests shave their whole body every third day, that no impurity may be found upon them when engaged in the service of the gods. The priests wear linen only, and shoes of byblus, and are not permitted to wear any other garments, or other shoes. They wash themselves in cold water twice every day and twice every night, and use a great number of ceremonies. On the other hand, they enjoy no slight advantages, for they do not consume or expend any of their private property; but sacred food is cooked for them, and a great quantity of beef and geese is allowed each of them every day, with wine from the grape; but they must not taste of fish. Beans the Egyptians do not sow at all in their country, nor do they eat those that happen to grow there. The priests abhor the sight of that pulse, accounting it impure. The service of each god is performed, not by one, but by many priests, of whom one is chief; and, when one of them dies, his son is put in his place. The male kine they deem sacred to Epaphus, and to that end prove them in the following manner: If the examiner finds one black hair upon him, he adjudges him to be unclean; one of the priests appointed for this purpose makes this examination, both when the animal is standing up and lying down; and he draws out the tongue, to see if it is pure as to the prescribed marks, which I shall mention in another part of my history. He also looks at the hairs of his tail, to see whether they grow naturally. If the beast is found pure in all these respects, he marks it by rolling a piece of byblus round the horns, and then having put on it some sealing earth, he impresses it with his signet; and so they drive him away. Any one who sacrifices one that is unmarked is punished with death. The established mode of sacrifice is this : they lead the victim, properly marked, to the altar where they intend to sacrifice, and kindle a fire ; then having poured wine upon the altar, near the victim, they invoke the god, and kill it ; then cut off the head, and flay the body of the animal. Having pronounced many imprecations on the head, they who have a market and Greek merchants dwelling amongst them, carry it there and sell it ; but those who have no Greeks amongst them throw it into the river ; and they pronounce the following imprecations on the head : " If any evil is about to befall either those that now sacrifice, or Egypt in general, may it be averted on this head." But a different mode of disembowelling and burning the victims prevails in different sacrifices. The practice with regard to the goddess whom they consider the greatest, and in whose honor they celebrate the most magnificent festival, is this : When they have flayed the bullocks, having first offered up prayers, they take out all the intestines, and leave the vitals with the fat in the carcass : they then cut off the legs and the extremity of the hip, with the shoulders and neck, and fill the body of the bullock with fine bread, honey, raisins, figs, frankincense, myrrh, and other perfumes, and burn it, pouring on it a great quantity of oil. They sacrifice after they have fasted ; and while the sacred things are being burnt, they all beat themselves ; after which they spread a banquet of what remains of the victims.

All the Egyptians sacrifice the pure male kine and calves, but they are not allowed to sacrifice the females, for they are sacred to Isis ; the image of Isis is made in the form of a woman with the horns of a cow, as the Greeks represent Io ; and all Egyptians alike pay a far greater reverence to cows than to any other cattle. No Egyptian man or woman will kiss a Greek on the mouth ; or use the knife, spit, or cauldron of a Greek, or taste of the flesh of a pure ox that has been divided by a Greek knife. They bury the kine that die in the following manner : The females they throw into the river, and the males they inter in the suburbs, with one horn, or both, appearing above the

ground, for a mark.   When it is putrified, and the appointed time
arrives, a raft comes to each city from the island called Prosopitis,
in the Delta, which is nine schœni in circumference.   Now in this
island Prosopitis there are several cities ; but that from which the
rafts come to take away the bones of the oxen, is called Atar-
bechis ; in it a temple of Venus has been erected.   From this city
then many persons go about to other towns ; and having dug up
the bones, carry them away, and bury them in one place ; and
they bury all other cattle that die in the same way that they do
the oxen ; for they do not kill any of them.   All those who have
a temple erected to Theban Jupiter, or belong to the Theban district, abstain from sheep, and sacrifice goats only.   For the Egyptians do not all worship the same gods in the same manner, except
Isis and Osiris, who, they say, is Bacchus.   On the other hand,
those who frequent the temple of Mendes, and belong to the Mendesian district, abstain from goats, and sacrifice sheep.   The
Thebans say that this custom was established among them in the
following way : that Hercules was very desirous of seeing Jupiter,
but Jupiter was unwilling to be seen by him ; at last, however, as
Hercules persisted, Jupiter flayed a ram, cut off the head, and held
it before himself, and then having put on the fleece, showed himself to Hercules.   From this circumstance the Egyptians make
the image of Jupiter with a ram's face ; and the Ammonians, who
are a colony of Egyptians and Ethiopians, and who speak a language between both, have adopted the same practice ; and, as I
conjecture, the Ammonians thus derived their name, for the Egyptians call Jupiter, Ammon.   The Thebans then do not sacrifice
rams, being for this reason accounted sacred by them ; on one day
in the year, however, at the festival of Jupiter, they kill and flay
one ram, put it on this image of Jupiter, and bring an image of
Hercules to it ; then all who are in the temple beat themselves in
mourning for the ram, and bury him in a sacred vault.

Of this Hercules I have heard that he is one of the twelve
gods ; but of the other Hercules, who is known to the Greeks, I
could never hear in any part of Egypt.   That the Egyptians did

not derive the name of Hercules from the Greeks, but rather the Greeks from the Egyptians, I have many proofs to show. The parents of this Hercules, Amphitryon and Alcmene, were both of Egyptian descent, and the Egyptians say they do not know the names of Neptune and the Dioscuri, yet if they had derived the name of any deity from the Greeks, they would certainly have mentioned these above all others, since even at that time they made voyages, and some of the Greeks were sailors. But Hercules is one of the ancient gods of the Egyptians; and they say themselves it was seventeen thousand years before the reign of Amasis, when the number of their gods was increased from eight to twelve, of whom Hercules was accounted one. Being desirous of obtaining certain information from whatever source I could, I sailed to Tyre in Phœnicia, having heard that there was there a temple dedicated to Hercules; and I saw it richly adorned with a great variety of offerings, and in it were two pillars, one of fine gold, the other of emerald stone, both shining exceedingly at night. Conversing with the priests of this god, I inquired how long this temple had been built, and I found that they did not agree with the Greeks. For they said that the temple was built at the time when Tyre was founded, and that two thousand three hundred years had elapsed since the foundation of Tyre. In this city I also saw another temple dedicated to Hercules by the name of Thasian; I went therefore to Thasos, and found there a temple of Hercules built by the Phœnicians, who founded Thasos, when they sailed in search of Europa, and this occurred five generations before Hercules the son of Amphitryon appeared in Greece. The researches then that I have made evidently prove that Hercules is a god of great antiquity, and therefore those Greeks appear to me to have acted most correctly, who have built two kinds of temples sacred to Hercules, and who sacrifice to one as an immortal, under the name of Olympian, and paid honor to the other as a hero. The Mendesians pay reverence to all goats; at the death of a he-goat public mourning is observed throughout the whole Mendesian district.

The Egyptians consider the pig to be an impure beast, and therefore if a man in passing by a pig should touch him only with his garments, he forthwith goes to the river and plunges in ; and in the next place, swineherds, although native Egyptians, are the only men who are not allowed to enter any of their temples ; neither will any man give his daughter in marriage to one of them, nor take a wife from among them; but the swineherds intermarry among themselves. The Egyptians do not think it right to sacrifice swine to any deities but the moon and Bacchus. In this sacrifice of pigs to the moon, when the sacrificer has slain the victim, he puts together the tip of the tail, with the spleen and the caul, covers them with the fat found about the belly of the animal, and consumes them with fire : the rest of the flesh they eat during the full moon in which they offer the sacrifices ; but on no other day would any one even taste it. The poor amongst them, through want of means, form pigs of dough, and having baked them, offer them in sacrifice.

Whence each of the gods sprung, whether they existed always, and of what form they were, was, so to speak, unknown till yesterday. For I am of opinion that Hesiod and Homer lived four hundred years before my time, and not more, and these were they who framed a theogony for the Greeks, and gave names to the gods, and assigned to them honors and arts, and declared their several forms.

The Egyptians were also the first who introduced public festivals, processions, and solemn supplications ; and the Greeks learned these from them. The Egyptians hold public festivals several times in a year ; that which is best and most rigidly observed is in the city of Bubastis, in honor of Diana ; the second, in the city of Busiris, is in honor of Isis ; the largest temple of Isis is in this city, in the middle of the Egyptian Delta. Isis is in the Grecian language called Demeter. The third festival is held at Sais, in honor of Minerva ; the fourth, at Heliopolis, in honor of the sun ; the fifth, at the city of Buto, in honor of Latona ; the sixth, at the city of Papremis, in honor of Mars. When they are assembled at the sacrifice, in the city of Sais, they all on a certain night kindle a great number of lamps in the open air, around their houses ; the lamps are flat vessels filled with salt and oil, the wick floats on the surface and burns all night ; hence the festival is named " the lighting of lamps." The Egyptians who do not come to this public assembly observe the rite of sacrifice, and all kindle lamps, not only in Sais, but throughout all Egypt.

Egypt, though bordering on Libya, does not abound in wild beasts ; but all that they have are accounted sacred. Superintendents, consisting both of men and women, are appointed to feed every kind separately ; and the son succeeds the father in this office. All the inhabitants of the cities perform their vows to the superintendents. Having made a vow to the god to whom the animal belongs, they shave either the whole heads of their children, or a half, or a third part of the head, and then weigh the hair in a scale against silver, and whatever the weight may be, they give to the superintendent of the animals ; she in return cuts up some fish, and gives it as food to the animals ; such is the usual mode of feeding them. Should any one kill one of these beasts, if wilfully, death is the punishment ; if by accident, he pays such fine as the priests choose to impose. But whoever kills an ibis or a hawk, whether wilfully or by accident, must necessarily be put to death. When a conflagration takes place, a supernatural impulse seizes on the cats. The Egyptians, standing at a distance, take care of the cats, and neglect to put out the fire ; but the cats often make their escape, leap over the men, and throw themselves into the fire ; when this happens great lamentations are made among the Egyptians. In whatever house a cat dies of a natural death, all the family shave their eyebrows ; but if a dog die, they shave the whole body and the head. All cats that die are carried to certain sacred houses, where they are first embalmed, and then buried in the city of Bubastis. All persons bury their dogs in sacred vaults within their own city ; and ichneumons are buried in the same manner as the dogs ; but field-mice and hawks they carry to the city of Buto ; the ibis to Hermopolis ; the bears, which are few in number, and

the wolves, which are not much larger than foxes, they bury
wherever they are found lying.

This is the nature of the crocodile :—During the four coldest
months it eats nothing, and though it has four feet, it is amphibi-
ous.   It lays its eggs on land, and there hatches them.   It spends
the greater part of the day on the dry ground, but the whole
night in the river ; for the water is then warmer than the air and
dew.   Of all living things with which we are acquainted, this, from
the least beginning, grows to be the largest.   For it lays eggs little
larger than those of a goose, and the young is at first in proportion
to the egg ; but when grown up it reaches to the length of seventeen cubits (25½ feet), and even more.   It has the eyes of a
pig, large teeth, and projecting tusks : it is the only animal that
has no tongue ; it does not move the lower jaw, but is the only

THE TROCHILUS.

animal that brings down its upper jaw to the under one.   It has
strong claws, and a skin covered with scales, that cannot be broken
on the back.   It is blind in the water, but very quick-sighted on
land ; and because it lives for the most part in the water,
its mouth is filled with leeches.   All other birds and beasts
avoid him, but he is at peace with the trochilus, because he
receives benefit from that bird.   For when the crocodile gets out
of the water on land, and then opens its jaws, which it does most
commonly toward the west, the trochilus enters its mouth and
swallows the leeches : the crocodile is so well pleased with this
service that it never hurts the trochilus.   With some of the Egyptians crocodiles are sacred ; with others not, but they treat them as
enemies.   Those who dwell about Thebes, and Lake Mœris con-

sider them to be very sacred ; and they each of them train up a
crocodile, which is taught to be quite tame ; and put crystal and
gold ear-rings into their ears, and bracelets on their fore paws ;
they give them appointed and sacred food, and treat them as well
as possible while alive, and when dead they embalm them, and
bury them in sacred vaults. But the people who dwell about the
city of Elephantine eat them, not considering them sacred. They
are not called crocodiles by the Egyptians, but " champsæ " ; the
Ionians gave them the name of crocodiles, because they thought
they resembled lizards, which are also so called, and which are
found in the hedges of their country. The modes of taking the
crocodile are many and various, but I shall only describe that

SPEARING THE CROCODILE.

which seems to me most worthy of relation. When the fisherman
has baited a hook with the chine of a pig, he lets it down into the
middle of the river, and holding a young live pig on the brink of
the river, beats it ; the crocodile, hearing the noise, goes in its
direction, and meeting with the chine, swallows it, and the men
draw it to land ; when it is drawn out on shore, the sportsman first
of all plasters its eyes with mud, after which he manages it very
easily ; but until he has done this, he has a great deal of trouble.
The hippopotamus is esteemed sacred in the district of Papremis, but
not so by the rest of the Egyptians. It is a quadruped, cloven-
footed, with the hoofs of an ox, snub-nosed, has the mane of a
horse, projecting tusks, and the tail and neigh of a horse. In size

he is equal to a very large ox : his hide is so thick that spear-handles are made of it when dry. Otters are also met with in the river, which are deemed sacred ; and amongst fish, they consider that which is called the lepidotus, and the eel, sacred ; these they say are sacred to the Nile ; and among birds, the vulpanser.

There is also another sacred bird, called the phœnix, which I have never seen except in a picture ; for it makes its appearance amongst them only once in five hundred years, as the Heliopolitans affirm : they say that it comes on the death of its sire. If he is like the picture, he is of the following size and description : the plumage of his wings is partly golden-colored, and partly red ; in outline and size he is like an eagle. They tell this incredible story about him :—They say that he comes from Arabia, and brings the body of his father, enclosed in myrrh, to the temple of the sun, and there buries him in the temple. He brings him in this manner : first he moulds an egg of myrrh as large as he thinks himself able to carry ; then he tries to carry it, and when he has made the experiment, he hollows out the egg, puts his parent into it, and stops up with some more myrrh the hole through which he introduced the body, so when his father is put inside, the weight is the same as before ; then he carries him to the temple of the sun in Egypt.

In the neighborhood of Thebes there are sacred serpents not at all hurtful to men : they are diminutive in size, and carry two horns that grow on the top of the head. When these serpents die they bury them in the temple of Jupiter, for they say they are sacred to that God. There is a place in Arabia, situated very near the city of Buto, to which I went, on hearing of some winged serpents ; there I saw bones and spines of serpents in such quantities as it would be impossible to describe : there were heaps upon heaps, some large, some smaller, scattered in a narrow pass between two mountains, which leads into a spacious plain, contiguous to the plain of Egypt : it is reported that at the beginning of spring, winged serpents fly from Arabia toward Egypt ; but that ibises, a sort of bird, meet them at the pass, and do not allow the serpents to go by, but kill them : for this service the Arabians say that the ibis is highly reverenced by the Egyptians; and the Egyptians acknowledge it. The ibis is all over a deep black; it has the legs of a crane, its beak is much curved, and it is about the size of the crex. Such is the form of the black ones, that fight with the serpents. But those that are best known, for there are two species, are bare on the head and the whole neck, have white plumage, except on the head, the throat, and the tips of the wings and extremity of the tail; in all these parts they are of a deep black; in their legs and beak they are like the other kind. The form of the serpent is like that of the water-snake; but he has wings without feathers, and as like as possible to the wings of a bat. This must suffice for the description of sacred animals.

Of the Egyptians, those who inhabit that part of Egypt which is sown with corn, cultivate the memory of past events more than any other people, and are the best-informed men I ever met. Their manner of life is this: They purge themselves every month for three days successively, seeking to preserve health by emetics and clysters, for they suppose that all diseases to which men are subject proceed from the food they use. And indeed in other respects the Egyptians, next to the Libyans, are the most healthy people in the world, as I think, on account of the seasons, because they are not liable to change; for men are most subject to disease at periods of change, and above all others at the change of the seasons. They feed on bread made into loaves of spelt, which they call cyllestis; and they use wine made of barley, for they have no vines in that country. Some fish they dry in the sun and eat raw, others salted with brine; and of birds they eat quail, ducks, and smaller birds raw, salting them first. All other things, whether birds or fishes, that they have, except such as are accounted sacred, they eat either roasted or boiled. At their convivial banquets, among the wealthy classes, when they have finished supper, a man carries round in a coffin the image of a dead body carved in wood, made as perfect a counterfeit as possible in color and workmanship, and in size generally about one or two cubits in length; and showing this to each of the company, he says: " Look upon this, then drink and enjoy yourself; for when dead you will be like this."

They observe their ancient customs and acquire no new ones. Among other memorable customs they have just one song called " Linus," which is sung in Phœnicia, Cyprus, and elsewhere ; in different nations it bears a different name, but it agrees almost exactly with the same which the Greeks sing, under the name of Linus.   So that among the many wonderful things in Egypt, the greatest wonder of all is where they got this Linus ; for they seem to have sung it from time immemorial.   The " Linus " in the Egyptian language is called Maneros ; and the Egyptians say that he was the only son of the first king of Egypt, and that happening to die prematurely, he was honored by the Egyptians in this mourning dirge, the first and only song they have.   In the following particular the Egyptians resemble the Lacedæmonians only among all the Greeks : the young men, when they meet their elders, give way and turn aside ; and rise from their seats when they approach. But, unlike any nation of the Greeks, instead of addressing one another in the streets, they salute by letting the hand fall down as far as the knee.   They wear linen tunics fringed round the legs, which they call calasiris, and over these they throw white woollen mantles ; woollen clothes, however, are not carried into the temples, nor are they buried with them, as this is accounted profane— agreeing in this respect with the worshippers of Orpheus and Bacchus, who are Egyptians and Pythagoreans : for they consider it profane for one who is initiated in these mysteries to be buried in woollen garments for some religious reason or other.   The Egyptians have discovered more prodigies than all the rest of the world. They have amongst them oracles of Hercules, Apollo, Minerva, Diana, Mars, and Jupiter ; but that which they honor above all others is the oracle of Latona in the city of Buto.   The art of medicine is divided amongst them into specialties, each physician applying himself to one disease only.   All places abound in physicians, some for the eyes, others for the head, others for the teeth, others for cutaneous diseases, and others still for internal disorders.

Their manner of mourning and burying is as follows : When a man of any consideration dies, all the women of that family be-smear their heads and faces with mud, leave the body in the house, and wander about the city, beating themselves, having their clothes girt up, their neck and breast exposed, and all their relations accompany them. The men, too, beat themselves in the same way. When they have done this, they carry out the body to be embalmed. There are persons who are specially appointed for this purpose ; when the dead body is brought to them, they show to the bearers wooden models of corpses, skilfully painted to illustrate the various methods of embalming. They first show the most expensive man-ner of embalming ; then the second, which is inferior and less ex-pensive ; and lastly, the third and cheapest. The relations stipu-late which style they prefer, agree on the price, and depart. To embalm a body in the most expensive manner, they first draw out the brains through the nostrils with an iron hook, perfecting the operation by the infusion of drugs. Then with a sharp Ethiopian stone they make an incision in the side, and take out all the bowels ; and having cleansed the abdomen and rinsed it with palm-wine, they next sprinkle it with pounded perfumes. Then they fill the belly with pure myrrh pounded, and cassia, and other per-fumes, frankincense excepted, and sew it up again ; this done, they steep it in natrum, leaving it under for seventy days ; a longer time than which it is not lawful to steep it. At the expiration of the seventy days they wash the corpse, and wrap the whole body in bandages of flaxen cloth, smearing it with gum, which the Egyp-tians commonly use instead of glue. After this the relations take the body back again, make a wooden case in the shape of a man, enclose the body in it, and store it in a sepulchral chamber, setting it upright against the wall. For those who, to avoid great expense, desire the middle way, they prepare in the following manner. Charging syringes with oil made from cedar, they fill the abdomen of the corpse without making any incision or taking out the bowels, but inject it at the fundament ; and having prevented the injection from escaping, they steep the body in natrum for the prescribed

number of days, on the last of which they let out from the abdomen
the oil of cedar which has such power that it brings away the intestines and vitals in a state of dissolution ; the natrum dissolves
the flesh, and nothing of the body remains but the skin and the
bones. The operation is then complete. The third method of
embalming, which is used only for the poorer sort, consists in
thoroughly rinsing the abdomen in syrmæa, and steeping it with
natrum for the seventy days. Should any person, whether Egyptian or stranger, be found to have been seized by a crocodile, or
drowned in the river, to whatever city the body may be carried,
the inhabitants are by law compelled to have the body embalmed,
and adorned in the handsomest manner, and buried in the sacred
vaults. Nor is it lawful for any one else, whether relations or
friends, to touch him ; but the priests of the Nile bury the corpse
with their own hands, as being something more than human.

They avoid using Grecian customs ; and, in a word, the customs
of all other people whatsoever.

The Egyptians who dwell in the morasses, have the same
customs as the rest of the Egyptians, and each man has
but one wife, like the Greeks. But to obtain food more
easily, they have the following inventions : when the river is
full, and has made the plains like a sea, great numbers of lilies,
which the Egyptians call lotus, spring up in the water : these they
gather and dry in the sun ; then having pounded the middle of
the lotus, which resembles a poppy, they make bread of it and
bake it. The root also of this lotus is fit for food, and is tolerably
sweet ; it is round, and of the size of an apple. There are also
other lilies, like roses, that grow in the river, the fruit of which is
contained in a separate pod, that springs up from the root in form
very much like a wasp's nest ; in this there are many berries fit to
be eaten, of the size of an olive stone, and they are eaten both fresh
and dried. The byblus, an annual plant, is found in the fens. They
cut off the top and put it to some other uses, but the lower part
that is left, to the length of a cubit, they eat and sell. Those who
are anxious to eat the byblus dressed in the most delicate manner,
stew it in a hot pan and then eat it.

The Egyptians who live about the fens use an oil drawn from the fruit of the sillicypria, which they call cici : they plant and cultivate these sillicypria, which in Greece grow spontaneous and wild, on the banks of the rivers and lakes : under cultivation these bear an abundance of fruit, though of an offensive smell. Some bruise it and press out the oil ; others boil and stew it, and collect the liquid that flows from it ; this is fat, and no less suited for lamps than olive oil ; but it emits a disgusting smell. They contrive in various ways to protect themselves from the mosquitoes, which are very abundant. Towers are of great service to those who inhabit the upper parts of the marshes ; for the mosquitoes are prevented by the winds from flying high : but those who live round the marshes have contrived another expedient. Every man has a net, with which in the daytime he takes fish, and at night, in whatever bed he sleeps, he throws the net around it, and crawls in underneath ; if he should wrap himself up in his clothes or in linen, the mosquitoes would bite through them, but they never attempt to bite through the net.

Their ships in which they convey merchandise are made of the acacia, which in shape is much like the Cyrenæan lotus, and exudes a gum. From this acacia they cut planks about two cubits in length and join them together like bricks, building their ships in the following manner : They fasten the planks of two cubits length round stout and long ties : when they have thus built the hulls, they lay benches across them. They make no use of ribs, but caulk the seams inside with byblus. They make only one rudder, and that is driven through the keel. They use a mast of acacia, and sails of byblus. These vessels are unable to sail up the stream unless a fair wind prevails, but are towed from the shore. They are thus carried down the stream : there is a hurdle made of tamarisk, wattled with a band of reeds, and a stone with a hole in the middle, of about two talents in weight ; of these two, the hurdle is fastened to a cable, and let down at the prow of the vessel to be carried on by the stream ; and the stone by another cable at the stern ; and by this means the hurdle, by the stream bearing hard upon it, moves quickly and draws along " the baris " (for this is the name given to these vessels), but the stone being dragged at the stern, and sunk to the bottom, keeps the vessel in its course. They have very many of these vessels, and some of them carry many thousand talents. When the Nile inundates the country, the cities alone are seen above its surface, like the islands dotting the Ægean Sea. When this happens, they navigate no longer by the channel of the river, but straight across the country.

CHAPTER III.

GOD-KINGS PRIOR TO MENES.

In former time, the priests of Jupiter did to Hecatæus the historian, when he was tracing his own genealogy, and connecting his family with a god in the sixteenth degree, the same as they did to me, though I did not endeavor to trace my genealogy. Conducting me into the interior of a spacious edifice, and showing me four hundred and forty-five wooden colossuses, they counted them over; for every high-priest places an image of himself there during his lifetime; the priests pointed out that the succession from father to son was unbroken. But when Hecatæus traced his own genealogy, and connected himself with a god in the sixteenth degree, they controverted his genealogy by computation, not admitting that a man could be born from a god; and said that each of the colossuses was a Piromis, sprung from a Piromis; until they pointed out the three hundred and forty-five colossuses, each a Piromis, sprung from a Piromis, and they did not connect them with any god or hero. Piromis means, in the Grecian language, "a noble and good man." They said that these were very far from being gods; but before the time of these men, gods had been the rulers of Egypt, and had dwelt amongst men; and that one of them always had the supreme power, and that Orus, the son of Osiris, was the last who reigned over it. Now, Osiris in the Greek language means Bacchus, and Orus is the equivalent of Apollo.

All the revenue from the city of Anthylla, which is of much importance, is assigned to purchase shoes for the wife of the reigning king of Egypt.

CHAPTER IV.

FIRST LINE OF 330 KINGS, ONLY THREE MENTIONED.

THE priests informed me, that Menes, who first ruled over Egypt, in the first place protected Memphis by a mound; for the whole river formerly ran close to the sandy mountain on the side of Libya; but Menes, beginning about a hundred stades above Memphis, filled in the elbow toward the south, dried up the old channel, and conducted the river into a canal, so as to make it flow between the mountains. This bend of the Nile is still carefully upheld by the Persians, and made secure every year; for if the river should break through and overflow in this part, there would be danger lest all Memphis should be flooded. When the part cut off had been made firm land by this Menes, who was first king, he built on it the city that is now called Memphis; and outside of it he excavated a lake from the river toward the north and the west; for the Nile itself bounds it toward the east. In the next place, they relate that he built in it the temple of Vulcan, which is vast and well worthy of mention. After this the priests enumerated from a book the names of three hundred and thirty other kings. In so many generations of men, there were eighteen Ethiopians and one native queen, the rest were Egyptians. The name of this woman who reigned, was the same as that of the Babylonian queen, Nitocris: they said that she avenged her brother, whom the Egyptians had slain, while reigning over them. After they had slain him, they delivered the kingdom to her; and she, to avenge him, destroyed many of the Egyptians by this stratagem: she caused an extensive apartment to be made underground, and pretended that she was going to consecrate it, then inviting those of the Egyptians whom she knew to have been principally concerned in the murder, she gave them a great banquet, and in the midst of the feast let in the river upon them, through a large concealed channel. Of the other kings they did not say that they were in any

HEAD OF RAMESES II.

respect renowned, except the last, Mœris; he accomplished some memorable works, as the portal of Vulcan's temple, facing the north wind; and dug a lake, and built pyramids in it, the size of which I shall mention when I come to speak of the lake itself.

CHAPTER V.

FROM SESOSTRIS TO SETHON.

I SHALL next mention king Sesostris. The priests said that he was the first who, setting out in ships of war from the Arabian Gulf, subdued those nations that dwell by the Red Sea ;

There are also in Ionia two images of this king, carved on rocks, one on the way from Ephesia to Phocæa, the other from Sardis to Smyrna. In both places a man is carved, four cubits and a half high, holding a spear in his right hand, and a bow in his left, and the rest of his equipment in unison, for it is partly Egyptian and partly Ethiopian ; from one shoulder to the other across the breast extend sacred Egyptian characters engraved, which have the following meaning : " I ACQUIRED THIS REGION BY MY OWN SHOULDERS."

The priests tell a yarn of this Egyptian Sesostris, that returning and bringing with him many men from the nations whose territories he had subdued, when he arrived at the Pelusian Daphnæ, his brother, to whom he had committed the government of Egypt, invited him to an entertainment, and his sons with him, and caused wood to be piled up round the house and set on fire : but that Sesostris, being informed of this, immediately consulted with his wife, for he had taken his wife with him ; she advised him to extend two of his six sons across the fire, and form a bridge over the burning mass, and that the rest should step on them and make their escape. Sesostris did so, and two of his sons were in this manner burned to death, but the rest, together with their father, were saved. Sesostris having returned to Egypt, and taken revenge on his brother, employed the multitude of prisoners whom he brought from the countries he had subdued in many remarkable works : these were the men who drew the huge stones which, in the time of this king, were conveyed to the temple of Vulcan ; they, too, were compelled to dig all the canals now seen in Egypt ; and thus by their involuntary labor made Egypt, which before was throughout practicable for horses and carriages, unfit for these purposes. But the king intersected the country with this network of canals for the reason that such of the Egyptians as occupied the inland cities, being in want of water when the river receded, were forced to use a brackish beverage unfit to drink, which they drew from wells. They said also that this king divided the country

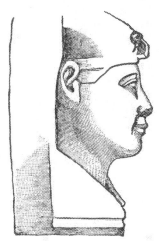

BUST OF THOTHMES I.

amongst all the Egyptians, giving an equal square allotment to each ; and thence drew his revenues by requiring them to pay a fixed tax every year ; if the river happened to take away a part of any one's allotment, he was to come to him and make known what had happened ; whereupon the king sent persons to inspect and measure how much the land was diminished, that in future he might pay a proportionate part of the appointed tax. Land-measuring appears to me to have had its beginning from this act, and to have passed over into Greece ; for the pole[1] and the sun-

---

[1] By the Greek word Πόλος Herodotus means "a concave dial," shaped like the vault of heaven.

dial, and the division of the day into twelve parts, the Greeks learned from the Babylonians. This king was the only Egyptian that ever ruled over Ethiopia; he left as memorials in front of Vulcan's temple statues of stone: two of thirty cubits, of himself and his wife; and four, each of twenty cubits, of his sons. A long time after, the priest of Vulcan would not suffer Darius the Persian to place his statue before them, saying, "that deeds had not been achieved by him equal to those of Sesostris the Egyptian: for Sesostris had subdued other nations, not fewer than Darius had done, and the Scythians besides; but that Darius was not able to conquer the Scythians; wherefore it was not right for one who had not surpassed him in achievements to place his statue before his offerings." They relate, however, that Darius pardoned these observations.

After the death of Sesostris, his son Pheron succeeded to the kingdom; he undertook no military expedition, and happened to become blind through the following occurrence: the river having risen to a very great height for that time, eighteen cubits, it overflowed the fields, a storm of wind arose, and the river was tossed about in waves; whereupon they say that the king with great arrogance laid hold of a javelin, and threw it into the midst of the eddies of the river; and that immediately afterward he was seized with a pain in his eyes, and became blind. He continued blind for ten years; but in the eleventh, having escaped from this calamity, he dedicated offerings throughout all the celebrated temples, the most worthy of mention being two stone obelisks to the temple of the sun, each consisting of a single block of granite, and each a hundred cubits in length and eight cubits in breadth.

A native of Memphis succeeded him in the kingdom, whose name in the Grecian language is Proteus; there is to this day an enclosure sacred to him at Memphis, which is very beautiful and richly adorned, situated to the south side of the temple of Vulcan. The priests told me that when Paris had carried Helen off from Sparta, violent winds drove him out of his course in the Ægean into the Egyptian Sea, and from there (for the gale did not abate) he came to Egypt, and in Egypt to that which is now called the Canopic mouth of the Nile.

And Homer appears to me to have heard this relation ; but as it was not so well suited to epic poetry as the other which he has made use of, he·rejected it.   He has told in the Iliad the wanderings of Paris ; how, while he was carrying off Helen, he was driven out of his course, and wandered to other places, and how he arrived at Sidon of Phœnicia ; and in the exploits of Diomede, his verses are as follows : " Where were the variegated robes, works of Sidonian women, which god-like Paris himself brought from Sidon, sailing over the wide sea, along the course by which he conveyed high-born Helen." [1]   He mentions it also in the Odyssey, in the

PARIS CARRYING AWAY HELEN.

following lines : " Such well-chosen drugs had the daughter of Jove, of excellent quality, which Polydamna gave her, the Egyptian wife of Thonis, where the fruitful earth produces many drugs, many excellent when mixed, and many noxious." [2]   Menelaus also says the following to Telemachus : " The gods detained me in Egypt, though anxious to return hither, because I did not offer perfect hecatombs to them." [3] He shows in these verses, that he was acquainted with the wandering of Paris in Egypt ; for Syria borders on Egypt, and the Phœnicians, to whom Sidon belongs, inhabit Syria.   From these verses, and this first passage especially, it is clear that Homer was not the author of the Cyprian verses, but some other person. For in the Cyprian verses it is said, that Paris reached Ilium from

[1] Iliad, vi., 289.   [2] Odyssey, iv., 227.   [3] Odyssey, iv., 351.

Sparta on the third day, when he carried off Helen, having met with a favorable wind and a smooth sea ; whereas Homer in the Iliad says that he wandered far while taking her with him.

Rhampsinitus succeeded Proteus in the kingdom : He left as a monument the portico of the temple of Vulcan, fronting to the west ; and erected two statues before the portico, twenty-five cubits high. Of these, the one standing to the north the Egyptians call Summer ; and that to the south, Winter : and the one that they call Summer, they worship and do honor to ; but the one called Winter, they treat in a quite contrary way.

This king, they said, possessed a great quantity of money, such as no one of the succeeding kings was able to attain. Wishing to treasure up his wealth in safety, he built a chamber of stone, one of the walls of which adjoined the outside of the palace. But the builder, forming a plan against it, devised the following contrivance ; he fitted one of the stones so that it might be easily taken out by two men, or even one. When the chamber was finished, the king laid up his treasures in it ; in the course of time the builder, finding his end approaching, called his two sons to him, and described to them how he had provided when he was building the king's treasury that they might have abundant sustenance ; and having clearly explained to them every thing relating to the removal of the stone, he gave them its dimensions, and told them, if they would observe his instructions, they would be stewards of the king's riches. He died, and the sons were not long in applying themselves to the work ; coming by night to the palace, they found the stone in the building, easily removed it, and carried off a great quantity of treasure. When the king happened to open the chamber, he was astonished at seeing the vessels deficient in treasure ; but was not able to accuse any one, as the seals were unbroken, and the chamber well secured. When on opening it two or three times, the treasures were always evidently diminished (for the thieves did not cease plundering), he adopted the following plan : he ordered traps to be made, and placed them round the vessels in which the treasures were. But when the thieves came as before, and one of them had entered, as soon as he went near a vessel, he was straightway caught in the trap ; perceiving, therefore, in what a predicament he was, he immediately called to his brother, and told him what had happened, and bade him enter as quick as possible, and cut off his head, lest, if he was seen and recognized, he should ruin him also : the other thought that he spoke well, and did as he was advised ; then, having fitted in the stone, he returned home, taking with him his brother's head. When day came, the king entered the chamber, and was astonished at seeing the body of the thief in the trap without the head, but the chamber secure, and without any means of entrance or exit. In this perplexity he con- trived another plan : he hung up the body of the thief on a public wall, and having placed sentinels there, ordered them to seize and bring before him whomsoever they should see weeping or express- ing commiseration at the spectacle. The mother was greatly grieved at the body being suspended, and coming to words with her surviving son, commanded him, by any means he could, to contrive how he might take down and bring away the corpse of his brother; and if he should neglect to do so, she threatened to go to the king, and inform him that he had the treasures. Having got some asses, and filled some skins with wine, he put them on the asses, and then drove them along ; but when he came near the sentinels that guarded the suspended corpse, he drew out two or three of the necks of the skins that hung down, and loosened them ; and, as the wine ran out, he beat his head, and cried out aloud, as if he knew not to which of the asses he should turn first. The sentinels, when they saw wine flowing in abundance, ran into the road, with vessels in their hands, caught the wine that was being spilt, thinking it all their own gain; but the man, feigning anger, railed bitterly against them all; however, as the sentinels soothed him, he at length pretended to be pacified ; and at last drove his asses out of the road, and set them to rights again. When more conversation passed, and one of the sentinels joked with him and set him laughing, he gave them another of the skins ; and they, just as they were, lay down and set to to drink, and invited him to stay and drink with them. He was persuaded, and remained with them; and as they treated him kindly during the drinking, he gave them another of the skins; and the sentinels, having taken very copious draughts, became royally drunk, and, overpowered by the wine, fell asleep on the spot. Then he took down the body of his brother, and having by way of insult shaved the right cheeks of all the sentinels, laid the corpse on the asses, and drove home, having performed his mother's injunctions. The king, upon being informed that the body of the thief had been stolen, was exceedingly indignant, but being unable by any means to find out the contriver of this artifice, he grew so astonished at the shrewdness and daring of the man, that at last, sending throughout all the cities, he caused a proclamation to be made, offering a free pardon, and promising great reward to the man, if he would discover himself. The thief, relying on this promise, went to the king's palace; and Rhampsinitus greatly admired him, and gave him his daughter in marriage, accounting him the most knowing of all men; for while the Egyptians were superior to all others, he was superior to the Egyptians.

After this, they said that this king descended alive into the place which the Greeks call Hades, and there played at dice with Ceres, and sometimes won, and other times lost; and that he came up again and brought with him as a present from her a napkin of gold. Any person to whom such things appear credible may adopt the accounts given by the Egyptians; it is my object, however, throughout the whole history, to write what I hear from each people. The Egyptians say that Ceres and Bacchus hold the chief sway in the infernal regions; and the Egyptians were also the first who asserted the doctrine that the soul of man is immortal, and that when the body perishes the soul enters into some other animal, constantly springing into existence; and when it has passed through the different kinds of terrestrial, marine, and aërial beings, it again enters into the body of a man that is born; and that this revolution is made in three thousand years.

Now, they told me that down to the reign of Rhampsinitus

there was a perfect distribution of justice, and that all Egypt was in a high state of prosperity; but that after him Cheops, coming to reign over them, plunged into every kind of wickedness. For, having shut up all the temples, he first of all forbade them to offer sacrifice, and afterward ordered all the Egyptians to work for him; some, accordingly, were appointed to draw stones from the quarries in the Arabian mountain down to the Nile, others he ordered

BES AND HI.

to receive the stones when transported in vessels across the river, and to drag them to the mountain called the Libyan. And they worked to the number of a hundred thousand men at a time, each party during three months. The time during which the people were thus harassed by toil lasted ten years on the road which they constructed, along which they drew the stones, a work, in my opinion, not much less than the pyramid: for its length is five stades, and its width ten orgyæ, and its height, where it is the highest, eight orgyæ; and it is of polished stone, with figures carved on it: ten years, then, were expended on this road, and in forming the subterraneous apartments on the hill, on which the pyramids stand, which he had made as a burial vault for himself, in an island, formed by draining a canal from the Nile. Twenty years were spent in erecting the pyramid itself: of this, which is square, each face is eight plethra, and the height is the same; it is composed of polished stones, and joined with the greatest exactness; none of the stones are less than thirty feet in length. This pyramid was built in the form of steps, which some call crossæ, others bomides. When they had first built it in this manner, they raised the stones for covering the surface by machines made of short pieces of wood: having lifted them from the ground to the first range of steps, when the stone arrived there it was put on another machine that stood ready on the first range; from this it was drawn to the second range on another machine; for the machines were equal in number to the ranges of steps; or they removed the machine, which was only one, and portable, to each range in succession, whenever they wished to raise the stone higher; for I should relate it in both ways, as it was related to me. The highest parts of it were first finished, and last of all the parts on the ground. On the pyramid is shown an inscription, in Egyptian characters, how much was expended in radishes, onions, and garlic for the workmen; which the interpreter, as I well remember, reading the inscription, told me amounted to one thousand six hundred talents of silver. If this be really the case, how much more was probably expended in iron tools, in bread, and in clothes for the laborers, since they occupied in building the works the time which I mentioned, and no short time besides, as I think, in cutting and drawing the stones, and in forming the subterraneous excavation. It is related that Cheops in his cruelty subjected his daughter to every sort of disgrace, but she contrived to leave a monument of herself, and asked every one that she met to give her a stone toward the edifice she designed: of these stones they said the

THE GREAT PYRAMID, WITHOUT THE SURFACE STONE.

pyramid was built that stands in the middle of the three, before the great pyramid, each side of which is a plethron and a half in length. The Egyptians say that this Cheops reigned fifty years; and when he died, his brother Chephren succeeded to the kingdom; and he followed the same practices as the other, both in other respects, and in building a pyramid. This does not come up to the dimensions of his brother's, for I myself measured them; nor has it subterraneous chambers; nor does a channel from the Nile flow to it, as to the other; but this flows through an artificial aqueduct round an island within, in which they say the body of Cheops is laid. Having laid the first course of variegated Ethiopian stones, less in height than the other by forty feet, he built it near the large pyramid. They both stand on the same hill, which is about a hundred feet high. Chephren, they said, reigned fifty-six years. Thus one hundred and six years are reckoned, during which the Egyptians suffered all kinds of calamities, and for this length of time the temples were never opened. From the hatred they bear them the Egyptians are not very willing to mention their names; but call the pyramids after Philition, a shepherd, who at that time kept his cattle in those parts.

They said that after him, Mycerinus, son of Cheops, reigned over Egypt; that the conduct of his father was displeasing to him; and that he opened the temples, and permitted the people, who were worn down to the last extremity, to return to their employments, and to sacrifices; and that he made the most just decisions of all their kings. On this account, of all the kings that ever reigned in Egypt, they praise him most, for he both judged well in other respects, and moreover, when any man complained of his decision, he used to make him some present out of his own treasury and pacify his anger. To this beneficent Mycerinus, the beginning of misfortunes was the death of his daughter, who was his only child; whereupon he, extremely afflicted, and wishing to bury her in a more costly manner than usual, caused a hollow wooden image of a cow to be made and covered with gold, into which he put the body of his deceased daughter. This cow was not interred in the

ground, but even in my time was exposed to view in the city of
Sais, placed in the royal palace, in a richly furnished chamber.
They burn near it all kinds of aromatics every day, and a lamp is
kept burning by it throughout each night.

The cow is covered with a purple cloth, except the head and
the neck, which are overlaid with very thick gold ; and the orb of
the sun imitated in gold is placed between the horns.   The cow is
kneeling ; in size equal to a large, living cow.

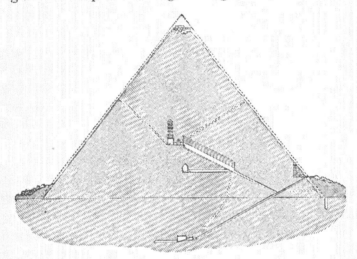

SECTION OF THE GREAT PYRAMID.

After the loss of his daughter, a second calamity befell this king :
an oracle reached him from the city of Buto, importing, " that he
had no more than six years to live, and should die in the seventh."
Thinking this very hard, he sent a reproachful message to the god,
complaining, " that his father and uncle, who had shut up the
temples, and paid no regard to the gods, and moreover had
oppressed men, had lived long ; whereas he who was religious
must die so soon."   But a second message came to him from the
oracle, stating, " that for this very reason his life was shortened,
because he had not done what he ought to have done ; for it was
needful that Egypt should be afflicted during one hundred and fifty
years ; and the two who were kings before him understood this,

but he did not." When Mycerinus heard this, and saw that this
sentence was now pronounced against him, he ordered a great
number of lamps to be made, which were lighted whenever night
came on, and he drank and enjoyed himself, never ceasing night
or day, roving about the marshes and groves, wherever he could
hear of places most suited for pleasure. He had recourse to this
artifice for the purpose of convicting the oracle of falsehood, that
by turning the nights into days, he might have twelve years instead
of six.

This king also left a pyramid, but much smaller than that of his
father, being on each side twenty feet short of three plethra ; it is
quadrangular, and built half way up of Ethiopian stone.

After Mycerinus, the priests said, that Asychis became king of
Egypt, and that he built the eastern portico to the temple of Vulcan, which is by far the largest and most beautiful in its wealth of
sculptured figures and infinite variety of architecture. This king,
being desirous of surpassing his predecessors, left a pyramid, as a
memorial, made of bricks ; on which is an inscription carved on
stone, in the following words : " Do not despise me in comparison
with the pyramids of stone, for I excel them as much as Jupiter, the
other gods. For by plunging a pole into a lake, and collecting
the mire that stuck to the pole, men made bricks, and in this manner built me."

After him there reigned a blind man of the city of Anysis, whose
name was Anysis. During his reign, the Ethiopians and their king,
Sabacon, invaded Egypt with a large force ; whereupon this blind
king fled to the fens ; and the Ethiopian reigned over Egypt for fifty
years, during which time he performed the following actions : When
any Egyptians committed any crime, he would not have any of them
put to death, but passed sentence upon each according to the magnitude of his offence, enjoining them to heap up mounds of earth,
each offender against his own city, and by this means the cities
were made much higher ; for first of all they had been raised
considerably by those who dug the canals in the time of king
Sesostris. Although other cities in Egypt were carried to a

great height, in my opinion the greatest mounds were thrown up about the city of Bubastis, in which is a beautiful temple of Bubastis corresponding to the Grecian Diana. Her sacred precinct is thus situated : all except the entrance is an island ; for two canals from the Nile extend to it, not mingling with each other, but each reaches as far as the entrance to the precinct, one flowing round it on one side, the other on the other. Each is a hundred feet broad, and shaded with trees. The portico is ten orgyæ in height, and is adorned with figures six cubits high, that are deserving of notice. This precinct, being in the middle of the city, is visible on every side to a person going round it ; for while the

SECTION OF GALLERY IN PYRAMID.

city has been mounded up to a considerable height, the temple has not been moved, so that it is conspicuous as it was originally built. A wall sculptured with figures runs round it ; and within is a grove of lofty trees, planted round a large temple in which the image is placed. The width and length of the precinct is each way a stade. Along the entrance is a road paved with stone, four plethra in width and about three stades in length, leading through the square eastward toward the temple of Mercury ; on each side of the road grow trees of enormous height. They told me that the final departure of the Ethiopian occurred in the following manner : it appeared to him in a vision that a man, standing by him, advised him to assemble all the priests in Egypt, and to cut them in two down the middle ; but he, fearing that the gods held out this as a pretext to him, in order that he, having been guilty of impiety in reference to sacred things, might draw down some evil on himself from gods or from men, would not do so ; but as the time had expired during which it was foretold that he should reign over Egypt, he departed hastily from the country. When Sabacon of his own accord had departed from Egypt, the blind king resumed the government, having returned from the fens, where he had lived fifty years, on an island formed of ashes and earth. For when any of the Egyptians came to him bringing provisions, as they were severally ordered to do unknown to the Ethiopian, he bade them bring some ashes also as a present. The kings who preceded Amyrtæus were unable, for more than seven hundred years, to find out where this island was. It was called Elbo, and was about ten stades square.

After him reigned a priest of Vulcan, whose name was Sethon : he held in no account the military caste of the Egyptians, as not having need of their services ; and accordingly, among other in-dignities, he took away their lands ; to each of whom, under former kings, twelve chosen acres had been assigned. After this, when Sennacherib, king of the Arabians and Assyrians, marched a large army against Egypt, the Egyptian warriors refused to assist him ; and the priest, being reduced to a strait, entered the temple, and bewailed before the image the calamities he was in danger of suf-fering. While he was lamenting, sleep fell upon him, and it appeared to him in a vision, that the god stood by and encouraged him, assuring him that he should suffer nothing disagreeable in meeting the Arabian army, for he would himself send assistants to him. Confiding in this vision, he took with him such of the Egyp-tians as were willing to follow him, and encamped in Pelusium, at the entrance into Egypt ; but none of the military caste followed him, only tradesmen, mechanics, and sutlers. When they arrived there, a number of field mice, pouring in upon their enemies, de-voured their quivers and their bows, and the handles of their shields ; so that on the next day, when they fled bereft of their

arms, many of them fell. And to this day, a stone statue of this
king stands in the temple of Vulcan, with a mouse in his hand,

HALL OF COLUMNS IN THE GREAT TEMPLE OF KARNAK.

and an inscription to the following effect: " Whoever looks on
me, let him revere the gods."

The Egyptians and the priests show that from the first king to this priest of Vulcan who last reigned, were three hundred and forty-one generations of men ; and the same number of chief priests and kings. Now, three hundred generations are equal to ten thousand years, for three generations of men are one hundred years ; and the forty-one remaining generations that were over the three hundred, make one thousand three hundred and forty years. Thus, they say, in eleven thousand three hundred and forty years, no god has assumed the form of a man. They relate that during this time the sun has four times risen out of his usual quarter, and that he has twice risen where he now sets, and twice set where he now rises ; yet, that no change in the things in Egypt was occasioned by this, either in respect to the productions of the earth or the river, or to diseases or deaths.

CHAPTER VI.

WHAT things both other men and the Egyptians agree in saying occurred in this country, I shall now proceed to relate, and
shall add to them some things of my own observation. The
Egyptians having become free, after the reign of the priest of Vulcan, since they were at no time able to live without a king, divided all Egypt into twelve parts and established twelve others.
These contracted intermarriages, and agreed that they would
not attempt the subversion of one another, and would main-
tain the strictest friendship. They made these regulations and
strictly upheld them, for the reason that it had been foretold them
by an oracle when they first assumed the government, "that whoever among them should offer a libation in the temple of Vulcan
from a bronze bowl, should be king of all Egypt"; for they used
to assemble in all the temples. Now, being determined to leave
in common a memorial of themselves, they built a labyrinth, a little
above the lake of Mœris, situated near that called the city of Crocodiles; this I have myself seen, and found it greater than can be
described. For if any one should reckon up all the buildings
and public works of the Greeks, they would be found to have cost
less labor and expense than this labyrinth alone, though the temple
in Ephesus is deserving of mention, and also that in Samos. The
pyramids likewise were beyond description, and each of them comparable to many of the great Greek structures. Yet the labyrinth
surpasses even the pyramids. For it has twelve courts enclosed
with walls, with doors opposite each other, six facing the north,
and sixth the south, contiguous to one another; and the same
exterior wall encloses them. It contains two kinds of rooms, some

under ground and some above, to the number of three thousand, fifteen hundred of each. The rooms above ground I myself went through and saw, and relate from personal inspection. But the underground rooms I know only from report; for the Egyptians who have charge of the building would, on no account, show me them, saying that they held the sepulchres of the kings who originally built this labyrinth, and of the sacred crocodiles. I can therefore only relate what I have learnt by hearsay concerning the lower rooms; but the upper ones, which surpass all human works, I myself saw. The passages through the corridors, and the windings through the courts, from their great variety, presented a thousand occasions of wonder, as I passed from a court to the rooms, and from the rooms to halls, and to other corridors from the halls, and to other courts from the rooms. The roofs of all these are of stone, as also are the walls: but the walls are full of sculptured figures. Each court is surrounded with a colonnade of white stone, closely fitted. And adjoining the extremity of the labyrinth is a pyramid, forty orgyæ in height, on which large figures are carved, and a way to it has been made under ground.

Yet more wonderful than this labyrinth is the lake named from Mœris, near which this labyrinth is built; its circumference measures three thousand six hundred stades, or a distance equal to the sea-coast of Egypt. The lake stretches lengthways, north and south, being in depth in the deepest part fifty orgyæ. That it is made by hand and dry, this circumstance proves, for about the middle of the lake stand two pyramids, each rising fifty orgyæ above the surface of the water, and the part built under water extends to an equal depth; on each of these is placed a stone statue, seated on a throne. Thus these pyramids are one hundred orgyæ in height. The water in this lake does not spring from the soil, for these parts are excessively dry, but it is conveyed through a channel from the Nile, and for six months it flows into the lake, and six months out again into the Nile. And during the six months that it flows out it yields a talent of silver every day to the king's treasury from the fish; but when the water is flowing into it, twenty minæ. The people of the country told me that this lake discharges itself under ground into the Syrtis of Libya, running westward toward the interior by the mountain above Memphis. But when I did not see anywhere a heap of soil from this excavation, for this was an object of curiosity to me, I inquired of the people who lived nearest the lake, where the soil that had been dug out was to be found ; they told me where

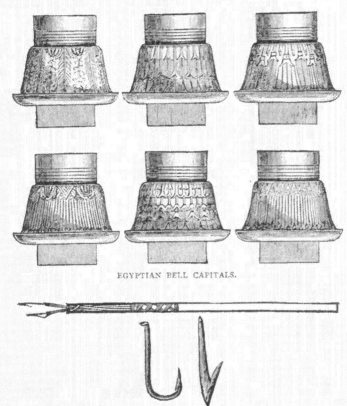

EGYPTIAN BELL CAPITALS.

HARPOON AND FISH HOOKS.

it had been carried, and easily persuaded me, because I had heard that a similar thing had been done at Nineveh, in Assyria. For certain thieves formed a design to carry away the treasures of Sardanapalus, King of Nineveh, which were very large, and preserved in subterraneous treasuries ; the thieves, therefore, beginning from their own dwellings, dug under ground by estimated measurement to the royal palace, and the soil that was taken out of the excavations, when night came on, they threw into the river Tigris, that flows by Nineveh ; and so they proceeded until they had effected their purpose. The same method I heard was adopted in digging the lake in Egypt, except that it was not done by night, but during the day ; for the Egyptians who dug out the soil carried it to the Nile, and the river receiving it, soon dispersed it.

While the twelve kings continued to observe justice, in course of time, as they were sacrificing in the temple of Vulcan, and were about to offer a libation on the last day of the festival, the high-priest, mistaking the number, brought out eleven of the twelve golden bowls with which he used to make the libation. Whereupon he who stood last of them, Psammitichus, since he had not a bowl, having taken off his helmet, which was of bronze, held it out and made the libation. All the other kings were in the habit of wearing helmets, and at that time had them on. Psammitichus therefore, without any sinister intention, held out his helmet ; but they having taken into consideration what was done by Psammitichus, and the oracle that had foretold to them, "that whoever among them should offer a libation from a bronze bowl, should be sole king of Egypt"; calling to mind the oracle, did not think it right to put him to death, since upon examination they found that he had done it by no premeditated design. But they determined to banish him to the marshes, having divested him of the greatest part of his power ; and they forbade him to leave the marshes, or have any intercourse with the rest of Egypt. With the design of avenging himself on his persecutors, he sent to the city of Buto to consult the oracle of Latona, the truest oracle that the Egyptians have, and the answer was returned " that vengeance would come from the sea, when men of bronze should appear." He was very incredulous that men of bronze would come to assist him ; but not long after a stress of weather compelled some Ionians and Carians, who had sailed out for the purpose of piracy, to bear away to Egypt ; and when they had disembarked and were clad in bronze armor, an Egyptian, who had never before seen men clad in such manner, went to the marshes to Psammitichus, and told him that men of bronze had arrived from the sea, and were ravaging the plains. He felt at once that the oracle was accomplished, and treated these Ionians and Carians in a friendly manner, and by promising them great things, persuaded them to join with him ; and, with their help and that of such Egyptians as were well disposed toward him, he overcame the other kings.

Psammitichus, now master of all Egypt, constructed the portico to Vulcan's temple at Memphis that faces the south wind; he built a court for Apis, in which he is fed whenever he appears, opposite the portico, surrounded by a colonnade, and full of sculptured figures ; and instead of pillars, statues twelve cubits high are placed under the piazza. Apis, in the language of the Greeks, means Epaphus. To the Ionians, and those who with them had assisted him, Psammitichus gave lands opposite each other, with the Nile flowing between. These bear the name of " Camps." He royally fulfilled all his promises; and he moreover put Egyptian children under their care to be instructed in the Greek lan-

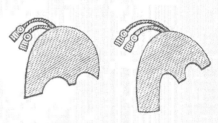

EGYPTIAN HELMETS.

guage; from whom the present interpreters in Egypt are descended. The Ionians and the Carians continued for a long time to inhabit these lands, situated near the sea, a little below the city of Bubastis. They were the first people of a different language who settled in Egypt. The docks for their ships, and the ruins of their buildings, were to be seen in my time in the places from which they had removed.

Psammitichus reigned in Egypt fifty-four years ; during twenty-nine of which he sat down before and besieged Azotus, a large city of Syria, until he took it. This Azotus, of all the cities we know of, held out against a siege the longest period. Neco was son of Psammitichus, and became king of Egypt: he first set about the canal that leads to the Red Sea, which Darius the Persian afterward completed. Its length is a voyage of four days, and in width it was dug so that two triremes might sail rowed abreast. The water is drawn into it from the Nile, and enters it a little above the city Bubastis. The canal passes near the Arabian city Patumos, and reaches to the Red Sea. In the digging of it one hundred and twenty thousand Egyptians perished in the reign of Neco.

Psammis his son reigned only six years over Egypt. He made an expedition into Ethiopia, and shortly afterward died, Apries his son succeeding to the kingdom. He, next to his grandfather Psammitichus, enjoyed greater prosperity than any of the former kings, during a reign of five and twenty years, in which period he marched an army against Sidon, and engaged the Tyrians by sea. But it was destined for him to meet with adversity. For, having sent an army against the Cyrenæans, he met with a signal defeat. And the Egyptians, complaining of this, revolted from him, suspecting that Apries had designedly sent them to certain ruin, in order that they might be destroyed, and he might govern the rest of the Egyptians with greater security. Both those that returned and the friends of those who perished, being very indignant at this, openly revolted against him. Apries, having heard of this, sent Amasis to appease them by persuasion. But when he had come to them, and was urging them to desist from their enterprise, one of the Egyptians, standing behind him, placed a helmet on his head, and said : "I put this on you to make you king." And this action was not at all disagreeable to Amasis, as he presently showed. When Apries heard of this, he armed his auxiliaries and marched against the Egyptians with Carian and Ionian auxiliaries to the number of thirty thousand. They met near the city Momemphis, and prepared to engage with each other. Apries had a palace in the city of Sais that was spacious and magnificent.

There are seven classes of people among the Egyptians— priests, warriors, herdsmen, swineherds, tradesmen, interpreters, and pilots. Their warriors are called Calasiries or Hermotybies.

The Hermotybies number, when they are most numerous, a hundred and sixty thousand. None of these learn any business or mechanical art, but apply themselves wholly to military affairs. The Calasiries number two hundred and fifty thousand men : nor are these allowed to practise any art, but they devote themselves to military pursuits alone, the son succeeding to his father.

When Apries, leading his auxiliaries, and Amasis, all the Egyptians, met together at Momemphis, the foreigners fought well, but being far inferior in numbers, were, on that account, defeated. Apries is said to have been of opinion that not even a god could deprive him of his kingdom, so securely did he think himself established ; but he was beaten, taken prisoner, and carried back to Sais, to that which was formerly his own palace, but which now belonged to Amasis : here he was maintained for some time in the royal palace, and Amasis treated him well. But at length the Egyptians complaining that he did not act rightly in preserving a man who was the greatest enemy both to them and to him, he delivered Apries to the Egyptians. They strangled him, and buried him in his ancestral sepulchre, in the sacred precinct of Minerva, very near the temple, on the left hand as you enter.

Apries being thus dethroned, Amasis, who was of the Saitic district, reigned in his stead ; the name of the city from which he came was Siuph. At first the Egyptians held him in no great estimation, as having been formerly a private person, and of no illustrious family ; but afterward he conciliated them by an act of address, without any arrogance. He had an infinite number of treasures among them a golden foot-pan, in which Amasis himself and all his guests were accustomed to wash their feet. This he broke in pieces, had the statue of a god made from it, and placed it in the most suitable part of the city. The Egyptians flocked to the image and paid it the greatest reverence. Thus, Amasis called the Egyptians together and said : " This statue was made out of the foot-pan in which the Egyptians formerly spat and washed their feet, and which they then so greatly reverenced ; now, the same has happened to me as to the foot-pan ; for though I was be-

fore but a private person, I now am your king ; you must therefore honor and respect me." By this means he won over the
Egyptians, so that they thought fit to obey him. He adopted the
following method of managing his affairs : early in the morning,
until the time of full-market, he assiduously despatched the business
brought before him ; after that he drank and jested with his companions, and talked loosely and sportively. But his friends, offended at this, admonished him, saying : " You do not, O king, control yourself properly. in making yourself too common. For it
becomes you, who sit on a venerable throne, to pass the day in
transacting public business ; thus the Egyptians would know that
they are governed by a great man, and you would be better
spoken of. But now you act in a manner not at all becoming a
king." But he answered them : "They who have bows, when
they want to use them, bend them ; but when they have done
using them, they unbend them ; for if the bow were to be kept
always bent, it would break. Such is the condition of man ; if he
should incessantly attend to serious business, and not give himself
up sometimes to sport, he would shortly become mad or stupefied.
I, being well aware of this, give up a portion of my time to each.

He built an admirable portico to the temple of Minerva at Sais,
far surpassing all others both in height and size, as well as in the
dimensions and quality of the stones ; he likewise dedicated large
statues, and huge andro-sphinxes, and brought other stones of a
prodigious size for repairs : some from the quarries near Memphis ;
but those of greatest magnitude, from the city of Elephantine, distant from Sais a passage of twenty days. But that which I rather
the most admire, is this : he brought a building of one stone from
the city of Elephantine, and two thousand men, who were appointed to convey it, were occupied three whole years in its transport, and these men were all pilots. The length of this chamber,
outside, is twenty-one cubits, the breadth fourteen, and the height
eight. But inside, the length is eighteen cubits and twenty digits,
the width twelve cubits, and the height five cubits. This chamber is placed near the entrance of the sacred precinct ; for they

say that he did not draw it within the precinct for the following
reason : the architect, as the chamber was being drawn along,

THE GREAT SPHINX.

heaved a deep sigh, being wearied with the work, over which so
long a time had been spent ; whereupon Amasis, making a re-

ligious scruple of this, would not suffer it to be drawn any farther. Some persons however say, that one of the men employed
at the levers was crushed to death by it, and that on that account
it was not drawn into the precinct. Amasis dedicated in all the
most famous temples, works admirable for their magnitude ; and
amongst them, at Memphis, the reclining colossus before the
temple of Vulcan, of which the length is seventy-five feet ; and
on the same base stand two statues of Ethiopian stone, each twenty
feet in height, one on each side of the temple. There is also at
Sais another similar statue, lying in the same manner as that at
Memphis. It was Amasis also who built the temple to Isis at
Memphis, which is spacious and well worthy of notice.

Under the reign of Amasis, Egypt is said to have enjoyed the
greatest prosperity, both in respect to the benefits derived from
the river to the land, and from the land to the people ; and it is
said to have contained at that time twenty thousand inhabited
cities. Amasis it was who established the law among the Egyptians, that every Egyptian should annually declare to the governor
of his district, by what means he maintained himself ; and if he
failed to do this, or did not show that he lived by honest means,
he should be punished with death. Solon the Athenian brought
this law from Egypt and established it at Athens. Amasis, being
partial to the Greeks, bestowed other favors on various of the
Greeks, and gave the city of Naucratis for such as arrived in
Egypt to dwell in ; and to such as did not wish to settle there, but
only to trade by sea, he granted places where they might erect
altars and temples to the gods. Now, the most spacious of these
sacred buildings, which is also the most renowned and frequented,
called the Hellenium, was erected at the common charge of the
following cities : of the Ionians,—Chios, Teos, Phocæa, and Clazomenæ ; of the Dorians,—Rhodes, Cnidus, Halicarnassus, Phaselis ;
and of the Æolians,—Mitylene alone. So that this temple belongs
to them, and these cities appoint officers to preside over the mart :
and whatever other cities claim a share in it, claim what does not
belong to them. Besides this, the people of Ægina built a temple

to Jupiter for themselves ; and the Samians another to Juno, and the Milesians one to Apollo. Naucratis was anciently the only place of resort for merchants, and there was no other in Egypt : and if a man arrived at any other mouth of the Nile, he was obliged to swear " that he had come there against his will " ; and having taken such an oath, he must sail in the same ship to the Canopic mouth ; but if he should be prevented by contrary winds from doing so, he was forced to unload his goods and carry them in barges round the Delta until he reached Naucratis. So great were the privileges of Naucratis. When the Amphyctions contracted to build the temple that now stands at Delphi for three hundred talents—for the temple that was formerly there had been burned by accident, and it fell upon the Delphians to supply a fourth part of the sum—the Delphians went about from city to city to solicit contributions, and brought home no small amount from Egypt. For Amasis gave them a thousand talents of alum, and the Greeks who were settled in Egypt twenty minæ.

Amasis also dedicated offerings in Greece. In the first place, a gilded statue of Minerva at Cyrene, and his own portrait painted ; secondly, to Minerva in Lindus two stone statues and a linen corselet well worthy of notice ; thirdly, to Juno at Samos two images of himself carved in wood, which stood in the large temple even in my time, behind the doors. He was the first who conquered Cyprus, and subjected it to the payment of tribute.

BOOK III. THALIA.

CHAPTER I.

EXPEDITIONS OF CAMBYSES.

CAMBYSES, son of Cyrus, made war against Amasis, leading with him his own subjects, together with Greeks, Ionians and Æolians. The cause of the war was this : Cambyses sent a herald into Egypt to demand the daughter of Amasis. The suggestion was made by an Egyptian physician, who out of spite served Amasis in this manner, because Amasis had selected him out of all the physicians in Egypt, torn him from his wife and children, and sent him as a present to the Persians, when Cyrus had sent to Amasis, and required of him the best oculist in Egypt. The Egyptian therefore, having this spite against him, urged on Cambyses by his suggestions, bidding him demand the daughter of Amasis, in order that if he should comply he might be grieved, or if he refused he might incur the hatred of Cambyses. But Amasis, dreading the power of the Persians, resorted to a piece of deceit. There was a daughter of Apries, the former king, very tall and beautiful, the only survivor of the family, named Nitetis. This damsel, Amasis adorned with cloth of gold, and sent to Persia as his own daughter. After a time, when Cambyses saluted her, addressing her by her father's name, the damsel said to him : " O king, you do not perceive that you have been imposed upon by Amasis, who dressed me in rich attire, and sent me to you, presenting me as his own daughter; whereas, I am really the daughter of Apries, whom he put to death, after he had incited the Egyptians to revolt." These words enraged Cambyses, and led him to invade Egypt.

A circumstance that few of those who have made voyages to Egypt have noticed, I shall now proceed to mention. From every part of Greece, and also from Phœnicia, earthen vessels filled with wine are imported into Egypt twice every year, and yet not a single one of these wine jars is afterward to be seen. In what way, then, you may ask, are they disposed of? Every magistrate is obliged to collect all the vessels from his own city, and send them to Memphis; the people of that city fill them with water, and convey them to the arid parts of Syria; so that the earthen vessels continually imported and landed in Egypt, are added to those already in Syria. The Persians, as soon as they became masters of Egypt, facilitated the passage into that country, by sup-

EGYPTIAN POTTERY.

plying it with water in this manner. But as, at that time, water was not provided, Cambyses, by the advice of a Halicarnassian stranger, sent ambassadors to the Arabian, and requested a safe passage, which he obtained, giving to, and receiving from him, pledges of faith.

The Arabians observe pledges as religiously as any people : when any wish to pledge their faith, a third person, standing between the two parties, makes an incision with a sharp stone in the palm of the hand, near the longest fingers, of both the contractors ; then taking some of the nap from the garment of each, he smears seven stones, placed between them, with the blood ; and as he does this, he invokes Bacchus and Urania. When this ceremony is completed, the person who pledges his faith, binds his friends as sureties to the stranger, or the citizen, if the contract be made with a citizen, and the friends also hold themselves obliged to observe the engagement. They acknowledge no other gods than Bacchus and Urania, and they say that their hair is cut in the same way as Bacchus' is cut, in a circular form, banged round the temples. They call Bacchus, Orotal; and Urania, Alilat. When the Arabian had exchanged pledges with the ambassadors who came from Cambyses, he filled camels' skins with water, loaded them on all his living camels, and drove them to the arid region, and there awaited the army of Cambyses. This is the most credible of the accounts that are given; yet it is right that one less credible should be mentioned, since it is likewise affirmed. There is a large river in Arabia called Corys, which discharges itself into the Red Sea. From this river it is said that the king of the Arabians, having sewn together a pipe of ox-hides and other skins, reaching in length to the desert, conveyed the water through it; and that in the arid region he dug large reservoirs, to receive and preserve the water. It is a twelve days' journey from the river to the desert, yet he conveyed water through three pipes into three different places.

Amasis died after a reign of forty-four years, during which no great calamity had befallen him. He was embalmed and buried in the sepulchre within the sacred precinct, which he himself had built. During the reign of Psammenitus, son of Amasis, a most remarkable prodigy befell the Egyptians; rain fell at Egyptian Thebes, which had never happened before, nor since, to my time, as the Thebans themselves affirm. For no rain ever falls in the upper regions of Egypt; but at that time rain fell in drops at Thebes. The Persians, having marched through the arid region, halted near the Egyptians, as if with a design of engaging; there the auxiliaries of the Egyptians, consisting of Greeks and Carians, condemning Phanes because he had led a foreign army against Egypt, adopted the following expedient against him: Phanes had left his sons in Egypt; these they brought to the camp, within sight of their father, placed a bowl midway between the two armies, then dragging the children one by one, they slew them over the bowl, into which they also poured wine and water; then all the auxiliaries drank of the blood, and immediately joined battle. After a hard fight, when great numbers had fallen on both sides, the Egyptians were put to flight. Here I saw a very surprising fact, of which the people of the country informed me. As the bones of those who were killed in that battle lie scattered about separately, the bones of the Persians in one place, and those of the Egyptians in another, the skulls of the Persians were so weak that if you should hit one with a single pebble, you would break a hole in it; whereas those of the Egyptians are so hard, that you could scarcely fracture them by striking them with a stone. The cause of this, they told me (and I readily assented), is that the Egyptians begin from childhood to shave their heads, and the bone is thickened by exposure to the sun; from the same cause also they are less subject to baldness, and one sees fewer persons bald in Egypt than in any other country. But the Persians have weak skulls, because they shade them from the first, wearing tiaras for hats.

The Egyptians fled in complete disorder from the battle. When they had shut themselves up in Memphis, Cambyses sent a Mitylenæan bark up the river, with a Persian herald on board, to invite the Egyptians to terms. But when they saw the bark entering Memphis they rushed in a mass from the wall, destroyed the ship, and having torn the crew to pieces, limb by limb, they carried them into the citadel. After this the Egyptians were besieged, and at length surrounded. The neighboring Libyans, fearing what had befallen Egypt, gave themselves up without resistance, submitted to pay a tribute, and sent presents, which Cambyses received very graciously.

On the tenth day after Cambyses had taken the citadel of Memphis, he seated Psammenitus, the King of the Egyptians, who had reigned only six months, at the entrance of the city. And by way of insult, he dressed his daughter in the habit of a slave, and sent her with a pitcher to fetch water, with other maidens selected from the principal families, dressed in the same manner. As the girls, with loud lamentation and weeping, came into the presence of their fathers, all the other fathers answered them with wailing and weeping, when they beheld their children thus humiliated. But Psammenitus only bent his eyes to the ground. When these water-carriers had passed by, he next sent his son, with two thousand Egyptians of the same age, with halters about their necks, and a bridle in their mouths ; and they were led out to suffer retribution for those Mitylenæans who had perished at Memphis with the ship. For the royal judges had given sentence, that for each man ten of the principal Egyptians should be put to death. Yet, when he saw them passing by, and knew that his son was being led out to death, though all the rest of the Egyptians who sat round him wept and made loud lamentations, he did the same as he had done in his daughter's case. But just then it happened that one of his boon-companions, a man somewhat advanced in years, who had lost his all, and possessed nothing but such things as a beggar has, asking alms of the soldiery, passed by Psammenitus, and the Egyptians seated in the suburbs. Then, indeed, he wept bitterly, and calling his companion by name, smote his head. Cambyses, surprised at this behavior, sent a messenger to say : " Psammenitus, your master Cambyses inquires why, when you saw your daughter humiliated and your son led to execution, you did not bewail or lament ; and have been so highly concerned for a beggar, who is no way related to you, as he is informed." Psammenitus answered : " Son of Cyrus, the calamities of my family are too great to be expressed by lamentation ; but the griefs of my friend were worthy of tears, who, having fallen from abundance and prosperity, has come to beggary on the threshold of old age." When this answer was brought back by the messenger, it appeared to Cambyses to be well said ; and, as the Egyptians relate, Crœsus wept, for he had attended Cambyses into Egypt, and the Persians that were present wept also ; Cambyses himself, touched with pity, gave immediate orders to preserve his son out of those who were to perish, but those who were sent found the son no longer alive, having been the first that suffered ;

but Psammenitus himself they conducted to Cambyses, with whom he afterward lived, without experiencing any violence. And had it not been suspected that he was planning innovations, he would probably have recovered Egypt, so as to have the government intrusted to him. For the Persians are accustomed to honor the sons of kings, and even if they have revolted from them, sometimes bestow the government upon their children. Psammenitus, devising mischief, received his reward, for he was discovered inciting the Egyptians to revolt ; and when he was detected by Cambyses he was compelled to drink the blood of a bull, and died immediately.

Cambyses proceeded from Memphis to the city of Sais, and entering the palace of Amasis, commanded the dead body of Amasis to be brought out of the sepulchre ; he gave orders then to scourge it, to pull off the hair, to prick it, and to abuse it in every possible manner. But when they were wearied with this employment, for the dead body, since it was embalmed, resisted, and did not at all fall in pieces, Cambyses gave orders to burn it, commanding what is impious. For to burn the dead is on no account allowed by either nation : not by the Persians, for they consider fire to be a god, and say it is not right to offer to a god the dead body of a man ; nor by the Egyptians, as fire is held by them to be a living beast, which devours every thing it can lay hold of, and when it is glutted with food it expires with what it has consumed ; therefore, as it is their law on no account to give a dead body to wild beasts, for that reason they embalm them, that they may not lie and be eaten by worms.

Cambyses determined to send to Elephantine for some of the Ichthyophagi, who understood the Ethiopian language, that he might despatch them as spies to Ethiopia. When the Ichthyophagi came, he despatched them to the Ethiopians, having instructed them what to say, carrying presents, consisting of a purple cloak, a golden necklace, bracelets, an alabaster box of ointment, and a cask of palm wine. These Ethiopians, to whom Cambyses sent, are said to be the tallest and handsomest of all men ; and have customs different from those of other nations, especially with regard to the regal power; for they confer the sovereignty upon the man whom they consider to be of the largest stature, and to possess strength proportionate to his size.

When the Ichthyophagi arrived among this people, they gave the presents to the king, and addressed him as follows: "Cambyses, King of the Persians, desirous of becoming your friend and ally, has sent us to confer with you, and he presents you with these gifts, which are such as he himself most delights in." But the Ethiopian, knowing that they came as spies, spoke thus to them: "Neither has the king of the Persians sent you with presents to me, because he valued my alliance; nor do you speak the truth; for ye are come as spies of my kingdom. Nor is he a just man; for if he were just, he would not desire any other territory than his own; nor would he reduce people into servitude who have done him no injury. However, give him this bow, and say these words to him: 'The king of the Ethiopians advises the king of the Persians, when the Persians can thus easily draw a bow of this size, then to make war on the Macrobian Ethiopians with more numerous forces; but until that time let him thank the gods, who have not inspired the sons of the Ethiopians with a desire of adding another land to their own.'" Having spoken thus and unstrung the bow, he delivered it to the comers. Then taking up the purple cloak, he asked what it was, and how made; and when the Ichthyophagi told him the truth respecting the purple, and the manner of dyeing, he said that the men are deceptive, and their garments are deceptive also. Next he inquired about the necklace and bracelets, and when the Ichthyophagi explained to him their use as ornaments, the king, laughing, and supposing them to be fetters, said that they have stronger fetters than these. Thirdly, he inquired about the ointment; and when they told him about its composition and use, he made the same remark as he had on the cloak. But when he came to the wine, and inquired how it was made, being very much delighted with the draught, he further asked what food the king made use of, and what was the longest age to which a Persian lived. They answered, that he fed on bread, describing the nature of wheat ; and that the longest period of the life of a Persian was eighty years. Upon this the Ethiopian said, that he was not at all surprised if men who fed on earth lived so few years ; and he was sure they would not be able to live even so many years, if they did not refresh themselves with this beverage, showing the wine to the Ichthyophagi : for in this he admitted they were surpassed by the Persians. The Ichthyophagi inquiring in turn of the king concerning the life and diet of the Ethiopians, he said, that most of them attained to a hundred and twenty years, and some even exceeded that term, and that their food was boiled flesh, and their drink milk. When the spies expressed their astonishment at the number of years, he led them to a fountain, by washing in which they became more sleek, as if it had been of oil, and an odor proceeded from it as of violets. The water of this fountain, the spies said, is so weak, that nothing is able to float upon it, neither wood, nor such things as are lighter than wood ; but every thing sinks to the bottom. If this water is truly such as it is said to be, it may be they are long-lived by reason of the abundant use of it. Leaving this fountain, he conducted them to the common prison, where all were fettered with golden chains ; for among these Ethiopians bronze is the most rare and precious of all metals. After this, they visited last of all their sepulchres, which are said to be prepared from crystal in the following manner. When they have dried the body, either as the Egyptians do, or in some other way, they plaster it all over with gypsum, and paint it, making it as much as possible to resemble real life ; they then put round it a hollow column made of crystal, which they dig up in abundance, and is easily wrought. The body being in the middle of the column is plainly seen, and it does not emit an unpleasant smell, nor is it in any way offensive ; and it is all visible [1] as the body itself. The nearest relations keep the column in their houses for a year, offering to it the first-fruits of all, and

---

[1] The Egyptian mummies could only be seen in front, the back being covered by a box or coffin ; the Ethiopian bodies could be seen all round, as the column of glass was transparent.

performing sacrifices ; after that time they carry it out and place it somewhere near the city.

When the spies returned home and reported all that had passed, Cambyses, in a great rage, immediately marched against the Ethiopians, without making any provision for the subsistence of his army, or once considering that he was going to carry his arms to the remotest parts of the world ; but, as a madman, and not in possession of his senses, as soon as he heard the report of the Icthyophagi, he set out on his march, ordering the Greeks who were present to stay behind, and taking with him all his land forces. When the army reached Thebes, he detached about fifty thousand men, and ordered them to reduce the Ammonians to slavery, and to burn the oracular temple of Jupiter, while he with the rest of his army marched against the Ethiopians. But before the army had passed over a fifth part of the way, all the provisions that they had were exhausted, and the beasts of burden themselves were eaten. Now if Cambyses had at this juncture altered his purpose, and had led back his army, he would have proved himself to be a wise man. But he obstinately continued advancing. The soldiers supported life by eating herbs as long as they could gather any from the ground ; but when they reached the sands, some of them had recourse to a dreadful expedient, for taking one man in ten by lot, they devoured him : when Cambyses heard this, shocked at their eating one another, he abandoned his expedition against the Ethiopians, marched back and reached Thebes, after losing a great part of his army. From Thebes he went down to Memphis, and suffered the Greeks to sail away. Thus ended the expedition against the Ethiopians. Those who had been sent against the Ammonians, after having set out from Thebes, under the conduct of guides, are known to have reached the city Oasis, which is inhabited by Samians, distant seven days' march from Thebes, across the sands. This country in the Greek language is called the Island of the Blessed. But afterward none, except the Ammonians and those who have heard their report, are able to give any account of them ; for they neither reached the Ammonians, nor re-

A CAMEL RACE.

turned back. But the Ammonians make the following report: When they had advanced from this Oasis toward them across the sands, and were about half-way between them and Oasis, as they were taking dinner, a vehement south wind blew, carrying with it heaps of sand, and completely destroyed the whole army.

When Cambyses arrived at Memphis, Apis, whom the Greeks call Epaphus, appeared to the Egyptians; and when this manifestation took place, the Egyptians immediately put on their richest apparel, and kept festive holiday. Cambyses, seeing them thus occupied, and concluding that they made these rejoicings on account of his ill success, summoned the magistrates of Memphis; and when they came into his presence, he asked " why the Egyptians had done nothing of the kind when he was at Memphis before, but did so now, when he had returned with the loss of a great part of his army." They answered, that their god appeared to them, who was accustomed to manifest himself at intervals, and that when he did appear, then all the Egyptians were accustomed to rejoice and keep a feast. Cambyses, having heard this, said they were liars, and put them to death. Then he summoned the priests into his presence, and when the priests gave the same account, he said, that he would find out whether a god so tractable had come among the Egyptians; and commanded the priests to bring Apis to him. This Apis, or Epaphus, the Egyptians say, is the calf of a cow upon which the lightning has descended from heaven. It is black, and has a square spot of white on the forehead; on the back the figure of an eagle; and in the tail double hairs; and on the tongue a beetle. When the priests brought Apis, Cambyses, like one almost out of his senses, drew his dagger, meaning to strike the belly of Apis, but hit the thigh; then falling into a fit of laughter, he said to the priests: " Ye blockheads, are there such gods as these, consisting of blood and flesh, and sensible of steel? This, truly, is a god worthy of the Egyptians. But you shall not mock me with impunity." Then he gave orders to scourge the priests, and kill all the Egyptians who should be found feasting. Apis, wounded in the thigh, lay and languished in the temple; and at length, when he had died of the wound, the priests buried him without the knowledge of Cambyses.

But Cambyses, as the Egyptians say, immediately became mad in consequence of this atrocity, though he really was not of sound mind before. His first crime he committed against his brother Smerdis, who was born of the same father and mother; him he sent back from Egypt to Persia through envy, because he alone of all the Persians had drawn the bow, which the Ichthyophagi brought from the Ethiopian, within two fingers' breadth; of the other Persians no one was able to do this. After the departure of Smerdis for Persia, Cambyses saw the following vision in his sleep: he imagined that a messenger arrived from Persia and informed him that Smerdis was seated on the royal throne, and touched the heavens with his head. Upon this, fearing for himself, lest his brother should kill him, and reign, he sent Prexaspes, the most faithful to him of the Persians, to Persia, with orders to kill Smerdis. Having gone up to Susa, he killed Smerdis; some say, when he had taken him out to hunt; but others, that he led him to the Red Sea and drowned him. This they say was the first of the crimes of Cambyses; the second was that of marrying his own sister, who had accompanied him into Egypt.

The Greeks say, that one day Cambyses made the whelp of a lion fight with a young dog; and this wife was also looking on; the dog being over-matched, another puppy of the same litter broke his chain, and came to his assistance, and thus the two dogs united got the better of the whelp. Cambyses was delighted at the sight, but she, sitting by him, shed tears. Cambyses, observing this, asked her why she wept. She answered, that she wept seeing the puppy come to the assistance of his brother, remembering Smerdis, and knowing that there was no one to avenge him. The Greeks say, that for this speech she was put to death by Cambyses. But the Egyptians say, that as they were sitting at table, his wife took a lettuce, stripped off its leaves, and then asked her husband "whether the lettuce stripped of its leaves, or thick with foliage, was the handsomer." He said: "When thick with foliage." Whereupon she remarked: "Then you have imitated this lettuce, in dismembering the house of Cyrus." Whereupon he, in rage, kicked her and inflicted such injuries that she died.

Thus madly did Cambyses behave toward his own family; whether on account of Apis, or from some other cause, from which, in many ways, misfortunes are wont to befall mankind. For Cambyses is said, even from infancy, to have been afflicted with a certain severe malady, which some called the sacred disease.[1] In that case, it was not at all surprising that, when his body was so diseased, his mind should not be sound. And toward the other Persians he behaved madly in the following instances: for it is reported that he said to Prexaspes, whom he highly honored, and whose office it was to bring messages to him, whose son was cup-bearer to Cambyses, no trifling honor by any means, he is reported to have said: "Prexaspes, what sort of a man do the Persians think me? and what remarks do they make about me?" He answered: "Sir, you are highly extolled in every other respect, but they say you are too much addicted to wine." The king enraged cried out: "Do the Persians indeed say that, by being addicted to wine, I am beside myself, and am not in my senses? then their former words were not true." For, on a former occasion, when the Persians and Crœsus were sitting with him, Cambyses asked, what sort of a man he appeared to be in comparison with his father Cyrus; they answered, that he was superior to his father, because he held all that Cyrus possessed, and had acquired besides Egypt and the empire of the sea. Crœsus, who was not pleased with this decision, spoke thus to Cambyses: "To me, O son of Cyrus, you do not appear comparable to your father, for you have not yet such a son as he left behind him." Cambyses was delighted at hearing this, and commended the judgment of Crœsus. So, remembering this, he said in anger to Prexaspes: "Observe now yourself, whether the Persians have spoken the truth, or whether they who say such things are not out of their senses: for if I shoot that son of yours who stands under the portico, and hit

---

[1] Epilepsy.

him in the heart, the Persians will appear to have said nothing to
the purpose ; but if I miss, then say that the Persians have spoken
the truth, and that I am not of sound mind." Having said this,
and bent his bow, he hit the boy ; and when the boy had fallen,
he ordered them to open him and examine the wound ; and when
the arrow was found in the heart, he said to the boy's father,
laughing: " Prexaspes, it has been clearly shown to you that I am
not mad, but that the Persians are out of their senses. Now tell
me, did you ever see a man take so true an aim?" But Prexaspes,
perceiving him to be out of his mind, and being in fear for his own
life, said : " Sir, I believe that a god himself could not have shot
so well." At another time, having, without any just cause, seized
twelve Persians of the first rank, he had them buried alive up to
the head.

While he was acting in this manner, Crœsus the Lydian
thought fit to admonish him in the following terms : " O king, do
not yield entirely to your youthful impulses and anger, but possess
and restrain yourself. It is a good thing to be provident, and wise
to have forethought. You put men to death who are your own
subjects, having seized them without any just cause ; and you slay
their children. If you persist in such a course, beware lest the
Persians revolt from you. Your father Cyrus strictly charged me
to admonish you, and suggest whatever I might discover for your
good." He thus manifested his good-will, in giving this advice ;
but Cambyses answered : " Do you presume to give me advice,
you, who so wisely managed your own country ; and so well advised my father, when you persuaded him to pass the river Araxes,
and advance against the Massagetæ, when they were willing to
cross over into our territory? You have first ruined yourself by
badly governing your own country, and then ruined Cyrus, who
was persuaded by your advice. But you shall have no reason to
rejoice ; for I have long wanted to find a pretext against you."
So saying, he took up his bow for the purpose of shooting him ;
but Crœsus jumped up and ran out. Cambyses, unable to shoot
him, commanded his attendants to seize him, and put him to death.

But the attendants, knowing his temper, concealed Crœsus for the following reason, that if Cambyses should repent, and inquire for Crœsus, they, by producing him, might receive rewards for preserving him alive; or if he should not repent, or sorrow for him, then they would put him to death. Not long afterward Cambyses did regret the loss of Crœsus, whereupon the attendants acquainted him that he was still living; on which Cambyses said : " I am rejoiced that Crœsus is still alive ; they, however, who disobeyed my orders and saved him, shall not escape with impunity, but I will have them put to death." And he made good his word.

He committed many such mad actions, both against the Persians and his allies, while he stayed at Memphis opening ancient sepulchres, and examining the dead bodies ; he also entered the temple of Vulcan, and derided the image, for the image of Vulcan is very much like the Phœnician Pataici, which the Phœnicians place at the prows of their triremes, and is a representation of a pigmy. He likewise entered the temple of the Cabeiri, (into which it is unlawful for any one except the priest to enter,) and these images he burnt, after he had ridiculed them in various ways : these also are like that of Vulcan ; and they say that they are the sons of this latter. It is in every way clear to me that Cambyses was outrageously mad ; otherwise he would not have attempted to deride sacred things and established customs. For if any one should propose to all men, to select the best institutions of all that exist, each, after considering them all, would choose his own ; so certain is it that each thinks his own institutions by far the best. It is not therefore probable, that any but a madman would make such things the subject of ridicule. That all men are of this mind respecting their own institutions may be inferred from many proofs, but is well illustrated by the following incident : Darius once summoned some Greeks under his sway, and asked them " for what sum they would feed upon the dead bodies of their parents." They answered, that they would not do it for any sum. Then Darius called to him some of the Indians called Callatians, who are accustomed to eat their parents, and asked them, in the presence of the Greeks, "for what sum they would consent to burn their fathers when they die." But they made loud exclamations and begged he would speak words of good omen. Such then is the effect of custom: and Pindar appears to me to have said rightly "that custom is the king of all men."

ATTACK ON FORT.

Whilst Cambyses was invading Egypt, the Lacedæmonians made an expedition against Polycrates, who had made an insurrection and seized on Samos. At first, having divided the state into three parts, he had shared it with his brothers Pantagnotus and

Syloson; but afterward, having put one of them to death, and expelled Syloson, the younger, he held the whole of Samos, and
made a treaty of friendship with Amasis, King of Egypt, sending
presents, and receiving others from him in return. In a very short
time the power of Polycrates increased, and was noised abroad
throughout Ionia and the rest of Greece ; for wherever he turned
his arms, every thing turned out prosperously. He had a hundred
fifty-oared galleys, and a thousand archers. And he plundered all
without distinction ; for he said that he gratified a friend more by
restoring what he had seized, than by taking nothing at all. He
accordingly took many of the islands, and many cities on the continent; he moreover overcame in a sea-fight, and took prisoners,
the Lesbians, who came to assist the Milesians with all their forces ;
these, being put in chains, dug the whole trench that surrounds the
walls of Samos.

The Lacedæmonians, arriving with a great armament, besieged
Samos, attacked the fortifications, and passed beyond the tower
that faced the sea near the suburbs ; but afterward, when Polycrates himself advanced with a large force, they were driven back,
and after forty days had been spent in besieging Samos, finding
their affairs were not at all advanced, they returned to Peloponnesus ;
though a groundless report got abroad, that Polycrates coined a
large quantity of the money of the country in lead, had it gilt, and
gave it it to them ; whereupon they took their departure. This
was the first expedition that the Lacedæmonian Dorians undertook
against Asia.

Those of the Samians who had fomented the war against Polycrates set sail for Siphnus when the Lacedæmonians were about to
abandon them, for they were in want of money. The Siphnians
were at that time the richest of all the islanders, having such gold
and silver mines, that from the tenth of the money accruing from
them, a treasure was laid up at Delphi equal to the richest ; and
they used every year to divide the product of the mines. When
they established this treasure, they asked the oracle, whether their
present prosperity would continue with them for a long time ; but

the Pythian answered as follows: "When the Prytaneum in Siphnus shall be white, and the market white-fronted, then shall there be need of a prudent man to guard against a wooden ambush and a crimson herald." The market and Prytaneum of the Siphnians were then adorned with Parian marble. As soon as the Samians reached Siphnus, they sent ambassadors to the city in a ship which, like all ships at that time, was painted red. And this was what the Pythian meant by a wooden ambush and a crimson herald.

THE OBELISK.

These ambassadors requested the Siphnians to lend them ten talents; the Siphnians refused the loan, and the Samians proceeded to ravage their territory. The Siphnians were beaten, and compelled to give a hundred talents.

I have dwelt longer on the affairs of the Samians, because they have the three greatest works that have been accomplished by all the Greeks. The first is a mountain, one hundred and fifty orgyæ in height, in which is dug a tunnel, beginning from the base, with an opening at each side.   The length of the excavation is seven stades, and the height and breadth eight feet each; through the whole length of it is dug another excavation twenty cubits deep, and three feet broad, through which the water conveyed by pipes reaches the city, drawn from a copious fountain. The architect of this excavation was a Megarian, Eupalinus, son of Naustrophus.   The second work is a mound in the sea round the harbor, in depth about one hundred orgyæ; and in length more than two stades.   The third is a temple, the largest of all we have ever seen; of this, the architect was Rhœcus, son of Phileus, a native.

CHAPTER II.

WHILE Cambyses, son of Cyrus, tarried in Egypt, and was acting madly, two magi, who were brothers, revolted. One of these, Cambyses had left steward of his palace, the other was a person very much like Smerdis, son of Cyrus, whom Cambyses, his own brother, had put to death. The magus Patizithes, having persuaded this man that he would manage every thing for him, set him on the throne; and sent heralds in various directions, particularly to Egypt, to proclaim to the army, that they must in future obey Smerdis, son of Cyrus, and not Cambyses. The herald who was appointed to Egypt, finding Cambyses and his army at Ecbatana in Syria, stood in the midst and proclaimed what had been ordered by the magus. Cambyses, believing that he spoke the truth, and that he had himself been betrayed by Prexaspes, and that he, when sent to kill Smerdis, had not done so, looked toward Prexaspes, and said: " Prexaspes, hast thou thus performed the business I enjoined upon thee?" But he answered: " Sire, it is not true that your brother Smerdis has revolted against you, nor that you can have any quarrel, great or small, with him. For I myself put your order into execution, and buried him with my own hands. I think I understand the whole matter, O king: the magi are the persons who have revolted against you,—Patizithes, whom you left steward of the palace, and his brother Smerdis." When Cambyses heard the name of Smerdis, the truth of this account and of the dream struck him: for he fancied in his sleep that some one announced to him that Smerdis, seated on the royal throne, touched the heavens with his head. Perceiving, therefore, that he had destroyed his brother without a cause, he wept bitterly for him, deplored the whole calamity, and leapt upon his horse, resolving with all speed to march to Susa against the magus. But as he was leaping on his horse, the chape of his sword's scabbard fell off, and the blade, being laid bare, struck the thigh ; wounding him in that part where he himself had formerly smitten the Egyptian god Apis. Mortally wounded, he asked what was the name of the city. They said it was Ecbatana. And it had been before prophesied to him from the city of Buto, that he should end his life in Ecbatana. He had imagined that he should die an old man in Ecbatana of Media, where all his treasures were ; but the oracle in truth meant in Ecbatana of Syria. When he had thus been informed of the name of the city, though smitten by misfortune, he returned to his right mind; and comprehending the oracle, said: " Here it is fated that Cambyses, son of Cyrus, should die."

Twenty days later he summoned the principal men of the Persians who were with him, told them his vision and his great mistake, shed bitter tears, and charged them never to permit the government to return into the hands of the Medes. When the Persians saw their king weep, all rent the garments they had on, and gave themselves up to lamentation. Soon the bone became infected, the thigh mortified, and Cambyses, son of Cyrus, died, after he had reigned in all seven years and five months, having never had any children. Great incredulity stole over the Persians who were present, as to the story that the magi had possession of the government, and agreed that it must be Smerdis, son of Cyrus, who had risen up and seized the kingdom. Prexaspes, moreover, vehemently denied that he had killed Smerdis; for it was not safe for him, now that Cambyses was dead, to own that he had killed the son of Cyrus with his own hand.

The magus, after the death of Cambyses, relying on his having the same name as Smerdis the son of Cyrus, reigned securely during the seven months that remained to complete the eighth year of Cambyses ; in which time he treated all his subjects with such beneficence, that at his death, all the people of Asia, except the Persians, regretted his loss. For the magus, on assuming the sovereignty, despatched messengers to every nation he ruled over, and proclaimed a general exemption from military service and tribute for the space of three years. But in the eighth month he was discovered in the following manner. Otanes, son of Pharnaspes, was by birth and fortune equal to the first of the Persians. This Otanes first suspected the magus not to be Smerdis the son of Cyrus, from the fact, that he never went out of the citadel, and that he never summoned any of the principal men of Persia to his presence. Having conceived suspicion of him, he contrived the following artifice. Cambyses had married his daughter, whose name was Phædyma; the magus of course had her as his wife, as well as all the rest of the wives of Cambyses. Otanes therefore, sending to his daughter, inquired whether her husband was Smerdis, son of Cyrus, or some other person; she sent back word to him, saying that she did not know. Otanes sent a second time, saying: "If you do not yourself know Smerdis, son of Cyrus, then inquire of Atossa, for she must of necessity know her own brother." To this his daughter replied: "I can neither have any conversation with Atossa, nor see any of the women who used to live with me; for as soon as this man, whoever he is, succeeded to the throne, he dispersed us all, assigning us separate apartments." When Otanes heard this, the matter appeared much more plain; and he sent a third message to her in these words: "Daughter, it becomes you, being of noble birth, to undertake any peril that your father may require you to incur. For if this Smerdis is not the son of Cyrus, but the person whom I suspect, it is not fit that he should escape with impunity, but suffer the punishment due to his offences. Now follow my directions: watch your opportunity, and whenever you discover him to be sound asleep, touch his ears; and if you find he has ears, be assured that he is Smerdis, son of Cyrus; but if he has none, then he is Smerdis the magus." To this message Phædyma answered, saying "that she should incur very great danger by doing so; for he kept the sides of his head concealed, and if he had no ears, and she should be discovered touching him, she well knew that he would put her to death; nevertheless she would make the attempt." Cyrus, during his reign, had cut off the ears of this Smerdis the magus, for some grave offence. Phædyma, therefore, determining to execute all that she had promised her father, catching the magus sound asleep on his couch one day felt for his ears, and perceiving without any difficulty that the man had no ears, as soon as it was day, she sent and made known to her father what the case was.

Thereupon Otanes, having taken with him Aspathines and Gobryas, who were the noblest of the Persians, and persons on whom he could best rely, related to them the whole affair; and they agreed that each should associate with himself a Persian in whom he could place most reliance. Otanes accordingly introduced Intaphernes; Gobryas, Megabyzus; and Aspathines, Hydarnes. Just at this time Darius, son of Hystaspes, arrived at Susa from Persia, where his father was governor, and the six Persians determined to admit Darius to the confederacy. These seven met, exchanged pledges with each other, and conferred together. When it came to the turn of Darius to declare his opinion, he addressed them as follows : " I thought that I was the only person who knew that it was the magus who reigns, and that Smerdis, son of Cyrus, is dead; and for this very reason I hastened hither in order to contrive the death of the magus. But since it proves that you also are acquainted with the fact, it appears to me that we should act immediately." Otanes said to this : " Son of Hystaspes, you are born of a noble father, and show yourself not at all inferior to him; do not, however, so inconsiderately hasten this enterprise, but set about it with more caution; for we must increase our numbers, and then attempt it." Darius replied to this : " Be assured, ye men who are here present, if you adopt the plan proposed by Otanes, you will all miserably perish; for some one will discover it to the magus, consulting his own private advantage; indeed, you ought to have carried out your project immediately, without communicating it to any one else; but since you have thought fit to refer it to others, and have disclosed it to me, let us carry it out this very day, or be assured, that if this day passes over, no one shall be beforehand with me and become my accuser, but I myself will denounce you to the magus." Otanes, seeing Darius so eager, replied : " Since you compel us to precipitate our enterprise, and will not permit us to defer it, tell us in what way we are to enter the palace and attack him ; for you yourself know that guards are stationed at intervals ; and how shall we pass them ?" " There are many things," said Darius, " that can not be made clear by words, but may by action ; and there are other things that seem practicable in description, but no signal effect proceeds from them. Be assured that the guards stationed there will not be at all difficult to pass by : for in the first place, seeing our rank, there is no one who will not allow us to pass, partly from respect, and partly from fear ; and in the next place, I have a most specious pretext by which we shall gain admission, for I will say that I have just arrived from Persia, and wish to report a message to the king from my father. For when a lie must be told, let it be told. Whoever of the doorkeepers shall willingly let us pass, shall be rewarded in due time ; but whoever offers to oppose us must instantly be treated as an enemy." After this Gobryas said : " Friends, shall we ever have a better opportunity to recover the sovereign power, or if we shall be unable to do so, to die? seeing we who are Persians, are governed by an earless Medic magus. Those among you who were present with Cambyses when he lay sick, well remember the imprecations he uttered at the point of death against the Persians, if they should not attempt to repossess themselves of the sovereign power : we did not then believe this story, but thought that Cambyses spoke from ill-will. I give my voice that we yield to Darius, and that on breaking up this conference we go direct to the magus." And all assented to his proposal.

Meantime the magi, on consultation, determined to make Prexaspes their friend : both because he had suffered grievous wrong from Cambyses, who shot his son dead with an arrow ; and because he alone of all the Persians knew of the death of Smerdis, son of Cyrus, as he had despatched him with his own hand ; and moreover, Prexaspes was in high repute with the Persians. Therefore, having sent for Prexaspes, they endeavored to win his friendship, binding him by pledges and oaths, that he would never divulge to any man the cheat they had put upon the Persians, assuring him that in return they would give him every thing his heart could desire. When Prexaspes had promised that he would do as the magi wished, they made a second proposal, saying, that they would assemble all the Persians under the walls of the palace, and desired that he would ascend a tower, and assure them that they were governed by Smerdis, son of Cyrus. Prexaspes assented, and the magi, having convoked the Persians, placed him on the top of a turret, and commanded him to harangue the people. But he purposely forgot what they desired him to say, and, beginning from Achæmenes, described the genealogy of Cyrus' family ; told them what great benefits Cyrus had done the Persians ; and finally declared the whole truth, saying that he had before concealed it, as it was not safe for him to tell what had happened ; but that in the present emergency necessity constrained him to make it known. He accordingly told them that he, being compelled by Cambyses, had put Smerdis, son of Cyrus, to death, and that it was the magi who then reigned. After he had uttered many imprecations against the Persians, if they should not recover back the sovereign power, and punish the magi, he threw himself headlong from the tower. Thus died Prexaspes, a man highly esteemed during the course of his whole life.

The seven Persians, resolving to attack the magi without delay, had offered prayers to the gods, and were in the midst of their way when they were informed of all that Prexaspes had done, whereupon they again conferred together ; and some, with Otanes, strongly advised to defer the enterprise while affairs were in such a ferment ; but others, with Darius, urged to proceed at once. While hotly disputing there appeared seven pairs of hawks pursuing two pairs of vultures, and plucking and tearing them. The seven, on seeing this, all approved the opinion of Darius, and forthwith proceeded to the palace, emboldened by the omen. When they approached the gates, it happened as Darius had supposed ; for the guards, out of

respect for men of highest rank among the Persians, and not suspecting any such design on their part, let them pass by, moved as they were by divine impulse; nor did any one question them. But when they reached the hall, they fell in with the eunuchs appointed to carry in messages, who inquired of them for what purpose they had come; and at the same time that they questioned them they threatened the doorkeepers for permitting them to pass, and endeavored to prevent the seven from proceeding any farther. They instantly drew their daggers, stabbed all that opposed their passage on the spot, and then rushed to the men's apartment. The magi happened to be both within at the time, and were consulting about the conduct of Prexaspes. But seeing the eunuchs in confusion, and hearing their outcry, they hurried out, and put themselves on the defensive. One snatched up a bow, and the other a javelin, and the parties engaged with each other. The one who had taken up the bow, seeing his enemies were near and pressing upon them, found it of no use; but the other made resistance with his spear, and first wounded Aspathines in the thigh, and next Intaphernes in the eye; and Intaphernes lost his eye from the wound, but did not die. The other magus, when he found his bow of no service, fled to a chamber adjoining the men's apartment, purposing to shut to the door, and two of the seven, Darius and Gobryas, rushed in with him; and as Gobryas was grappling with the magus, Darius standing by was in perplexity, fearing that he should strike Gobryas in the dark; but Gobryas, seeing that he stood by inactive, asked him why he did not use his hand. He answered: "Fearing for you, lest I should strike you." "Never mind," said Gobryas, "drive your sword through both of us." Darius obeyed, thrust with his dagger, and by good fortune hit the magus.

Having slain the magi, and cut off their heads, they left the wounded of their own party there, as well on account of their exhaustion as to guard the acropolis; but the other five of them, carrying the heads of the magi, ran out with shouting and clamor, and called upon the rest of the Persians, relating what they had done, and showing them the heads; and at the same time they slew every one of the magi that came in their way. The Persians, informed of what had been done by the seven, and of the fraud of the magi, determined themselves also to do the like ; and having drawn their daggers, they slew every magus they could find ; and if the night coming on had not prevented, they would not have left a single magus alive. This day the Persians observe in common more than any other, and in it they celebrate a great festival, which they call " The Slaughter of the Magi." On that day no magus is allowed to be seen in public.

When the tumult had subsided, and five days had elapsed, those who had risen up against the magi deliberated on the state of affairs. Otanes advised that they should commit the government to the Persians at large, " for," said he, " how can a monarchy be a well-constituted government, where one man is allowed to do whatever he pleases without control?" Megabyzus advised them to intrust the government to an oligarchy, and said : " Let us choose an association of the best men, and commit the sovereign power to them, for among them we ourselves shall be included, and it is reasonable to expect that the best counsels will proceed from the best men." Darius expressed his opinion the third, saying : " What Megabyzus has said concerning the people was spoken rightly, but if three forms are proposed, and each the best in its kind, democracy, oligarchy, and monarchy, I contend that the last is far superior. For nothing can be found better than one man, who is the best; since acting upon equally wise plans, he would govern the people without blame, and would keep his designs most secret from the ill-affected. But in an oligarchy, whilst many are exerting their energies for the public good, strong private enmities commonly spring up ; for each wishing to be chief, and to carry his own opinions, they come to deep animosities one against another, whence seditions arise ; and from seditions, murder ; and from murder recourse is always had to a monarchy ; and thus it is proved that this form of government is the best. Also when the people rule, it is impossible that evil should not spring up, and powerful combinations, for they who injure the commonwealth act in concert ; and this lasts until some one of the people stands forward and puts them down ; and on this account, being admired by the people, he becomes a monarch ; this again shows that a monarchy is best. Moreover, we should not subvert the institutions of our ancestors, when we see how good they are."

Four of the seven adhered to this opinion. Then said Otanes : " Associates, since it is evident that some one of us must be made king, I will not enter into competition with you ; for I wish neither to govern nor be governed. But on this condition I give up all claim to the government, that neither I nor any of my posterity may be subject to any one of you." The six agreed to these terms, and he withdrew from the assembly ; and this family alone, of all the Persians, retains its liberty to this day, and yields obedience only so far as it pleases, but without transgressing the laws of the Persians. The rest of the seven consulted how they might appoint a king on the most equitable terms ; and they determined that Otanes and his posterity forever should be given a Median vest yearly, by way of distinction, together with all such presents as are accounted most honorable among the Persians, for he first advised the enterprise, and associated them together. And they made the resolution that every one of the seven should have liberty to enter into the palace without being introduced, and that the king should not be allowed to marry a wife out of any other family than of the conspirators. With regard to the kingdom, they determined that he whose horse should first neigh in the suburbs at sunrise, while they were mounted, should have the kingdom.

Darius had a groom, a shrewd man, whose name was Œbares, to whom, when the assembly had broken up, Darius said : " Œbares, we have determined that he whose horse shall neigh first at sunrise, when we ourselves are mounted, is to have the kingdom. Now, if you have any ingenuity, contrive that I may obtain this honor, and not another." Œbares answered : "If, sir, it depends on this, whether you shall be king or not, keep up your spirits ; for no one else shall be king before you ; I know a trick that will make him neigh." At dawn of day, the six, as they had agreed, met together on horseback ; and as they were riding round the suburbs, Darius' horse, at the signal from Œbares, ran forward and neighed, and at that instant lightning and thunder came from a clear sky. These things consummated the auspices, as if done by appointment, and the others, dismounting from their horses, did obeisance to Darius as king.

Accordingly Darius, son of Hystaspes, was declared king, and

EGYPTIAN WAR CHARIOT, WARRIOR AND HORSES.

all the people of Asia, except the Arabians, were subject to him. The Arabians never submitted to the Persian yoke, but were on friendly terms, and gave Cambyses a free passage into Egypt ; for without the consent of the Arabians the Persians could not have penetrated into Egypt. Darius contracted his first marriages with Persians ; he married two daughters of Cyrus, Atossa and Artystona ; Atossa, you remember, had been before married to her brother Cambyses, and afterward to the magus. He married another also, daughter of Smerdis, son of Cyrus, whose name was Parmys; and he had besides, the daughter of Otanes who detected the magus. His power was fully established on all sides. He erected a stone statue, representing a man on horseback; and he had engraved on it the following inscription: "Darius, son of Hystaspes, by the sagacity of his horse, (here mentioning the name,) and by the address of Œbares, his groom, obtained the empire of the Persians." In Persia, he constituted twenty governments, which they call satrapies; set governors over them, and appointed tributes to be paid to him from each. In consequence of this imposition of tribute, and other things of a similar kind, the Persians say Darius was a trader, Cambyses a master, and Cyrus a father. The first, because he made profit of every thing; the second, because he was severe and arrogant; the last, because he was mild, and always aimed at the good of his people. If the total of all his revenues is computed together, fourteen thousand five hundred and sixty Euboic talents were collected by Darius as an annual tribute, [1] passing over many small sums which I do not mention. This tribute accrued to Darius from Asia and a small part of Libya; but in the course of time another revenue accrued from the islands, and the inhabitants of Europe as far as Thessaly. This treasure the king melts and pours into earthen jars, and knocking away the earthen mould when he wants money he cuts off as much as he has occasion to use.

The Cilicians were required to send each year to Darius three hundred and sixty white horses, one for every day. The Persian territory alone was not subject to tribute; but the Persians brought gifts. The Ethiopians bordering on Egypt, whom Cambyses subdued when he marched against the Macrobian Ethiopians, and who dwell about the sacred city of Nysa, celebrate festivals of Bacchus, use the same grain as the Calantian Indians, and live in subterraneous dwellings. These brought every third year two chœnices of unmolten gold, two hundred blocks of ebony, five Ethiopian boys, and twenty large elephants' tusks.

---

[1] Nearly $18,000,000 in all.

CHAPTER III.

THAT part of India toward the rising sun is all sand ; for of the people with whom we are acquainted, and of whom any thing certain is told, the Indians live the farthest toward the east of all the inhabitants of Asia ; and the Indians' country toward the east is a desert, by reason of the sands. There are many nations of Indians, and they do not all speak the same language ; some of them are nomads, and they inhabit the marshes of the river, and feed on raw fish, which they take going out in boats made of bamboo, one joint of which makes a boat. These Indians wear a garment made of rushes cut from the river, beaten flat, platted like a mat, and worn as a corselet. Other Indians, living to the east of these, are nomads, and eat raw flesh ; they are called Padæans. When any one of this community is sick, if it be a man, the men who are his nearest connections put him to death, alleging that if he wasted by disease his flesh would be spoiled ; and no matter if he denies that he is sick, they are not likely to agree with him, but kill and feast upon him. And if a woman be sick, the women who are most intimate with her do the same as the men. And whoever reaches to old age, they sacrifice and feast upon ; but few among them succeed in growing old, for before that, every one that falls into any distemper is put to death. Other Indians have different customs : they neither kill any thing that has life, nor sow any thing, nor are they wont to have houses, but they live upon herbs, and have a grain of the size of millet, in a pod, which springs spontaneously from the earth ; this they gather, and boil and eat it with the pod. When any one of them falls ill, he goes and lies down in the desert, and no one takes any thought about him, whether dead or sick. All these Indians whom I have mentioned have a complexion closely resembling the Ethiopians. They are situated very far from the Persians, toward the south, and were never subject to Darius.

Those who border on the city of Caspatyrus and the country of Pactyica are the most warlike of the Indians, and these are they who are sent to procure the gold. In this desert, and in the sand, there are ants in size somewhat less indeed than dogs, but larger than foxes. Some of them which were taken there, are in the possession of the king of the Persians. These ants, forming their habitations under ground, heap up the sand, as the ants in Greece do, and in the same manner; and they are very much like them in shape. The sand thus heaped up is mixed with gold. The Indians go to the desert to get this sand, each man having three camels, on either side a male harnessed to draw by the side, and a female in the middle; this last the man mounts himself, having taken care to yoke one that has been separated from her young as recently born as possible; for camels are not inferior to horses in swiftness, and are much better able to carry burdens. What kind of figure the camel has I shall not describe to the Greeks, as they are acquainted with it; but what is not known respecting it I will mention. A camel has four thighs and four knees in his hinder legs. The Indians then, adopting such a plan of harnessing, set out for the gold, having before calculated the time, so as to be engaged in their plunder during the hottest part of the day, for during the heat the ants hide themselves under ground. Amongst these people the sun is hottest in the morning, and not, as with us, at mid-day; during this time it scorches much more than at mid-day in Greece; so that, it is said, they then refresh themselves in water. But as the day declines, the sun becomes to them as it is in the morning to others; and after this, as it proceeds it becomes still colder, until sunset, then it is very cold. When the Indians arrive at the spot with their sacks, they fill them with the sand, and return as fast as possible. For the ants, as the Persians say, immediately discovering them by the smell, pursue them, and they are equalled in swiftness by no other animal, so that if the Indians did not get the start of the ants while they were assembling, not a man of them could be saved. Now the male camels (for they are inferior in speed to the females) would otherwise slacken their pace, dragging on, not both equally ; but the females, mindful of the young they have left, do not slacken their pace. Thus the Indians obtain the greatest part of their gold.

The extreme parts of the inhabited world somehow possess the most excellent products ; while Greece enjoys by far the best-tempered climate. In India, the farthest part of the inhabited world toward the east, all animals, both quadrupeds and birds, are much larger than they are in other countries, with the exception of horses ; in this respect they are surpassed by the Medic breed called the Nysæan horses. Then there is an abundance of gold there, partly dug, partly brought down by the rivers, and partly seized in the manner I have described. And certain wild trees there bear wool instead of fruit, which in beauty and quality excels that of sheep ; and the Indians make their clothing from these trees. Again, Arabia is the farthest of inhabited countries toward the south ; and this is the only region in which grow frankincense, myrrh, cassia, cinnamon, and ledanum. All these, except myrrh, the Arabians gather with difficulty. The frankincense they gather by burning styrax, which the Phœnicians import into Greece. Winged serpents, small in size, and various in form, guard the trees that bear frankincense, a great number round each tree. These are the same serpents that invade Egypt. They are driven from the trees by nothing else but the smoke of the styrax. Vipers are found in all parts of the world ; but flying serpents in Arabia, and nowhere else ; there they appear to be very numerous.

MILITARY DRUM.

The Arabians obtain the cassia, which grows in marshes or shallow lakes, by covering their whole body and face, except the eyes, with hides and skins, and thus avoiding the attacks of the winged animals, like bats, which infest the marshes, and screech fearfully, and are exceedingly fierce. The cinnamon they collect

in a still more wonderful manner.   Where it grows and what land
produces it they are unable to tell ; except that some say it grows
in those countries in which Bacchus was nursed.   Large birds
bring those rolls of bark, which we, from the Phœnicians, call cinnamon, for their nests, which are built with clay, against precipitous
mountains, where there is no access for man.   The Arabians, to
surmount this difficulty, cut up into large pieces the limbs of dead
oxen, and asses, and other beasts of burden, carry them to these
spots, lay them near the nests, and retire to a distance.   The birds
fly down and carry up the limbs of the beasts to their nests, which
not being strong enough to support the weight, break and fall to
the ground.   Then the men, coming up, gather the cinnamon,
much of which they export to other countries.   Still more wonderful is the fragrant ledanum.   For it is found sticking like gum to
the beards of he-goats, which collect it from the wood.   It is useful
for many ointments, and the Arabians burn it very generally as a
perfume.   They are famous for their perfumes ; and there breathes
from Arabia, as it were, a divine odor.   They have two kinds of
sheep worthy of admiration, which are seen nowhere else.   One
kind has large tails, not less than three cubits in length, which, if
suffered to trail, would ulcerate, by the tails rubbing on the ground.
But every shepherd knows enough of the carpenter's art to prevent this, for they make little carts and fasten them under the tails,
binding the tail of each separate sheep to a separate cart.   The
other kind of sheep have broad tails, even to a cubit in breadth.
Where the meridian declines[1] toward the setting sun, the Ethiopian
territory extends, being the extreme part of the habitable world.
It produces much gold, huge elephants, wild trees of all kinds,
ebony, and men of large stature, very handsome, and long-lived.

Such are the extremities of Asia and Libya.   Concerning the
western extremities of Europe I am unable to speak with certainty,
for I do not admit that there is a river, called by barbarians Eridanus, which discharges itself into the sea toward the north, from
which amber is said to come ; nor am I acquainted with the

---

[1] That is, " southwest."

Cassiterides islands, whence our tin comes. For in the first place, the name Eridanus shows that it is Grecian and not barbarian, and coined by some poet ; in the next place, though I have diligently inquired, I have never been able to hear from any man who has himself seen it, that there is a sea on that side of Europe. However, both tin and amber come to us from the remotest parts. Toward the north of Europe there is evidently a very great quantity of gold, but how procured I am unable to say with certainty ; though it is said that the Arimaspians, a one-eyed people, steal it from the griffins. Nor do I believe this, that any men are born with one eye, and yet in other respects resemble the rest of mankind. However, the extremities of the world seem to surround and enclose the rest of the earth, and to possess those productions which we account most excellent and rare.

CHAPTER IV.

Of the seven men that conspired against the magus, it happened that one of them, Intaphernes, by an act of insolence, lost his life shortly after the revolution. He wished to enter the palace in order to confer with Darius; but the door-keeper and the messenger would not let him pass, saying, that the king was engaged, but Intaphernes, suspecting they told a falsehood, drew his scimetar, cut off their ears and noses, and having strung them to straps taken from his bridle, hung them round their necks, and dismissed them. They presented themselves to the king, and told him the cause for which they had been so treated. Darius, fearing lest the six had done this in concert, sent for them, one by one, and endeavored to discover whether they approved of what had been done. When he found that Intaphernes had not done this with their knowledge, he seized Intaphernes himself, and his children, and all his family, having many reasons to suspect that he, with his relations, would raise a rebellion against him. And he bound them as for death: but the wife of Intaphernes, going to the gates of the palace, wept and lamented aloud; and prevailed on Darius to have compassion on her. He therefore sent a messenger to say as follows: "Madam, king Darius allows you to release one of your relations who are now in prison, whichever of them all you please." She deliberated, and answered: "Since the king grants me the life of one, I choose my brother from them all." Darius, wondering at her choice, asked: "Madam, the king inquires the reason why, leaving your husband and children, you have chosen that your brother should survive; who is not so near related to you as your children, and less dear to you than your husband?"

"O king," she answered, "I may have another husband if God will, and other children if I lose these; but as my father and

Signs in common use.	Signs employed more rarely.	Equivalent in English.
	—	A (as in father).
	— —	I (sounded as ee in see).
	—	U (sounded as oo in food).
		B
		P
		F
		G (deep guttural).
		K
		KH (sounded like the Hebrew ח).
		D
		T
		M
		N
		L
		S
		SH
		H
		J

ALPHABET.

mother are no longer alive, I cannot by any means have another brother; for this reason I spoke as I did." This pleased Darius so well that he granted to her the one whom she asked, and also her eldest son; all the rest he put to death.

It happened not long after this that Darius, in leaping from his horse while hunting, twisted his foot with such violence that the ankle-bone was dislocated. At first thinking he had about him Egyptians who had the first reputation for skill in the healing art, he made use of their assistance. But they, by twisting the foot, and using force, made the evil worse; and from the pain which he felt, Darius lay seven days and seven nights without sleep. On the eighth day, as he still continued in a bad state, some one who had before heard at Sardis of the skill of Democedes the Crotonian, made it known to Darius; and he ordered them to bring him to him as quickly as possible. They found him among the slaves altogether neglected; and brought him forward, dragging fetters behind him, and clothed in rags. As he stood before him, Darius asked him whether he understood the art. He denied that he did, fearing lest, if he discovered himself, he should be altogether precluded from returning to Greece. But he appeared to Darius to dissemble, although he was skilled in the art; he therefore commanded those who had brought him thither to bring out whips and goads. Whereupon he owned up, saying that he did not know it perfectly, but having been intimate with a physician, he had some poor knowledge of the art. Upon which Darius put himself under his care, and by using Grecian medicines, and applying lenitives after violent remedies, he caused him to sleep, and in a little time restored him to his health, though Darius had begun to despair of ever recovering the use of his foot. After this cure, Darius presented him with two pairs of golden fetters; but Democedes asked him, if he purposely gave him a double evil because he had restored him to health. Darius, pleased with the speech, introduced him to his wives, with the remark that this was the man who had saved the king's life; whereupon each of them dipped a goblet into a chest of gold, and presented it brimful to Democedes—so munificent a gift, that a servant named Sciton, following behind, picked up enough staters that fell from the goblets to make him a rich man.

This Democedes had been so harshly treated at Crotona by his father, who was of a severe temper, that he left him and went to Ægina ; having settled there, in the first year, though he was un-provided with means, and had none of the instruments necessary for the exercise of his art, he surpassed the most skilful of their physicians. In the second year, the Æginetæ engaged him for a talent out of the public treasury ; and in the third year the Athenians, for a hundred minæ ; and in the fourth year Polycrates, for two talents ; thus he came to Samos. From this man the Crotonian physicians obtained a great reputation ; for at this period the physicians of Crotona were said to be the first through-out Greece, and the Cyrenæans the second. At the same time the Argives were accounted the most skilful of the Greeks in the art of music. Democedes, having completely cured Darius at Susa, had a very large house, and a seat at the king's table ; and he had every thing he could wish for, except the liberty of returning to Greece. He obtained from the king a pardon for the Egyptian physicians who first attended the king, and were about to be em-paled, because they had been outdone by a Greek physician ; and in the next place he procured the liberty of a prophet of Elis, who had attended Polycrates, and lay neglected among the slaves. In short, Democedes had great influence with the king.

Not long after Atossa, daughter of Cyrus, and wife to Darius, had a tumor on her breast ; after some time it burst, and spread considerably. As long as it was small, she concealed it, and from delicacy informed no one of it ; when it became dangerous, she sent for Democedes and showed it to him. He said that he could cure her, but exacted a solemn promise, that she in return would perform for him whatever he should require of her, but added that he would ask nothing which might bring disgrace on her. When therefore he had healed her, and restored her to health, Atossa, in-structed by Democedes, addressed Darius, in the following words : " O king, you, who possess so great power, sit idle, and do not add any nation or power to the Persians. It is right that a man who is both young and master of such vast treasures should render himself considerable by his actions, that the Persians may know that they are governed by a man. Two motives should influence you, to such a course : first, that the Persians may know that it is a worthy man who rules over them ; and secondly, that they may be worn in war, and not tempted by too much ease to plot against you. You must perform some illustrious action while you are in the flower of your age ; for the mind grows with the growth of the body, and as it grows old, grows old with it, and dull for every action." She spoke thus according to her instructions, and he answered : " Lady, you have mentioned the very things that I myself propose to do ; for I have determined to make a bridge and march from this continent to the other, against the Scythians ; and this shall shortly be put in execution." Atossa replied : " Give up the thought of marching first against the Scythians, for they will be in your power whenever you choose ; but take my advice, and lead an army into Greece ; for from the account I have heard, I am anxious to have Lacedæmonian, Argive, Athenian, and Corinthian attendants : and you have the fittest man in the world to show and inform you of every thing concerning Greece ; I mean the person who cured your foot." Said Darius : " Well, since you think I ought to make my first attempt against Greece, I think it better first to send some Persians thither as spies with the man you mention ; they, when they are informed of and have seen every particular, will make a report to me ; and then, being thoroughly informed, I will turn my arms against them." No sooner said than done ; for as soon as day dawned, he summoned fifteen eminent Persians, and commanded them to accompany Democedes along the maritime parts of Greece ; and to take care that Democedes did not escape from them, but they must by all means bring him back again. He next summoned Democedes himself, and requested that when he should have conducted the Persians through all Greece, and shown it to them, to return ; he also commanded him to take with him all his movables as presents to his father and brothers, promising to give him many times as much instead. Moreover, he said, that for the purpose of transporting the presents he would give a merchant-ship, filled with all kinds of precious things, which should accompany him on his voyage. Now Darius, in my opinion, promised him these things without any deceitful intention ; but Democedes, fearing lest Darius was making trial of him, received all that was given, without eagerness, but said that he would leave his own goods where they were, that he might have them on his return ; the merchant-ship he said he would accept.

In Sidon, a city of Phœnicia, they manned two triremes, and with them also a large trading vessel, laden with all kinds of precious things ; and set sail for Greece. Keeping to the shore, they surveyed the coasts, and made notes in writing ; at length, having inspected the greatest part of it, and whatever was most re-markable, they proceeded to Tarentum in Italy. There, out of kindness toward Democedes, Aristophilides, king of the Tarentines, took off the rudders of the Median ships, and shut up the Persians as spies. While they were in this condition Democedes went to Crotona and when he had reached his own home, Aristophilides set the Persians at liberty, and restored what he had taken from their ships. The Persians pursuing Democedes, arrived at Crotona, found him in the public market, and laid hands on him. Some of the Crotonians, dreading the Persian power, were ready to deliver him up ; but others seized the Persians in turn, and beat them with staves, though they expostulated in these terms : "Men of Crotona, have a care what you do, you are rescuing a man who is a run-away from the king ; how will king Darius endure to be thus in-sulted ? How can what you do end well, if you force this man from us ? What city shall we sooner attack than this ? What sooner shall we endeavor to reduce to slavery?" But they could not persuade the Crotonians ; so launching a small boat they sailed back to Asia ; nor, as they were deprived of their guide, did they attempt to explore Greece any further. At their departure Demo-cedes enjoined them to tell Darius that he had Milo's daughter affianced to him as his wife, for the name of Milo, the wrestler, stood high with the king ; and on this account it appears to me that Democedes spared no expense to hasten this marriage, that he might appear to Darius to be a man of consequence in his own country.

After these things, king Darius took Samos, first of all the cities, either Grecian or barbarian, and for the following reason. When Cambyses, son of Cyrus, invaded Egypt, many Greeks resorted thither; some, as one may conjecture, on account of trade; others, to serve as soldiers; others, to view the country. Of these, the last was Syloson, son of Æaces, brother to Polycrates, and an exile from Samos. The following piece of good luck befel this Syloson: having put on a scarlet cloak, he walked in the streets of Memphis; and Darius, who was one of Cambyses' guard, and as yet a man of no great account, took a fancy to the cloak, and coming up, wished to purchase it. But Syloson, perceiving that Darius was very anxious to have the cloak, impelled by a divine impulse, said: "I will not sell it for any sum, but I will give it you for nothing, if so it must needs be." Darius accepted his offer with thanks and took the cloak. Syloson thought afterward that he had lost it through his good nature, but when, in course of time, Cambyses died, and the seven rose up against the magus, and of the seven, Darius possessed the throne, Syloson heard that the kingdom had devolved on the man to whom he had given his cloak in Egypt on his requesting it; so he went up to Susa and seated himself at the threshold of the king's palace, and said he had been a benefactor to Darius. The porter reported it to the king; who said: "What Greek is my benefactor, to whom I owe a debt of gratitude, having so lately come to the throne? Scarcely one of them has as yet come here; nor can I mention any thing that I owe to a Greek. However, bring him in, that I may know the meaning of what he says." The porter introduced Syloson, who related the story of the cloak, and said that he was the person who gave it. "Most generous of men!" exclaimed the king, "art thou then the man who, when as yet I had no power, made me a present, small as it was? yet the obligation is the same as if I were now to receive a thing of great value. In return I will give thee abundance of gold and silver, so that thou shalt never repent having conferred a favor on Darius son of Hystaspes." To this Syloson replied : " O king, give me neither gold nor silver; but recover and give me back my country, Samos, which now, since my brother Polycrates died by the hands of Orœtes, a slave of ours has possssessed. Give me this without bloodshed and bondage." Then Darius sent an army under the conduct of Otanes, one of the seven, with orders to accomplish whatever Syloson should desire.

Mæandrius held the government of Samos, having had the administration intrusted to him by Polycrates : though he wished to prove himself the most just of men, he was unable to effect his purpose. For when the death of Polycrates was made known to him, he erected an altar to Jupiter Liberator, and marked round it the sacred enclosure, which is now in the suburbs. Afterward, he summoned an assembly of all the citizens, and said : " To me, as you know, the sceptre and all the power of Polycrates has been intrusted, and I am now able to retain the government. But what I condemn in another, I will myself, to the utmost of my ability, abstain from doing. For neither did Polycrates please me in exercising despotic power over men equal to himself, nor would any other who should do the like. Now Polycrates has accomplished his fate ; and I, surrendering the government into your hands, proclaim equality to all. I require, however, that the following remuneration should be granted to myself; that six talents should be given me out of the treasures of Polycrates ; and in addition, I claim for myself and my descendants for ever, the priesthood of the temple of Jupiter Liberator, to whom I have erected an altar, and under whose auspices I restore to you your liberties." But one of them rising up said, " You forsooth are not worthy to rule over us, being as you are a base and pestilent fellow ; rather think how you will render an account of the wealth that you have had the management of." Thus spoke a man of eminence among the citizens, whose name was Telesarchus. But Mæandrius, perceiving that if he should lay down the power, some other would set himself up as a tyrant in his place, no longer thought of laying it down. To which end, when he had withdrawn to the citadel, send-

ing for each one severally, as if about to give an account of the
treasures, he seized them and put them in chains. They were kept
in confinement; but after this, disease attacked Mæandrius; and
his brother, whose name was Lycaretus, supposing that he would
die, in order that he might the more easily possess himself of the
government of Samos, put all the prisoners to death; for, as it
seems, they were not willing to be free.

When the Persians arrived at Samos, bringing Syloson with
them, no one raised a hand against them, and the partisans of
Mæandrius, and Mæandrius himself, said they were ready to quit
the island under a treaty; and when Otanes had assented to this,
and had ratified the agreement, the principal men of the Persians,
having had seats placed for them, sat down opposite the citadel.
The tyrant Mæandrius had a brother somewhat out of his senses,
whose name was Charilaus; he, for some fault he had committed,
was confined in a dungeon; and having at that time overheard what
was doing, and having peeped through his dungeon, when he saw
the Persians sitting quietly down, he shouted and said that he
wished to speak with Mæandrius. Mæandrius commanded him to
be released, and brought into his presence; and as soon as he was
brought there, upraiding and reviling his brother, he urged him to
attack the Persians, saying: "Me, O vilest of men, who am your
own brother, and have done nothing worthy of bonds, you have
bound and adjudged to a dungeon; but when you see the Persians
driving you out and making you houseless, you dare not avenge
yourself, though they are so easy to be subdued. But if you are in
dread of them, lend me your auxiliaries, and I will punish them for
coming here, and I am ready also to send you out of the island."
Mæandrius accepted his offer, as I think, not that he had reached
such a pitch of folly as to imagine that his own power could overcome that of the king, but rather out of envy to Syloson, if without
a struggle he should possess himself of the city uninjured. Having
therefore provoked the Persians, he wished to make the Samian
power as weak as possible, and then give it up; being well assured
that the Persians, if they suffered any ill-treatment, would be exas-

perated against the Samians ; and knowing also that he himself had
a safe retreat from the island, whenever he chose, for he had had a
secret passage dug leading from the citadel to the sea. Accordingly
Mæandrius himself sailed away from Samos ; but Charilaus armed
all the auxilaries, threw open the gates, sallied out upon the Persians,
who did not expect any thing of the kind, and slew those of the
Persians who were seated in chairs, and who were the principal men
among them. But the rest of the Persian army came to their assistance, and the auxiliaries, being hard pressed, were shut up again
within the citadel. But Otanes, the general, when he saw that the
Persians had suffered great loss, purposely neglected to obey the
orders which Darius had given him at his departure, that he should
neither kill nor take prisoner any of the Samians, but deliver the
island to Syloson without damage; on the contrary, he commanded
his army to put to death every one they met with, both man and
child alike. Whereupon, one part of the army besieged the citadel, and the rest killed every one that came in their way, all they
met, as well within the temples as without. Mæandrius in the meantime sailed to Lacedæmon, and carried with him all his treasures.
One day when he had set out his silver and golden cups, his servants began to clean them; and he, at the same time, holding a
conversation with Cleomenes, son of Anaxandrides, then king of
Sparta, led him on to his house. When the king saw the cups, he
was struck with wonder and astonishment; upon which Mæandrius
bade him take whatever he pleased, and when Mæandrius had repeated this offer two or three times, Cleomenes showed himself a
man of the highest integrity, for he refused to accept what was offered; and being informed that by giving to other citizens he would
gain their support, he went to the Ephori, and said that it would be
better for Sparta that this Samian stranger should quit the Peloponnesus, lest he should persuade him or some other of the Spartans
to become base. They immediately banished Mæandrius by public
proclamation. The Persians, having drawn Samos as with a net,
delivered it to Syloson, utterly destitute of inhabitants. Afterward,
however, Otanes, the general, repeopled it, in consequence of a
vision in a dream.

Whilst the naval armament was on its way to Samos, the Babylonians revolted, having very well prepared themselves. For during all the time the magus reigned, and the seven were rising up
against him, they had made preparations for a siege, and somehow
in the confusion this had escaped observation. But when they openly
revolted they resorted to this extraordinary means of husbanding
their resources: gathering together all the women, except their
mothers, and one woman apiece, besides, whom each one chose from
his own family, they strangled them ; the one woman each man selected to cook his food, and they strangled the rest, that they might
not consume their provisions.   When Darius was informed of this,
he collected all his forces, and marched against Babylon.   But upon
laying siege to them he found that they were not at all solicitous
about the event, for the Babylonians mounted the ramparts, and
danced, and derided Darius and his army, and cried : "Why sit ye
there, Persians? will ye not be off?   It will be a long day before
you will take us."

When the nineteenth month of the siege had passed, Zopyrus,
son of that Megabyzus, who was one of the seven who dethroned
the magus, went to Darius and asked him whether he deemed the
taking of Babylon of very great importance. Learning that he
valued it at a high price, he went away and inflicted on himself
an irremediable mutilation, for he cut off his nose and ears, chopped
his hair in a disgraceful manner, scourged himself, and then presented himself before Darius. The latter was very much grieved
when he beheld a man of high rank so mutilated, and starting from
his throne, he shouted aloud and asked who had mutilated him,·
and for what cause. He answered : "O King, there is no man
except yourself who could have power to treat me thus ; no
stranger has done it, but I myself, deeming it a great indignity
that the Assyrians should deride the Persians." "Foolish man,"
said Darius, "because you are mutilated, will the enemy sooner
submit? Have you lost your senses, that you have thus ruined
yourself?" "If I had communicated to you what I was about to
do," he answered, "you would not have permitted me, but now, if

you are not wanting to your own interests, we shall take Babylon. For I, as I am, will desert to the city, and will tell them that I have been thus treated by you ; and I think that when I have persuaded them that such is the case, I shall obtain the command of their army. Do you then, on the tenth day after I shall have entered the city, station a thousand men of that part of your army whose loss you would least regret over against the gates called after Semiramis ; again, on the seventh day after the tenth, station two thousand more against the gate called from Nineveh ; and from the seventh day let an interval of twenty days elapse, and then place four thousand more against the gate called from the Chal-

INFANTRY DRILLED BY SERGEANT.

dæans ; but let them carry no defensive arms except swords. After the twentieth day, command the rest of the army to invest the wall on all sides, but station the Persians for me at those called the Belidian and Cissian gates ; for, as I think, when I have performed great exploits, the Babylonians will intrust every thing to me, and, moreover, the keys of the gates, and then it will be mine and the Persians' care to do what remains to be done.

Having given these injunctions, he went to the gates, turning round as if he were really a deserter. Those who were stationed in that quarter, seeing him from the turrets, ran down and opened one door of the gate a little, and asked him who he was, and for what purpose he came. He told them that he was Zopyrus, and had deserted to them : the door-keepers then conducted him to the assembly of the Babylonians, and standing before them he deplored his condition, saying that he had suffered from Darius these injuries, and that he was so treated because he had advised to raise the siege, since there appeared no means of taking the city. " Now, therefore," he said, " I come to you, O Babylonians, as your greatest blessing ; and to Darius, his army, and the Persians, the greatest mischief; for he shall not escape with impunity, having thus mutilated me ; and I am acquainted with all his designs." And the Babylonians, seeing a man of distinction among the Persians deprived of his ears and nose, and covered with stripes and blood, thoroughly believing that he spoke the truth, and that he had come as an ally to them, were ready to intrust him with whatever he should ask ; and he, having obtained the command of the forces, acted as he had preconcerted with Darius ; for on the tenth he led out the army of the Babylonians, and surrounded the thousand whom he had instructed Darius to station there, and cut them all in pieces. Then the Babylonians, perceiving that he performed deeds such as he promised, were ready to obey him in every thing. He then suffered the appointed number of days to elapse, and again selected a body of Babylonians, led them out, and slaughtered the two thousand of Darius' soldiers. The Babylonians witnessing this action also, all had the praises of Zopyrus on their tongues. Then he again, after the appointed number of days had elapsed, led out his troops according to the settled plan, surrounded the four thousand, and cut them in pieces. And when he had accomplished this, Zopyrus was every thing to the Babylonians, and was appointed commander-in-chief and guardian of the walls. But when Darius, according to agreement, invested the wall all round, then Zopyrus discovered his whole treachery ; for while the Babylonians, mounting the wall, repelled the army of Darius that was attacking them, Zopyrus opened the Cissian and Belidian gates and led the Persians within the wall. Those of the Babylonians who saw what was done, fled into the temple of Jupiter Belus; and those who did not see it, remained each at his post, until they also discovered that they had been betrayed.

Thus Babylon was taken a second time. But when Darius had made himself master of the Babylonians, first of all, he demolished the walls and bore away all the gates, for when Cyrus had taken Babylon before, he did neither of these things; and secondly, Darius impaled about three thousand of the principal citizens, and allowed the rest of the Babylonians to inhabit the city. And that the Babylonians might have wives to take the place of those they had strangled, Darius ordered the neighboring provinces to send women to Babylon, taxing each at a certain number, so that

LIGHT ARMED TROOPS MARCHING.

a total of fifty thousand women came together; and from these the Babylonians of our time are descended. No Persian, in the opinion of Darius, either of those who came after, or who lived before, surpassed Zopyrus in great achievements, Cyrus only excepted; for with him no Persian ever ventured to compare himself. It is also reported that Darius frequently expressed this opinion, that he would rather Zopyrus had not suffered such ignominious treatment than acquire twenty Babylons in addition to that he had. And he honored him exceedingly; for he every year presented him with those gifts which are most prized by the Persians, and he assigned him Babylon to hold free from taxes during his life.

BOOK IV. MELPOMENE.

CHAPTER I.

DESCRIPTION OF SCYTHIA AND THE NEIGHBORING NATIONS.

AFTER the capture of Babylon, Darius made an expedition against the Scythians, for as Asia was flourishing in men, and large revenues came in, Darius was desirous of revenging himself upon the Scythians, because they had formerly invaded the Median territory, and defeated in battle those that opposed them. For the Scythians ruled over Upper Asia for twenty-eight years. But when those Scythians returned to their own country, after such an interval, a task no less than the invasion of Media awaited them; for they found an army of no inconsiderable force ready to oppose them; the wives of the Scythians, seeing their husbands were a long time absent, had married their slaves. The Scythians deprive all their slaves of sight for the sake of the milk which they drink, doing as follows: when they have taken bone tubes very like flutes, they thrust them into the veins of the mares, and blow with their mouth; while some blow, others milk. They say they do this because the veins of the mare, being inflated, become filled, and the udder is depressed. When they have finished milking, they pour the milk into hollow wooden vessels, and having placed the blind men round about the vessels, they agitate the milk: then they skim off that which swims on the surface, considering it the most valuable, but that which subsides is of less value than the other. On this account the Scythians put out the eyes of every prisoner they take; for they are not agriculturists, but feeders of cattle. From these slaves then and the women a race of youths had grown up, who, when they knew their own extraction, opposed those who were returning from Media. And first they cut off the country by digging a wide ditch, stretching from Mount Taurus to the lake Mæotis, which is of great extent, and afterward encamping opposite, they came to an engagement with the Scythians, who were endeavoring to enter. When several battles had been fought, and the Scythians were unable to obtain any advantage, one of them said: "Men of Scythia, what are we doing? by fighting with our slaves not only are we ourselves by being slain becoming fewer in number, but by killing them we shall hereafter have fewer to rule over. So it seems to me that we should lay aside our spears and bows, and that every one, taking a horsewhip, should go directly to them; for so long as they saw us with arms, they considered themselves equal to us, and born of equal birth; but when they shall see us with our whips instead of arms, they will soon learn that they are our slaves, and will no longer resist." The Scythians adopted the advice on the spot; and the slaves, struck with astonishment, forgot to fight, and fled.

As the Scythians say, theirs is the most recent of all nations. The first man that appeared in this country, which was a wilderness, was named Targitaus; they say that the parents of this Targitaus, in my opinion relating what is incredible, were Jupiter and a daughter of the river Borysthenes; and that Targitaus had three sons, who went by the names of Lipoxais, Apovais, and Colaxais; that during their reign a plough, a yoke, an axe, and a bowl of golden workmanship, dropping down from heaven, fell on the Scythian territory; that the eldest, seeing them first, approached, intending to take them up, but as he came near, the gold began to burn; when he had retired the second went up, and it did the same again; but when the youngest approached, the burning gold became extinguished, and he carried the things home with him; and the elder brothers, in consequence of this, giving way, surrendered the whole authority to Alaxais the youngest. The Scythians reckon the whole number of years from their begin-

ning, from King Targitaus to the time that Darius crossed over
against them, to be just a thousand years. This sacred gold the
kings watch with the greatest care, and annually approach it with
magnificent sacrifices to render it propitious. If he who has the
sacred gold happens to fall asleep in the open air on the festival,
the Scythians say he cannot survive the year, and on this account
they give him as much land as he can ride round on horseback in
one day. The country being very extensive, Colaxais established
three of the kingdoms for his sons, and made that one the largest
in which the gold is 'kept. The parts beyond the north of the
inhabited districts the Scythians say can neither be seen nor passed
through, by reason of the feathers shed there; for the earth and
air are so full of feathers that the view is intercepted. With
respect to these feathers I entertain the following opinion: in the
upper parts of this country it continually snows, less in summer
than in winter, as is reasonable; now, whoever has seen snow
falling thick near him, will know what I mean; for snow is like
feathers; and on account of the winter being so severe, the northern parts of this continent are uninhabited.

Such is the account the Scythians give of themselves, and of
the country above them; but the Greeks who inhabit Pontus give
the following account: they say that Hercules, as he was driving
away the herds of Geryon, arrived in this country, which was then
a desert, and that Geryon, fixing his abode outside the Pontus,
inhabited the island which the Greeks call Erythia, situated near
Gades, beyond the columns of Hercules in the ocean. The ocean,
they say, beginning from the sunrise, flows round the whole earth,
that Hercules thence came to the country now called Scythia, and
as a storm and frost overtook him, he drew his lion's skin over
him, and went to sleep; and in the meanwhile, his mares, which
were feeding apart from his chariot, vanished by some divine
chance. They add that when Hercules awoke, he sought for
them; and that having gone over the whole country, he at length
came to the land called Hylæa; there he found a monster, having
two natures, half virgin, half viper, of which the upper parts resem-

bled a woman, and the lower parts a serpent : in astonishment he asked her if she had anywhere seen his strayed mares. She said that she herself had them, and would not restore them to him unless he would make her his wife. Hercules agreed. She, how- ever, delayed giving back the mares, out of a desire to detain Her- cules as long as she could ; but as he was desirous of recovering them and departing, she at last restored the mares, saying : "These mares that strayed hither I preserved for you, but now that you will go away and leave me, tell me what I must do with our three sons when they are grown up ; shall I establish them here, for I possess the rule over this coun- try, or shall I send them to you?" He replied : "When you see the children arrived at the age of men, you cannot err if you do this : whichever of them you see able thus to bend this bow, and thus girding himself with this girdle, make him an inhabitant of this country ; and whichever fails in these tasks which I enjoin, send out of the country. If you do this you will please yourself and do wisely." Then having drawn out one of his bows, for Hercules carried two at that time, and having shown her the belt, he gave her both the bow and the belt, which had a golden cup at the extremity of the clasp, and departed. When the sons had attained to the age of men she gave them names ; to the first, Agathyrsis, to the second, Gelonus, and to the youngest, Scythes ; and, in the next place, she did what had been enjoined ; and two of her sons, Agathyrsis and Gelonus, being unable to come up to the proposed task, left the country, being expelled by their mother ; but the youngest of them, Scythes, having accomplished it, re- mained there. From this Scythes, son of Hercules, are descended those who have been successively kings of the Scythians ; and from the cup, the Scythians even to this day wear cups hung from their belts.

Aristeas, of Proconnesus, says in his epic verses, that, inspired by Apollo, he came to the Issedones ; that beyond the Issedones dwell the Arimaspians, a people that have only one eye ; beyond them the gold-guarding griffins ; and beyond these the Hyper-

boreans, who reach to the sea : that all these, except the Hyperboreans, beginning from the Arimaspians, continually encroached
upon their neighbors ; that the Issedones were expelled from their
country by the Arimaspians, the Scythians by the Issedones, and
that the Cimmerians, who inhabited on the South Sea, being pressed
by the Scythians, abandoned their country.

No one knows with certainty what is beyond the country about
which this account speaks. But as far as we have been able to arrive
at the truth with accuracy from hearsay, the whole shall be related.
From the port of the Borysthenitæ, for this is the most central part
of the sea-coast of all Scythia, the first people are the Callipidæ,
being Greek-Scythians; beyond these is another nation called Alazones. These and the Callipidæ, in other respects, follow the usages,
of the Scythians, but they both sow and feed on wheat, onions, garlic,
lentils, and millet ; but beyond the Alazones dwell husbandmen,
who do not sow wheat for food but for sale. Beyond these the
Neuri dwell ; and to the north of the Neuri the country is utterly
uninhabited, as far as I know. These nations are by the side of
the river Hypanis, to the west of the Borysthenes. But if one
crosses the Borysthenes, the first country from the sea is Hylæa ;
and from this higher up live Scythian agriculturists, where the
Greeks settled on the river Hypanis. These Scythian husbandmen occupy the country eastward, for three days' journey, extending to the river whose name is Panticapes ; and northward a passage of eleven days up the Borysthenes. Beyond this region
the country is a desert for a great distance ; and beyond the
desert Androphagi dwell, who are a distinct people, not in any respect Scythian. Beyond this is really desert, and no nation of
men is found there, as far as we know. The country eastward of
these Scythian agriculturists, when one crosses the river Panticapes,
nomads occupy, who neither sow at all nor plough ; and all this
country is destitute of trees except Hylæa. The nomads occupy
a tract eastward for fourteen days' journey, stretching to the river
Gerrhus. Beyond the Gerrhus are the parts called the Royal, and
the most valiant and numerous of the Scythians, who deem all

other Scythians to be their slaves. These extend southward to Taurica, and eastward to the trench, which those sprung from the blind men dug, and to the port on the lake Mæotis, which is called Cremni, and some of them reach to the river Tanais. The parts above to the north of the Royal Scythians, the Melanchlæni inhabit, a distinct race, and not Scythian. But above the Melanchlæni are lakes, and an uninhabited desert, as far as we know.

After one crosses the river Tanais, it is no longer Scythian, but the first region belongs to the Sauromatæ, who, beginning from the recess of the lake Mæotis, occupy the country northward, for a fifteen days' journey, all destitute both of wild and cultivated trees. Above these dwell the Budini, occupying the second region, and possessing a country thickly covered with all sorts of trees. Above the Budini, toward the north, there is first a desert of seven days' journey, and next to the desert, if one turns somewhat toward the east, dwell the Thyssagetæ, a numerous and distinct race, and they live by hunting. Contiguous to these, in the same regions, dwell those who are called Iyrcæ, who also live by hunting in the following manner : the huntsman, having climbed a tree, lies in ambush (and the whole country is thickly wooded), and each man has a horse ready taught to lie on his belly, that he may not be much above the ground, and a dog besides. When he sees any game from the tree, having let fly an arrow, he mounts his horse, and goes in pursuit, and the dog keeps close to him. Above these, as one bends toward the east, dwell other Scythians, who revolted from the Royal Scythians, and so came to this country. As far as the territory of these Scythians, the whole country that has been described is level and deep-soiled ; but after this it is stony and rugged. When one has passed through a considerable extent of the rugged country, a people are found living at the foot of lofty mountains, who are said to be all bald from their birth, both men and women, and are flat-nosed, and have large chins ; they speak a peculiar language, wear the Scythian costume, and live on the fruit of a tree ; the name of the tree on which they live is called ponticon, and is about the size of a fig-

tree; it bears fruit like a bean, and has a stone. When this is
ripe they strain it through a cloth, and a thick and black liquor
flows from it, to which they give the name of aschy; this they suck,
and drink mingled with milk; from the thick sediment of the pulp
they make cakes to eat, for they have not many cattle in these
parts, as the pastures there are not good. Every man lives under
a tree, which, in the winter, he covers with a thick white woollen
covering. No man does any injury to this people, for they are
accounted sacred; nor do they possess any warlike weapon.
They determine by arbitration the differences that arise among
their neighbors; and whoever takes refuge among them is injured
by no one. They are called Argippæi.

As far, then, as these bald people, our knowledge respecting
the country and the nations before them is very good, for some
Scythians frequently go there from whom it is not difficult to obtain information, as well as some Greeks belonging to the ports in
Pontus. The Scythians who go to them transact business by
means of seven interpreters and seven languages, but beyond the
bald men no one can speak with certainty, for lofty and impassable
mountains form their boundary, which no one has ever crossed;
but these bald men say, what to me is incredible, that men with
goats' feet inhabit these mountains; and when one has passed beyond them, other men are found, who sleep six months at a time,
but this I do not at all admit. However, the country eastward of
the bald men is well known, being inhabited by Issedones, who
are said to observe this extraordinary custom. When a man's
father dies all his relations bring cattle, which they sacrifice, and,
having cut up the flesh, they cut up also the dead parent of their
host, and mingling all the flesh together, they spread out a banquet; then making bare and cleansing his head they gild it; and
afterward treat it as a sacred image, performing grand annual sacrifices to it. A son does this to his father, as the Greeks celebrate
the anniversary of their father's death. These people are likewise
accounted just; and the women have equal authority with the
men.

Above them, the Issedones affirm, are the men with only one eye, and the gold-guarding griffins. The Scythians repeat this account, having received it from them; and we have adopted it from the Scythians, and call them in the Scythian language, Arimaspi; for *Arima*, in the Scythian language, signifies one, and *Spou*, the eye. All this country which I have been speaking of is subject to such a severe winter, that for eight months the frost is intolerable, so that if you pour water on the ground you will not make mud, but if you light a fire you will. Even the sea freezes, and the whole Cimmerian Bosphorus; and the Scythians who live within the trench lead their armies and drive their chariots over the ice to the Sindians, on the other side. Thus winter continues eight months, and even during the other four it is cold there. And this winter is different in character from the winters in all other countries; for in this no rain worth mentioning falls in the usual season, but during the summer it never leaves off raining. At the time when there is thunder elsewhere there is none there, but in summer it is violent: if there should be thunder in winter, it is counted a prodigy to be wondered at. So, should there be an earthquake, whether in summer or winter, in Scythia it is accounted a prodigy. Their horses endure this cold, but asses and mules cannot endure it at all; whereas in other places in the world horses that stand exposed to frost become frost-bitten and waste away, but asses and mules endure it. On this account also the race of beeves appears to me to be defective there, and not to have horns; and the following verse of Homer, in his Odyssey, confirms my opinion: "And Libya, where the lambs soon put forth their horns," rightly observing, that in warm climates horns shoot out quickly; but in very severe cold, the cattle do not produce them at all, or with difficulty. Concerning the Hyperboreans, I do not relate the story of Abaris, who was said to have carried an arrow round the whole earth without eating any thing. But I smile when I see many persons describing the circumference of the earth, who have no sound reason to guide them; they describe the ocean as flowing around the earth, which is made circular as if by a lathe, and make Asia equal to Europe.

In length Europe extends along both Libya and Asia, but in respect to width, it is evidently much larger. Libya shows itself to be surrounded by water, except so much of it as borders upon Asia. Neco, King of Egypt, was the first whom we know of that proved this; when he had ceased digging the canal leading from the Nile to the Arabian Gulf, he sent certain Phœnicians in ships, with orders to sail back through the pillars of Hercules into the Mediterranean Sea, and so return to Egypt. The Phœnicians accordingly, setting out from the Red Sea, navigated the southern sea; when autumn came they went ashore and sowed the land, by whatever part of Libya they happened to be sailing, and waited for harvest; then having reaped the corn, they put to sea again. When two years had thus passed, in the third they doubled the pillars of Hercules, arrived in Egypt, and related what to me does not seem credible, but may to others, that as they sailed round Libya, they had the sun on their right hand.[1] Ever since that the Carthaginians say that Libya is surrounded by water.

A great part of Asia was explored under the direction of Darius. Being desirous to know where the Indus, which is the second river that produces crocodiles, discharges itself into the sea, he sent in ships Scylax of Caryanda and others on whom he could rely to make a true report. They accordingly set out from the city of Caspatyrus, sailed down the river toward the sunrise to the sea; then sailing on the sea westward, they arrived in the thirtieth month at that place where the king of Egypt despatched the Phœnicians, whom I before mentioned, to sail round Libya. After this Darius subdued the Indians, and frequented this sea. Thus the other parts of Asia, except toward the rising sun, are found to exhibit things similar to Libya.

Whether Europe is surrounded by water either toward the east or toward the north, has not been fully discovered by any man; but in length it is known to extend beyond both the other continents. Nor can I conjecture for what reason three different names have been given to the earth, which is but one, and why those

---

[1] Herodotus means that south of the equator the sun was in the north.

should be derived from the names of women, Libya is said by most of the Greeks to take its name from a native woman of the name of Libya ; and Asia, from the wife of Prometheus. But the Lydians claim this name, saying that Asia was so called after Asius, son of Cotys, son of Manes, and not after Asia the wife of Prometheus ; from whom also a tribe in Sardis is called the Asian tribe ; nor is it clear whence Europe received its name, nor who gave it, unless we say that the region received the name from the Tyrian Europa : yet she evidently belonged to Asia, and never came into the country which is now called Europe by the Greeks.

The Euxine Sea exhibits the most ignorant nations : for we are unable to mention any one nation of those on this side the Pontus that has any pretensions to intelligence ; nor have we ever heard of any learned man among them, except the Scythian nation and Anacharsis. By the Scythian nation one of the most important of human devices has been contrived more wisely than by any others whom we know ; their other customs, however, I do not admire. This device has been contrived so that no one who attacks them can escape ; and that, if they do not choose to be found, no one is able to overtake them. For they have neither cities nor fortifications, but carry their houses with them ; they are all equestrian archers, living not from the cultivation of the earth, but from cattle, and their dwellings are wagons,—how must not such a people be invincible, and difficult to engage with ? The country and the rivers aid them : for the country, being level, abounds in herbage and is well watered ; and rivers flow through it almost as numerous as the canals in Egypt. The Ister, which is the greatest of all the rivers we know, flows always with an equal stream both in summer and winter, and has five mouths.

In each district of the Scythians, in the place where the magistrates assemble, is erected a structure sacred to Mars, of the following kind. Bundles of faggots are heaped up to the length and breadth of three stades, but less in height ; on the top of this a square platform is formed ; and three of the sides are perpendicular, but on the fourth it is accessible. Every year they heap on it one hundred and fifty wagon-loads of faggots, for it is continually sinking by reason of the weather. On this heap an old iron scimetar is placed by each tribe, and this is the image of Mars; they bring yearly sacrifices of cattle and horses; and to these *scimetars* they offer more sacrifices than to the rest of the gods. Whatever enemies they take alive, of these they sacrifice one in a hundred, not in the same manner as they do the cattle, but in a different manner; for after they have poured a libation of wine on their heads, they cut the throats of the men over a bowl; then having carried *the bowl* on the heap of faggots, they pour the blood over the scimetar. Below at the sacred precinct, they do as follows: having cut off all the right shoulders of the men that have been killed, with the arms, they throw them into the air; and then, having finished the rest of the sacrificial rites, they depart; but the arm lies wherever it has fallen, and the body apart. Swine they never use, nor suffer them to be used in their country at all.

When a Scythian overthrows his first enemy, he drinks his blood; and presents the king with the heads of the enemies he has killed in battle; for if he brings a head, he shares the booty that they take; but not, if he does not bring one. He skins it in the following manner. Having made a circular incision round the ears and taking hold of the skin, he shakes it from the skull; then having scraped off the flesh with the rib of an ox, he softens the skin with his hands, makes it supple, and uses it as a napkin; each man hangs it on the bridle of the horse which he rides, and prides himself on it; for whoever has the greatest number of these skin napkins is accounted the most valiant man. Many of them make cloaks of these skins, to throw over themselves, sewing them together like shepherd's coats; and many, having flayed the right hands of their enemies that are dead, together with the nails, make coverings for their quivers; the skin of a man, which is both thick and shining, surpasses almost all other skins in the brightness of its white. Many, having flayed men whole, and stretched the skin on wood, carry it about on horseback. The heads themselves, not indeed of all, but of their greatest enemies, they treat as follows:

each, having sawn off all below the eye-brows, cleanses it, and if the man is poor, he covers only the outside with leather, and so uses it; but if he is rich, he covers it with leather, and gilds the inside, and so uses it for a drinking-cup. They do this also to their relatives, if they are at variance, and one prevails over another in the presence of the king. When strangers of consideration come to him, he produces these heads, and relates how, though they were his relatives, they made war against him, and he overcame them, considering this a proof of bravery. Once in every year, the governor of a district, each in his own district, mingles a bowl of wine, from which those Scythians drink by whom enemies have been captured; but they who have not achieved this, do not taste of this wine, but sit at a distance in dishonor; this is accounted the greatest disgrace: such of them as have killed very many men, having two cups at once, drink them together.

Soothsayers among the Scythians are numerous, who divine by the help of a number of willow rods, in the following manner. They lay large bundles of twigs on the ground and untie them; and having placed each rod apart, they utter their predictions; and whilst they are pronouncing them, they gather up the rods again, and put them together again one by one. This is their national mode of divination. But the Enarees, or Androgyni, say that Venus gave them the power of divining by means of the bark of a linden tree: when a man has split the linden-tree in three pieces, twisting it round his own fingers, and then untwisting it, he utters a response.

When the king of the Scythians is sick, he sends for three of the most famous of the prophets, who prophesy in the manner above mentioned. When any of these prophets are proved to have sworn falsely, they put them to death in the following manner: they fill a wagon with faggots, and yoke oxen to it, then tie the feet of the prophets, bind their hands behind them, gag them, and enclose them in the midst of the faggots; then having set fire to them, they terrify the oxen, and let them go. Many oxen are burnt with the prophets, and many escape very much scorched, when the pole has been burnt asunder. Of the children of those whom he puts to death, the king kills all the males, but does not hurt the females.

The sepulchres of the kings are in the country of the Gerrhi. There, when their king dies, they dig a large square hole in the ground, to receive the corpse. Then, having the body covered with wax, the belly opened and cleaned, filled with bruised cypress, incense, parsley and anise-seed, and sewn up again, they carry it in a chariot to another nation ; those who receive the corpse, brought to them, do the same as the Royal Scythians ; they cut off part of their ear, shave off their hair, wound themselves on the arms, lacerate their forehead and nose, and drive arrows through their left hand. Thence they carry the corpse of the king to another nation whom they govern ; and those to whom they first came accompany them. When they have carried the corpse round all the provinces, they arrive at the sepulchres among the Gerrhi, who are the most remote of the nations they rule over. Then, when they have placed the corpse in the grave on a bed of leaves, having fixed spears on each side of the dead body, they lay pieces of wood over it, and cover it over with mats. In the remaining space of the grave they bury one of the king's wives, having strangled her, and his cup-bearer, a cook, a groom, a page, a courier, and horses, and firstlings of every thing else, and golden goblets ; they make no use of silver or bronze. Then they all heap up a large mound, vieing with each other to make it as large as possible. At the expiration of a year, they take the most fitting of his remaining servants, all native Scythians ; for whomsoever the king may order serve him, and they have no servants bought with money. Now when they have strangled fifty of these servants, and fifty of the finest horses, they take out their bowels, cleanse them, fill them with chaff, and sew them up again. Then placing the half of a wheel, with its concave side uppermost, on two pieces of wood, and the other half on two other pieces of wood, and preparing many of these in the same manner, they thrust thick pieces of wood through the horses lengthwise, up to the neck, mount them on the half-wheels ; the foremost part of the half-wheels supporting the shoulders of the horses, and the hinder part the belly near the thighs, while the legs on both sides are suspended in the air ; then, having put bridles and bits on the horses, they stretch them in front, and fasten them to a stake ; they then mount upon each horse one of the fifty young men that have been strangled. They drive a straight piece of wood along the spine as far as the neck, and a part of this wood which projects from the bottom they fix into a hole bored in the other piece of wood that passes through the horse. The horsemen are then placed round the monument, and they depart.

When the other Scythians die, their nearest relations carry them about among their friends, laid in chariots ; each one receives and entertains the attendants, and sets the same things before the dead body, as before the rest. In this manner private persons are carried about for forty days, and then buried. After the burial the Scythians purify themselves by wiping and thoroughly washing their heads and bodies. They set up three pieces of wood leaning against each other, extend around them woollen cloths ; and having joined them together as closely as possible, they throw red-hot stones into a vessel placed in the middle of the pieces of wood and the cloths. They have a sort of hemp growing in this country, much like flax, except in thickness and height ; in this respect the hemp is far superior : it grows both spontaneously and from cultivation ; and from it the Thracians make garments like linen, nor would any one who is not well skilled in such matters distinguish whether they are made of flax or hemp, but a person who has never seen this hemp would think the garment was made of flax. The Scythians take seed of this hemp, creep under the cloths, and put the seed on the red-hot stones ; this smokes, and produces such a steam, as no Grecian vapor-bath could surpass. Transported with vapor, they shout aloud ; and this serves them instead of washing, for they never bathe the body in water. Their women pound on a rough stone pieces of cypress, cedar, and incense-tree, pouring on water ; and then this pounded matter, when it is thick, they smear over the whole body and face. This at the same time gives them an agreeable odor, and when they take off the cataplasm on the following day, they become clean and shining.

I have never been able to learn with accuracy the amount of the population of the Scythians. There is a spot between the river Borysthenes and the Hypanis, called Exampæus, containing a fountain of bitter water, which renders the Hypanis unfit to be drunk. In this spot lies a bronze cauldron, in size six times as large as the bowl at the mouth of the Pontus, which Pausanias, son of Cleombrotus, dedicated. For the benefit of any one who has never seen this, I will describe it : The cauldron easily contains six hundred amphoræ ; and is six fingers in thickness. The inhabitants say that it was made from the points of arrows ; for their king, Ariantas, wishing to know the population of the Scythians, commanded the Scythians to bring him each one point of an arrow, and threatened death on whosoever should fail to bring it. Accordingly, a vast number of arrow points were brought, and resolving to leave a monument made from them, he made this bronze bowl, and dedicated it at Exampæus. Their country has nothing wonderful, except the rivers, which are very large and very many in number, and the extensive plains. They show the print of the foot of Hercules upon a rock near the river Tyras ; it resembles the footstep of man, and is two cubits in length.

CHAPTER II.

INVASION OF SCYTHIA BY DARIUS.

WHILST Darius was making preparations against the Scythians, and sending messages to command some to contribute land forces, and others a fleet, and others to bridge over the Thracian Bosphorus, Artabanus, the son of Hystaspes, and brother of Darius, entreated him on no account to make an expedition against the Scythians, representing the poverty of Scythia ; but he could not persuade him. At that time Œobazus, a Persian, who had three sons all serving in the army, besought Darius that one might be left at home for him. The king answered him, as a friend, and one who had made a moderate request, that he would leave him all his sons ; he therefore was exceedingly delighted, hoping that his sons would be discharged from the army. But at Darius' command the proper officers put all the sons of Œobazus to death, and left them on the spot.

When Darius, marching from Susa, reached Chalcedon on the Bosphorus, a bridge was already laid across. There, sitting in the temple, he took a view of the Euxine Sea, which is worthy of admiration, for of all seas it is by nature the most wonderful.

Darius, pleased with the bridge, presented its architect, Mandrocles the Samian, with ten of every thing, and he painted a picture of the whole junction of the Bosphorus, with King Darius seated on a throne, and his army crossing over, and dedicated it as first fruits in the temple of Juno.

When Darius reached the river Tearus he was so delighted with it that he erected a pillar with this inscription : THE SPRINGS OF THE TEARUS YIELD THE BEST AND FINEST WATER OF ALL RIVERS ; AND A MAN, THE BEST AND FINEST OF ALL MEN, CAME TO THEM, LEAD-

ING AN ARMY AGAINST THE SCYTHIANS, DARIUS, SON OF HYSTASPES,
KING OF THE PERSIANS, AND OF THE WHOLE CONTINENT.

Before he reached the Ister, he subdued the Getæ, who think
themselves immortal, supposing that they themselves do not die,
but that the deceased go to the deity Zalmoxis. Every fifth year
they dispatch one of themselves, taken by lot, to Zalmoxis, with
orders to let him know on each occasion what they want. Their
mode of sending him is this. Some who are appointed hold three
javelins ; whilst others take up the man who is to be sent to Zalmoxis by the hands and feet, swing him round, and throw him into
the air, upon the points. If he is transfixed and dies, they think
the god is propitious to them ; if he does not die, they blame the
messenger himself, saying that he is a bad man, and dispatch another.

When Darius and his land forces reached the Ister and all had
crossed, Coes, general of the Mitylenians, advised the king to let
the bridge remain over it, leaving the men who constructed it as
its guard. "Not," said he, "that I am at all afraid that we shall be
conquered in battle by the Scythians, but rather that, being unable to find them, we may suffer somewhat in our wanderings."
"Lesbian friend," replied Darius, "when I am safe back in my
own palace, fail not to present yourself to me, that I may requite
you for good advice with good deeds." Tying sixty knots in a
thong, he summoned the Ionian commanders to his presence, and
said : "Men of Ionia, I have changed my resolution concerning
the bridge ; so take this thong, and as soon as you see me
march against the Scythians, untie one of these knots every day ;
and if I return not until the days numbered by the knots have
passed, sail away to your own country. Till that time, since I
have changed my determination, guard the bridge, and apply the
utmost care to preserve and secure it."

The Scythians determined to fight no battle in the open field,
because their allies did not come to their assistance ; but to retreat
and draw off covertly, and fill up the wells and the springs as
they passed by, and destroy the herbage on the ground. They

sent forward the best of their cavalry as an advanced guard; but the wagons, in which all their children and wives lived, they left behind.

Advancing with his army as quick as possible, he fell in with the Scythian divisions and pursued them, but they kept a day's march before him. The Scythians, for Darius did not relax his pursuit, fled, as had been determined, toward those nations that had refused to assist them. When this had continued for a considerable time, Darius sent a horseman to Indathyrsus, king of the Scythians, with the following message: "Most miserable of men, why dost thou continually fly, when it is in thy power to do one of these two other things? For if thou thinkest thou art able to resist my power, stand, and having ceased thy wanderings, fight; but if thou art conscious of thy inferiority, in that case also cease thy hurried march, and bringing earth and water as presents to thy master, come to a conference." To this Indathyrsus, the king of the Scythians, answered: "This is the case with me, O Persian; I never yet fled from any man out of fear, nor do I now so flee from thee; nor have I done any thing different now from what I am wont to do, even in time of peace; but why I do not forthwith fight thee, I will explain. We have no cities nor cultivated lands, for which we are under any apprehension lest they should be taken or ravaged. Yet, if it is by all means necessary to come to battle at once, we have the sepulchres of our ancestors, come, find these, and attempt to disturb them, then you will know whether we will fight for our sepulchres or not; but before that, unless we choose, we will not engage with thee. The only masters I acknowledge are Jupiter my progenitor, and Vesta, queen of the Scythians; but to thee, instead of presents of earth and water, I will send such presents as are proper to come to thee. And in answer to thy boast, that thou art my master, I bid thee weep." (This is a Scythian saying.) The herald therefore departed carrying this answer to Darius.

When the kings of the Scythians heard the name of servitude, they were filled with indignation; whereupon they sent the division united with the Sauromatæ, which Scopasis commanded, with orders to confer with the Ionians, who guarded the bridge over the Ister. Those who were left resolved no longer to lead the Persians about, but to attack them whenever they were taking their meals; accordingly, observing the soldiers of Darius taking their meals, they put their design in execution. The Scythian cavalry always routed the Persian cavalry, but the Persian horsemen in their flight fell back on the infantry, and the infantry supported them. The Scythians, having beaten back the cavalry, wheeled around through fear of the infantry. A very remarkable circumstance, that was advantageous to the Persians and adverse to the Scythians, when they attacked the camp of Darius, was the braying of the asses and the appearance of the mules, for Scythia produces neither ass nor mule; there is not in the whole Scythian territory a single ass or mule, by reason of cold. The asses, then, growing playful, put the Scythian horses into confusion; and frequently, as they were advancing upon the Persians, when the horses heard, midway, the braying of the asses, they wheeled round in confusion, and were greatly amazed, pricking up their ears, as having never before heard such a sound, nor seen such a shape; and this circumstance in some slight degree affected the fortune of the war.

When the Scythians saw the Persians in great commotion, to detain them longer in Scythia they left some of their own cattle in the care of the herdsmen and withdrew to another spot; and the Persians coming up, took the cattle and exulted in what they had done. When this had happened several times, Darius at last was in a great strait, and the kings of the Scythians, having ascertained this, sent a herald, bearing as gifts to Darius, a bird, a mouse, a frog, and five arrows. The Persians asked the bearer of the gifts the meaning of this present; but he answered that he had no other orders than to deliver them and return immediately; and he advised the Persians, if they were wise, to discover what the gifts meant. Darius' opinion was that the Scythians meant to give themselves up to him, as well as earth and water; forming

his conjecture thus : since a mouse is bred in the earth, and sub-
sists on the same food as a man ; a frog lives in the water ; a bird
is very like a horse ; and the arrows they deliver up as their whole
strength. But Gobryas, one of the seven who had deposed the
magus, did not coincide with this ; he conjectured that the presents
intimated : " Unless, O Persians, ye become birds and fly into the
air, or become mice and hide yourselves beneath the earth, or
become frogs and leap into the lakes, ye shall never return home
again, but be stricken by these arrows." And thus the other
Persians interpreted the gifts.

The rest of the Scythians, after they had sent the presents to
Darius, drew themselves up opposite the Persians with their foot
and horse, as if they intended to come to an engagement ; and as
the Scythians were standing in their ranks, a hare started in the
midst of them ; and each went in pursuit of it. The Scythians being
in great confusion, and shouting loudly, Darius asked the meaning
of the uproar in the enemy's ranks ; but when he heard that they
were pursuing a hare, he said to those he was accustomed to address on such occasions : " These men treat us with great contempt ; and I am convinced that Gobryas spoke rightly concerning
the Scythian presents. I feel that we have need of the best advice, how our return home may be effected in safety." To this
Gobryas answered : " O king, I was in some measure acquainted
by report with these men ; but I have learned much more since I
came hither, and seen how they make sport of us. My opinion
is, that as soon as night draws on we should light fires, as we are
accustomed to do, and having deceived and left behind those
soldiers who are least able to bear hardships, and having tethered
all the asses, should depart before the Scythians direct their march
to the Ister, for the purpose of destroying the bridge, or the
Ionians take any resolution which may occasion our ruin."
Darius acted on this opinion : the infirm amongst the soldiers, and
those whose loss would be of the least consequence, he left on the
spot in the camp. And he left the asses, that they might make a
noise ; and the men were left on this pretext, that he with the

strength of his army was about to attack the Scythians, and they, during that time, would defend the camp. So Darius laid these injunctions on those he was preparing to abandon, caused the fires to be lighted, and marched away with all speed toward the Ister. The asses, deserted by the multitude, began to bray much louder than usual ; so that the Scythians, hearing them, supposed of course that the Persians were still at their station. When day appeared, the men that were abandoned, discovering that they had been betrayed by Darius, extended their hands to the Scythians, and told them what had occurred ; when they heard this the divisions of the Scythians joined forces as quickly as possible and pursued the Persians straight toward the Ister. But as a great part of the Persian army consisted of infantry, and they did not know the way, there being no roads cut, and as the Scythian army consisted of cavalry, and knew the shortest route, they missed each other, and the Scythians arrived at the bridge much before the Persians. Finding that the Persians were not yet arrived, they spoke to the Ionians who were on board the ships in these terms : " Men of Ionia, the number of days appointed for your stay is already passed, and you do not as you ought in continuing here ; but if you remained before through fear, now break up the passage and depart as quickly as possible, rejoicing that you are free, and give thanks to the gods and the Scythians. As for the man who before was your master, we will so deal with him that he shall never hereafter make war on any people."

Upon this the Ionians held a consultation. The opinion of Miltiades the Athenian, who commanded and reigned over the Chersonesites on the Hellespont, was, that they should comply with the request of the Scythians, and restore liberty to Ionia. But Histiæus the Milesian was of a contrary opinion, and said, " that every one reigned over his own city through Darius ; and if Darius' power should be destroyed, neither would he himself continue master of Miletus, nor any of the rest of other places ; because every one of the cities would choose to be governed rather by a democracy than a tyranny. Histiæus had no sooner delivered this opinion, than all went over to his side, who had before assented to that of Miltiades. Approving of the opinion of Histiæus, they determined to add to it the following acts and words. To break up the bridge on the Scythian side, as far as a bow-shot might reach, that they might seem to do something, when in effect they did nothing ; and that the Scythians might not attempt to use violence and purpose to cross the Ister by the bridge ; and to say, while they were breaking up the bridge on the Scythian side, they would do every thing that might be agreeable to the Scythians. And, Histiæus delivered the answer in the name of all, saying as follows : " Men of Scythia, you have brought us good advice, and urge it seasonably ; you, on your part, have pointed out the right way to us, and we on ours readily submit to you ; for, as you see, we are breaking up the passage, and will use all diligence, desiring to be free. But while we are breaking it up, it is fitting you should seek for them, and having found them, avenge us and yourselves on them, as they deserve." The Scythians, believing a second time that the Ionians were sincere, turned back to seek the Persians ; but entirely missed the way they had taken. The Scythians themselves were the cause of this, as they had destroyed the pastures for the horses in this direction, and filled in the wells ; for if they had not done this, they might easily have found the Persians ; but now they erred in the very thing which they thought they had contrived for the best. For the Scythians sought the enemy by traversing those parts of the country where there was forage and water for the horses, thinking that they too would make their retreat by that way. But the Persians carefully observing their former track, returned by it, and thus with difficulty found the passage. As they arrived in the night, and perceived the bridge broken off, they fell into the utmost consternation, lest the Ionians had abandoned them. There was with Darius an Egytian, who had an exceedingly loud voice. This man Darius commanded to stand on the bank of the Ister, and called Histiæus the Milesian. He did so, and Histiæus, having heard the first shout, brought up all the ships to carry the army across, and joined the bridge. Thus the Persians escaped.

CHAPTER III.

BEGINNING from Egypt the Adrymachidæ are the first of the Libyans we meet with : they for the most part observe the usages of Egypt, but they wear the same dress as the other Libyans. The women wear a chain of bronze on each leg, and allow their hair to grow long. Next to these are the Giligammæ, who occupy the country westward, as far as the island Aphrodisias. Midway on this coast the island of Platea is situated, which the Cyrenæans colonized. The Asbystæ adjoin the Giligammæ westward; they inhabit the country above Cyrene, but do not reach to the sea ; for the Cyrenæans occupy the sea-coast. They drive four-horsed chariots, more than any of the Libyans, and endeavor to imitate most of the customs of the Cyrenæans. The Nasamones, a very numerous people, live to the westward. In summer they leave their cattle on the coast, and go up to the region of Augila, in order to gather the fruit of the palm-trees, which grow in great numbers to a large size, and are all productive. They catch locusts, dry them in the sun, reduce them to powder, and sprinkling them in milk, drink them. In their oaths and divinations they swear, laying their hands on the sepulchres of those who are generally esteemed to have been the most just and excellent persons among them ; and they divine, going to the tombs of their ancestors, and after having prayed, they lie down to sleep, and whatever dream they have, they avail themselves of. In pledging their faith, each party gives the other to drink out of his hand, and drinks in turn from the other's hand ; and if they have no liquid, they take up some dust from the ground and lick it.

Above these to the north, in a country abounding with wild

beasts, live the Garamantes, who avoid all men and the society of any others ; they do not possess any warlike weapon, nor do they know how to defend themselves. The Macæ adjoin them on the sea-coast, westward ; these shave their heads so as to leave a tuft, and allowing the middle hair to grow, keep both sides shaved close to the skin ; in war they wear the skins of ostriches for defensive armor. The river Cinyps, flowing through their country from a hill called the Graces, discharges itself into the sea. This hill of the Graces is thickly covered with trees, though all the rest of Libya is bare. From the sea to this hill is a distance of two hundred stades. The Lotophagi occupy the coast that projects to the sea in front ; they subsist only on the fruit of the lotus, which is equal in size to the mastic berry, and in sweetness resembles the fruit of the palm-tree. The Lotophagi make wine also from this fruit.

The Machlyes, who also use the lotus, but in a less degree than those before mentioned, adjoin the Lotophagi on the sea-coast. They extend as far as a large river called Triton, which discharges itself into the great lake Tritonis ; and in it is an island named Phla. They say that the Lacedæmonians were commanded by an oracle to colonize this island. The following story is also told : that Jason, when the building of the Argo was finished at the foot of Mount Pelion, having put a hecatomb on board, and a bronze tripod, sailed round the Peloponnesus, purposing to go to Delphi ; and as he was sailing off Malea, a north wind caught him and drove him to Libya ; and before he could descern the land, he found himself in the shallows of the lake Tritonis ; and as he was in doubt how to extricate his ship, the story goes that a Triton appeared to him, and bade Jason give him the tripod, promising that he would show them the passage, and conduct them away in safety. Jason consented, and the Triton showed them the passage out of the shallows, and placed the tripod in his own temple ; then pronouncing an oracle from the tripod, he declared to Jason and his companions all that should happen,—that "when one of the descendants of those who sailed with him in the Argo should carry away the tripod, then it was fated that a hundred Grecian cities should be built about the lake Tritonis." The neighboring nations of the Libyans, when they heard this, concealed the tripods. The Auses adjoin these Machlyes ; they, as well as the Machlyes, dwell round the lake Tritonis, and the Triton forms the boundary between them. The Machlyes let the hair grow on the back of the head, and the Auses on the front. At the annual festival of Minerva, their virgins, dividing themselves into two companies, fight together with stones and staves, affirming that they perform the ancient rites to their native goddess, whom we call Minerva ; and those of the virgins who die from their wounds they call false virgins. But before they leave off fighting, they, with one consent, deck the maiden that excels in beauty, with a Corinthian helmet, and a suit of Grecian armor, and placing her in a chariot conduct her round the lake. In what way they formerly decorated the maidens before the Greeks settled in their neighborhood, I am unable to say ; but I conjecture that they were decked in Egyptian armor, for I am of opinion that the shield and helmet were brought from Egypt into Greece.

Above these nomadic tribes, inland, Libya abounds in wild beasts ; beyond the wild-beast tract is a ridge of sand, stretching from the Egyptian Thebes to the columns of Hercules. At intervals of a ten days' journey in this ridge, there are pieces of salt in large lumps on hills ; and at the top of each hill, from the midst of the salt, cool, sweet water gushes up. The first people you come to after a ten days' journey from Thebes, are the Ammonians, who have a temple resembling that of Theban Jupiter. For the image of Jupiter at Thebes has the head of a ram. They have also another kind of spring water which in the morning is tepid, becomes colder about the time of full forum, and at midday is very cold ; at that time they water their gardens. As the day declines it generally loses its coldness, till the sun sets, then the water becomes tepid again, and continuing to increase in heat till midnight, it then boils and bubbles up ; when midnight is passed, it gets cooler until morning. This fountain is called after the sun.

Next to the Ammonians, along the ridge of sand, at the end of another ten days' journey, there is a hill of salt, like that of the Ammonians, and water, and men live round it ; the name of this region is Augila ; and thither the Nasamonians go to gather dates. From the Augilæ, at the end of another ten days' journey, is another hill of salt and water, and many fruit-bearing palm-trees, as also in other places ; and men inhabit it who are called Garamantes, a very powerful nation ; they lay earth upon the salt, and then sow their ground. From these to the Lotophagi the shortest route is a journey of thirty days ; amongst them cattle that feed backwards are met with, having horns that are so bent forward, that they are unable to feed forwards, because their horns would stick in the ground. They differ from other kine in no other respect, except that their hide is thicker and harder. These Garamantes hunt the Ethiopian Troglodytes in four-horse chariots ; these Ethiopian Troglodytes are the swiftest of foot of all men of whom we have heard any account given. The Troglodytes feed upon serpents and lizards, and such kinds of reptiles ; they speak a language like no other, but screech like bats.

At the distance of another ten days' journey from the Garamantes is another hill of salt and water, around which a people live who are called Atarantes ; they are the only race we know of who have not personal names. For the name Atarantes belongs to them collectively, and to each one of them no name is given. They curse the sun as he passes over their heads, and moreover utter against him the foulest invectives, because he consumes by his scorching heat, the men themselves and their country. Afterward, at the end of still another ten days' journey, there is one more hill of salt and water, and men live round it, near a mountain called Atlas ; it is narrow and circular on all sides, and is said to be so lofty that its top can never be seen ; it is never free from clouds, either in summer or winter. The inhabitants say that it is the Pillar of Heaven. From this mountain the men derive their appellation, for they are called Atlantes. They are said neither to eat the flesh of any animal, nor to see visions. As far,

then, as these Atlantes, I am able to mention the names of the
nations that inhabit this ridge, but not beyond them. This ridge,
however, extends as far as the pillars of Hercules, and even beyond; and there is a mine of salt in it at intervals of ten days'
journey, and men dwelling there. The houses of them all are built
of blocks of salt, for in these parts of Libya no rain falls; walls
being of salt could not of course stand long if rain did fall. The
salt dug out there is white and purple in appearance. Above this
ridge, to the south and interior of Libya, the country is a desert,
without water, without animals, without rain, and without wood;
and there is no kind of moisture in it.

Westward of lake Tritonis, the Libyans are no longer nomads,
nor do they follow the same customs, with respect to their children,
as the nomads are accustomed to do; for the nomadic Libyans,
whether all I am unable to say with certainty, but many of them,
when their children are four years old, burn the veins on the
crown of their heads, with uncleaned sheep's wool; and some of
them do so on the veins in the temples; to the end that humors
flowing down from the head may not injure them as long as they
live: and, for this reason, they say they are so very healthy, for
the Libyans are in truth the most healthy of all men with whom
we are acquainted. But I simply repeat what the Libyans themselves say. From the Libyan women the Greeks derived the attire and ægis of Minerva's statues; for, except that the dress of
the Libyan women is leather, and the fringes that hang from the
ægis are not serpents, but made of thongs, they are otherwise
equipped in the same way; and, moreover, the very name proves
that the garb of the Palladia comes from Libya; for the Libyan
women throw over their dress, goats' skins without the hair,
fringed and dyed with red. From these goats' skins the Greeks
have borrowed the name of Ægis. And the howlings in the
temples were, I think, first derived from there; for the Libyan
women practise the same custom, and do it well. The Greeks
also learnt from the Libyans to yoke four horses abreast. All the
nomads, except the Nasamonians, inter their dead in the same

manner as the Greeks ; these bury them in a sitting posture, watching when one is about to expire, that they may set him up, and he may not die supine. Their dwellings are compacted of the asphodel shrub, interwoven with rushes, and are portable.

To the west of the river Triton, Libyans who are husbandmen next adjoin the Auses ; they are accustomed to live in houses, and are called Maxyes. They let the hair grow on the right side of the head, and shave the left ; and bedaub the body with vermilion : they say that they are descended from men who came from Troy. This region, and all the rest of Libya westward, is much more infested by wild beasts and more thickly wooded than the country of the nomads ; for the eastern country of Libya, which the nomads inhabit, is low and sandy, as far as the river Triton ; but the country westward of this, which is occupied by agriculturists, is very mountainous, woody, and abounds with wild beasts. For amongst them there are enormous serpents, and lions, elephants, bears, asps, asses with horns, and monsters with dogs' heads and without heads, who have eyes in their breasts, at least as the Libyans say, together with wild men and wild women. None of these things are found among the nomads, but others of the following kind : pygargi, antelopes, buffaloes, and asses, not such as have horns, but others that never drink ; and oryes, from the horns of which are made the elbows of the Phœnician citherns ; in size this beast is equal to an ox ; and foxes, hyænas, porcupines, wild rams, dictyes, thoes, panthers, boryes, and land crocodiles about three cubits long, very much like lizards ; ostriches, and small serpents, each with one horn. These, then, are the wild animals in that country, besides such as are met with elsewhere, except the stag and the wild boar ; but the stag and the wild boar are never seen in Libya. They have three sorts of mice there ; some called dipodes, or two-footed ; others, zegeries, this name is Libyan, and means the same as the word signifying hillocks in Greek ; and hedgehogs. There are also weasels produced in the silphium, like those at Tartessus.

The Zaveces adjoin the Maxyan Libyans ; their women drive

their chariots in war. The Gyzantes adjoin them ; amongst them bees make a great quantity of honey, and it is said that confectioners make much more. All these paint themselves with vermilion, and eat monkeys, which abound in their mountains. Near them, the Carthaginians say, lies an island called Cyraunis, two hundred stades in length, inconsiderable in breadth, easy of access from the continent, and abounding in olive trees and vines. In it is a lake, from the mud of which the girls of the country draw up gold dust by means of feathers daubed with pitch. Whether this is true I know not, but I write what is related ; it may be so, however, for I have myself seen pitch drawn up out of a lake and from water in Zacynthus ; and there are several lakes there, the largest of them is seventy feet every way, and two orgyæ in depth ; into this they let down a pole with a myrtle branch fastened to the end, and then draw up pitch adhering to the myrtle ; it has the smell of asphalt, but is in other respects better than the pitch of Pieria. They pour it into a cistern dug near the lake, and when they have collected a sufficient quantity, draw it off from the cistern into jars. All that falls into the lake passes under ground, and appears again upon the surface of the sea, which is about four stades distant from the lake. This account given of the island may probably be true. The Carthaginians further say, that beyond the pillars of Hercules there is an inhabited region of Libya ; when they arrive among these people and have unloaded their merchandise, they set it in order on the shore, go on board their ships, and make a great smoke ; the inhabitants, seeing the smoke, come down to the sea, deposit gold in exchange for the merchandise, and withdraw to some distance from the merchandise ; the Carthaginians then, going ashore, examine the gold, and if the quantity seems sufficient for the merchandise they take it up and sail away ; but if it is not sufficient, they go on board their ships again and wait ; the natives then approach and deposit more gold, until they have satisfied them ; neither party ever wrongs the other ; for they do not touch the gold before it is made adequate to the value of the merchandise, nor do the natives touch the merchandise before the other party has taken the gold.

No part of Libya appears to me so good in fertility as to be compared with Asia or Europe, except only the district of Cinyps ; for the land bears the same name as the river, and is equal to the best land for the production of corn ; nor is it at all like the rest of Libya ; for the soil is black, and well watered with springs, and it is neither affected at all by drought, nor is it injured by imbibing too much rain, which falls in this part of Libya. The proportion of the produce of this land equals that of Babylon. The land also which the Euesperides occupy is good ; for when it yields its best, it produces a hundred-fold ; but that in Cinyps three hundred-fold. The district of Cyrene, which is the highest of that part of Libya which the nomads occupy, has three seasons, a circumstance worthy of admiration ; for the first fruits near the sea swell so as to be ready for the harvest and vintage ; when these are gathered in, the fruits of the middle region, away from the sea, swell so as to be gathered in, these they call uplands ; and just as this middle harvest has been gathered in, that in the highest part becomes ripe and swells. So that when the first crop has been drunk and eaten, the last comes in. Thus harvest occupies the Cyrenæans during eight months. This may be sufficient to say concerning these things.

OLIVE TREES.

The Persians once upon a time, sent against the city of Barce, laid siege to it for nine months, digging passages under ground that reached to the walls, and making vigorous assaults. Now these excavations were discovered by a worker of bronze, carrying a bronze shield round within the wall, and applying it to the

ground within the city : in other places to which he applied it, it
made no noise, but at the parts that were excavated, the metal of
the shield sounded. The Barcæans, therefore, countermining them
in that part, slew the Persians who were employed in the excavation. When much time had been spent, and many had fallen on
both sides, and not the fewest on the side of the Persians, Amasis,
general of the land forces, had recourse to the following stratagem :
Finding that the Barcæans could not be taken by force, but might
be by artifice, he dug a wide pit by night, laid weak planks of
wood over it, and on the surface over the planks he spread a heap
of earth, making it level with the rest of the ground. At day-
break he invited the Barcæans to a conference ; they gladly assented,
thinking that at last they were pleased to come to terms : and they
made an agreement of the following nature, concluding the treaty
over the concealed pit : " That as long as this earth shall remain
as it is, the treaty should continue in force ; and that the Barcæans
should pay a reasonable tribute to the king, and that the Persians
should form no new designs against the Barcæans." After the
treaty the Barcæans, confiding in the Persians, went freely out of
the city, and allowed any one of the Persians who chose to pass
within the wall, throwing open all the gates. But the Persians,
having broken down the concealed bridge, rushed within the wall :
having not fully kept their oath. The Persians reduced the Barcæans to slavery and took their departure. But king Darius gave
them a village in the district of Bactria, to dwell in, and the name
of Barce was given to this village, which was still inhabited in my
time, in the Bactrian territory.

BOOK V. TERPSICHORE.

CHAPTER I.

CONQUESTS OF THE GENERALS OF DARIUS.

The Persians, left in Europe by Darius under the command of Megabazus, subdued the Perinthians first of the Hellespontines, who were unwilling to submit to Darius, and had been before roughly handled by the Pæonians. For an oracle had admonished the Pæonians to invade the Perinthians, and if the Perinthians, when encamped against them, should challenge them, shouting to them by name, then to attack, but if they should not shout out to them, not to attack. A threefold single combat took place between them according to a challenge ; for they matched a man with a man, a horse with a horse, and a dog with a dog. The Perinthians, victorious in two of these combats, through excess of joy sang the Pæon, whereupon the Pæonians conjectured that this was the meaning of the oracle, and said among themselves : " Now surely the oracle must be accomplished ; now it is our part to act." The Pæonians attacked the Perinthians as they were singing the Pæon, gained a complete victory, and left but few of them alive.

The nation of the Thracians is the greatest of all among men, except the Indians ; and if they were governed by one man, or acted in concert, they would, in my opinion, be invincible, and by far the most powerful of all nations. But as this is impracticable, and it is impossible that they should ever be united, they are weak.

Beyond the Ister appears to be an interminable desert, and the only men that I am able to hear of as dwelling there are those called

Sigynnæ, who wear the Medic dress ; their horses are shaggy all over the body, to five fingers in depth of hair ; they are small, flat-nosed, and unable to carry men ; but when yoked to chariots are very fleet.   They say that these people are a colony of Medes. How they can have been a colony of Medes I cannot comprehend ; but any thing may happen in the course of time.

There is a curious people who inhabit Lake Prasias itself, who were not at all subdued by Megabazus ;—they live upon the lake in dwellings erected upon planks fitted on lofty piles, which are driven in the middle of the lake, with a narrow entrance from the main land by a single bridge.   These piles that support the planks all the citizens anciently placed there at the common charge ; but afterward they established a law to the following effect : Whenever a man marries, for each wife he sinks three piles, bringing wood from a mountain called Orbelus : but every man has several wives. Each one has a hut on the planks, in which he dwells, with a trap-door closely fitted in the planks, and leading down to the lake. They tie the young children with a cord around the foot, for fear they should fall into the lake beneath.   To their horses and beasts of burden they give fish for fodder ; of which there is such an abundance, that you have simply to open your trap-door, let down an empty basket by a cord into the lake, when, after waiting a short time, you draw it up full of fish.

Megabazus, after conquering the Pæonians, arrived at the Hellespont, crossed over, and came to Sardis.   In the meantime, Histiæus the Milesian was building a wall around the place, which, at his own request, he had received from Darius as a reward for his services in preserving the bridge : this place was near the river Strymon, and its name Myrcinus.   Megabazus, upon learning what was being done by Histiæus, as soon as he reached Sardis said to Darius : " O king, what have you done, in allowing a crafty and subtle Greek to possess a city in Thrace, where there is an abundance of timber fit for building ships and plenty of wood for oars, and silver mines ?   A great multitude of Greeks and bar-barians dwell around, who, when they have obtained him as a leader, will do whatever he may command, both by day and by night. Put a stop therefore to the proceedings of this man, that you may not be harassed by a domestic war; send for him in a gentle manner, and stop him: and when you have him in your power, take care that he never returns to the Greeks." Magabazus easily persuaded Darius, since he wisely foresaw what was to happen. So Darius sent a messenger to Myrcinus, who spoke as follows: " Histiæus, King Darius says thus : I find on consideration that there is no man better affected to me and my affairs than thyself; and this I have learnt, not by words, but actions ; now, since I have great designs to put in execution, come to me by all means, that I may communicate them to thee." Histiæus, giving credit to these words, and at the time con-

sidering it a great honor to become a counsellor of the king, went to Sardis : when he arrived, Darius said, " Histiæus, I have sent for you on this occasion. As soon as I returned from Scythia, and you were out of my sight, I have wished for nothing so much as to see you and converse with you again ; being persuaded that a friend who is both intelligent and well affected, is the most valuable of all posses-

HEAD-DRESS OF A RIDING HORSE.

sions ; both of which I am able to testify from my own knowledge concur in you, as regards my affairs. You have done well in coming, and I make you this offer : Think no more of Miletus, nor of the new-founded city in Thrace ; but follow me to Susa, have the same that I have, and be the partner of my table and counsels." And Darius appointed Artaphernes, his brother by the same father, to be governor of Sardis, and departed for Susa, taking Histiæus with him. He first nominated Otanes to be general of the forces on the coast, whose father, Sisamnes, one of the roya' judges, King Cambyses had put to death and flayed, because he had given an unjust judgment for a sum of money. He had his skin torn off, and cut into thongs, and extended it on the bench on which he used to sit, when he pronounced judgment ; then Cambyses appointed as judge in the room of Sisamnes, whom he had slain and flayed, the son of Sisamnes, admonishing him to remember on what seat he sat to administer justice. This very Otanes, then, being now appointed successor to Megabazus in the command of the army, subdued the Byzantians and Chalcedonians, and took Antandros, which belongs to the territory of Troas, and Lamponium ; and obtaining ships from the Lesbians, he took Lemnos and Imbrus, both of which were then inhabited by Pelasgians. The Lemnians fought valiantly, and defended themselves for some time, but were at length overcome ; and over those who survived, the Persians set up Lycaretus as governor, the brother of Mæandrius, who had reigned in Samos. Otanes enslaved and subdued them all for various alleged reasons : some he charged with desertion to the Scythians ; others he accused of having harassed Darius' army in their return home from the Scythians.

Afterward, for the intermission from misfortune was not of long duration, evils arose a second time to the Ionians from Naxos and Miletus. For, on the one hand, Naxos surpassed all the islands in opulence ; and on the other, Miletus, at the same time, had attained the summit of its prosperity, and was accounted the ornament of Ionia. Some of the opulent men, exiled from Naxos by the people, went to Miletus : the governor of Miletus happened to be Aristagoras, son of Molpagoras, son-in-law and cousin of Histiæus, whom Darius detained at Susa. These Naxians arrived at Miletus, entreated Aristagoras, if he could, by any means, to give them some assistance so that that they might return to their own country. He, perceiving that if by his means they should return to their city, he might get the dominion of Naxos, used the friendship of Histiæus as a pretence, and addressed the following discourse to them : " I am not able of myself to furnish you with a force sufficient to reinstate you against the wishes of the Naxians, who are in possession of the city, for I hear that the Naxians have eight thousand heavy-armed men, and a considerable number of ships of war. Yet I will contrive some way, and use my best endeavors ; my scheme is this : Artaphernes happens to be my friend ; he is son of Hystaspes and brother of king Darius, and commands all the maritime parts of Asia, and has a large army and navy. This man, I am persuaded, will do whatever we desire." The Naxians urged Aristagoras to go about it in the best way he could, and bade him promise presents, and their expenses to the army, for they would repay it ; having great expectation that when they should appear at Naxos the Naxians would do whatever they should order, as also would the other islanders ; for of these Cyclades islands not one was as yet subject to Darius.

Accordingly Aristagoras journeyed to Sardis, and told Artaphernes, that Naxos was an island of no great extent, to be sure, but beautiful and fertile, and near Ionia, and in it was much wealth and many slaves. " Do send an army against this country, to reinstate those who have been banished ; and if you do this, I have, in the first place, a large sum of money ready, in addition to the expenses of the expedition, for it is just that we who lead you on should supply that ; and in the next, you will acquire for the king Naxos itself, and the islands dependent upon it, Paros, Andros, and the rest that are called Cyclades. Setting out from there you will easily attack Eubœa, a large and wealthy island, not less than Cyprus, and very easy to be taken. A hundred ships are sufficient to subdue them all." The reply was quickly given : " You propose things advantageous to the king's house, and advise every thing well, except the number of ships ; instead of one hundred, two hundred shall be ready at the commencement of the spring. But it is necessary that the king himself should approve of the design." Aristagoras, wild with delight, went back to Miletus. And Artaphernes, finding that Darius himself approved of the plan, made ready two hundred triremes, and a very numerous body of Persians and other allies : and he appointed Megabates general, a Persian of the family of the Archimenidæ, his own and Darius' nephew, whose daughter, if the report be true, was afterward betrothed to Pausanias, son of Cleombrotus the Lacedæmonian, who aspired to become tyrant of Greece. Artaphernes, having appointed Megabates general, sent forward the army to Aristagoras.

Megabates, with Aristagoras, the Ionian forces, and the Naxians, sailed professedly for the Hellespont; but when he arrived
at Chios, anchored at Caucasa, that he might cross over from there
to Naxos by a north wind. However, it was fated that the Naxians were not to perish by this armament, as the following event
occurred : As Megabates was going round the watches on board
the ships, he found no one on guard on board a Myndian ship ;
indignant at this, he ordered his body-guards to find the captain of
this ship, whose name was Scylax, and to bind him with his body
half-way through the lower row-lock of the vessel, so that his head
should be on the outside of the vessel, and his legs within. Some
one told Aristagoras that Megabates had bound and disgraced his
Myndian friend. He went therefore and interceded for him with
the Persian, but, when he found he could obtain nothing, went
himself and released him. Megabates, hearing of this, was very
indignant, and enraged at Aristagoras, and told him so ; " but,"
said Aristagoras, " what have you to do with these matters ? Did
not Artaphernes send you to obey me, and to sail wheresoever I
should command ? " Megabates, still more exasperated at this, as
soon as night arrived, dispatched men in a ship to Naxos, to inform the Naxians of the impending danger. The Naxians, who
had not a suspicion that this armament was coming against them,
immediately carried every thing from the fields into the town, and,
with plenty of food and drink, prepared to undergo a siege, so the
Persians had to attack men well fortified, and after besieging them
four months, consumed all the supplies they had brought with
them, together with large sums furnished by Aristagoras, and
wanting still more to carry on the siege, they were forced to build
a fortress for the Naxian exiles, and retire to the continent unsuccessful.

Aristagoras was thus unable to fulfil his promise to Artaphernes ;
while at the same time the expenses of the expedition pressed
heavily on him on account of the ill success of the army ; and having incurred the ill will of Megabates to such an extent that

he feared that he should be deprived of the government of Miletus, he meditated a revolt. It happened at the same time that a messenger with his head tattooed came from Susa from Histiæus, urging Aristagoras to revolt from the king. For Histiæus, being desirous to communicate to Aristagoras his wish for him to revolt, had no other means of signifying it with safety, because the roads were guarded; therefore, having shaved the head of the most trustworthy of his slaves, he marked it with a sharp iron, and waited till the hair had grown again, then sent him to Miletus without other instructions except that when he arrived at Miletus he should desire Aristagoras to shave off his hair and look upon his head: the punctures, as I have said before, signified a wish for him to revolt. Histiæus did this because he looked upon his detention at Susa as a great misfortune; while if a revolt should take place he had great hopes that he should be sent down to the coast; but if Miletus made no new attempt, he thought that he should never go there again. It was resolved to revolt, and messengers were sent to the force that had returned from Naxos, and which was at Myus, to seize the captains on board the ships. Aristagoras thus openly revolted, devising every thing he could against Darius. And first, in pretence, having laid aside the sovereignty, he established an equality in Miletus, in order that the Milesians might more readily join with him in the revolt. Afterward he effected the same throughout the rest of Ionia, expelling some of the tyrants; and he delivered up those whom he had taken from on board the ships that had sailed with him against Naxos, to the cities, in order to gratify the people, giving them up to the respective cities, from whence each came. The Mityleneans, as soon as they received Coes, led him out, and stoned him to death; but the Cymeans let their tyrant go; and in like manner most of the others let theirs go. Accordingly there was a suppression of tyrants throughout the cities. But Aristagoras enjoined them all to appoint magistrates in each of the cities, and went himself in a trireme as ambassador to Sparta, for it was necessary for him to procure some powerful alliance.

Aristagoras arrived at Sparta, when Cleomenes held the government ; and he went to confer with him, as the Lacedæmonians say, carrying a bronze tablet, on which was engraved the circumference of the whole earth, the whole sea, and all rivers. "Wonder not, Cleomenes," said Aristagoras, "at my eagerness in coming here, for it is a great sorrow to us that the children of Ionians should be slaves instead of free, and above all others it is a disgrace to you, inasmuch as you are at the head of Greece. I adjure you by the Grecian gods, rescue the Ionians, who are of your own blood, from servitude. It is easy for you to effect this, for the barbarians are not valiant ; whereas you, in matters relating to war, have attained to the utmost height of glory ; their mode of fighting is, with bows and short spears, and they engage in battle wearing loose trousers, and turbans on their heads, so that they are easy to be overcome. Besides, there are treasures belonging to those who inhabit that continent, such as are not possessed by all other nations together ; gold, silver, bronze, variegated garments, beasts of burden, and slaves ; all these you may have if you will. They live adjoining one another as I will show you. Next to these Ionians are the Lydians, who inhabit a fertile country, and abound in silver." As he said this he showed the map of the earth, which he had brought with him, engraved on a tablet. "Next to the Lydians," proceeded Aristagoras, "are these Phrygians to the eastward, who are the richest in cattle and in corn of all with whom I am acquainted. Next to the Phrygians are the Cappadocians, whom we call Syrians ; and bordering on them, the Cilicians, extending to this sea in which the island of Cyprus is situated ; they pay an annual tribute of five hundred talents to the king. Next to the Cilicians are these Armenians, who also abound in cattle ; and next to the Armenians are the Metienians, who occupy this country ; and next them this territory of Cissia, in which Susa is situated, on this river Choaspes, and here the great king resides, and here are his treasures of wealth. If you take this city, you may boldly contend with Jupiter in wealth. As it is, you carry on war for a country of small extent, and not very fertile, and of narrow limits, with the Messenians, who are your equals in valor, and with the Arcadians and Argives, who have nothing akin to gold or silver, the desire of which induces men to hazard their lives in battle. But when an opportunity is offered to conquer all Asia with ease, will you prefer any thing else?" "Milesian friend," said Cleomenes, "I defer to give you an answer until the third day." They met at the appointed time and place, and Cleomenes asked Aristagoras, how many days' journey it was from the sea of the Ionians to the king. Aristagoras, though he was cunning in other things, and had deceived him with much address, made a slip in this ; for he should not have told the real fact, if he wished to draw the Spartans into Asia ; whereas he told him frankly that it was a three months' journey up there. Cutting short the rest of the description which Aristagoras was proceeding to give of the journey, Cleomenes said : " My friend, from Miletus, depart from Sparta before sunset ; for you speak no agreeable language to the Lacedæmonians, in wishing to lead them a three months' journey from the sea ; " and Cleomenes went home. Aristagoras, nothing daunted, taking an olive-branch in his hand, went to the house of Cleomenes, entered in, as a suppliant, and besought Cleomenes to listen to him. The latter's little child, a daughter, whose name was Gorgo, stood by him ; she happened to be his only child, and was about eight or nine years of age. Cleomenes bade him say what he wished, and not mind the presence of the little girl. Thereupon Aristagoras promised him ten talents, if he would do as he desired ; and as Cleomenes refused, Aristagoras went on increasing his offers, until he promised fifty talents, when little Gorgo cried out, " Papa, this stranger will corrupt you, if you don't quickly depart." Cleomenes, pleased with the advice of the child, retired to another apartment ; and Aristagoras was forced to leave Sparta altogether, without ever getting another opportunity to give further particulars of the route to the city of the great king.

With respect to this road, the case is as follows : There are royal stations all along, and excellent inns, and the whole road is through an inhabited and safe country. There are twenty stations extending through Lydia and Phrygia, and the distance is ninety-four parasangs and a half. After Phrygia, the river Halys is met with, at which there are gates, which it is absolutely necessary to pass through, and thus to cross the river ; there is also a considerable fort on it. When you cross over into Cappadocia, and traverse that country to the borders of Cilicia, there are eight and twenty stations, and one hundred and four parasangs ; and on the borders of these people, you go through two gates, and pass by two forts. When you have gone through these and made the journey through Cilicia, there are three stations, and fifteen parasangs and a half. The boundary of Cilicia and Armenia is a river that is crossed in boats, called the Euphrates. In Arminia there are fifteen stations for resting-places, and fifty-six parasangs and a half ; there is also a fort at the stations. Four rivers that are crossed in boats flow through this country, which it is absolutely necessary to ferry over. First, the Tigris ; then the second and third have the same name, though they are not the same river, nor flow from the same source. For the first mentioned of these flows from the Armenians, and the latter from the Matienians. The fourth river is called the Gyndes, which Cyrus once distributed into three hundred and sixty channels. As you enter from Armenia into the country of Matiene, there are four stations ; and from thence as you proceed to the Cissian territory there are eleven stations, and forty-two parasangs and a half, to the river Choaspes, which also must be crossed in boats ; on this Susa is built. All these stations amount to one hundred and eleven,[1] as you go up from Sardis to Susa. Now if the royal road has been correctly measured in parasangs, and if the parasang is equal to thirty stades, as indeed it is, from Sardis to the royal palace, called Memnonia, is a distance of thirteen thousand five hundred stades, the parasangs being four hundred and fifty ; and by those who travel one hundred and fifty stades every day, just ninety days are spent on the journey. So Aristagoras spoke correctly when he stated the distance to Susa.

---

[1] The detail of stations above-mentioned gives only eighty-one instead of one hundred and eleven. The discrepancy can only be accounted for by a supposed defect in the manuscripts.

CHAPTER II.

ARISTAGORAS the Milesian, having been expelled from Sparta
by Cleomenes the Lacedæmonian, repaired to Athens ; for this
city was much more powerful than the rest. Presenting himself
before the people, he said the same that he had done at Sparta,
respecting the wealth of Asia and the Persian mode of warfare,
how they used neither shield nor spear, and could be easily conquered. He said also that the Milesians were a colony of the
Athenians, and it was but reasonable that they, having such great
power, should rescue them. And as there was nothing he did not
promise, being very much in earnest, at length he persuaded them.
It appears to be more easy to impose upon a multitude than one
man ; this schemer, you see, was not able to impose upon Cleomenes the Lacedæmonian singly, but did upon thirty thousand
Athenians. Twenty ships were sent to succor the Ionians, and
Melanthius commander over them, a citizen who was universally
esteemed. These ships proved the source of calamities both to
Greeks and barbarians. Aristagoras sailed first, arrived at Miletus,
and had recourse to a project from which no advantage could result to the Ionians ; nor did he employ it for that purpose, but
that he might vex king Darius. He sent a man into Phrygia, to
the Pæonians, who had been carried away captive by Megabazus,
from the river Strymon, and occupied a tract in Phrygia, and a
village by themselves. Arrived among the Pæonians, the messenger spoke as follows : " Men of Pæonia, Aristagoras, tyrant of
Miletus, has sent me to suggest to you a mode of deliverance, if
you will take his advice. For all Ionia has revolted from the king,
and offers you an opportunity of returning safe to your own coun-

try ; as far as to the coast take care of yourselves, and we will provide for the rest." When the Pæonians heard these words, they considered it a very joyful event, and taking with them their children and wives, fled to the coast ; though some of them, through fear, remained where they were. When the Pæonians reached the coast, they crossed over to Chios, when a large body of Persian cavalry came on their heels, and sent orders to Chios to.the Pæonians, commanding them to return. The Pæonians did not listen to the proposal ; but the Chians conveyed them to Lesbos, and the Lesbians forwarded them to Doriscus ; thence proceeding on foot they reached Pæonia.

The Athenians arrived with twenty ships, bringing with them five triremes of the Eretrians, who engaged in this expedition out of good-will to the Milesians, in order to repay a former obligation ; for the Milesians had formerly joined the Eretrians in the war against the Chalcidians. When these had arrived, and the rest of the allies had come up, Aristagoras resolved to make an expedition to Sardis. He himself did not march with the army, but remained at Miletus, and appointed as generals of the Milesians, his own brother Charopinus, and of the other citizens Hermophantus. The Ionians arrived at Ephesus with this force, left their ships at Coressus, in the Ephesian territory, and advanced with a numerous army, taking Ephesians for their guides ; and marching by the side of the river Cayster, they crossed Mount Tmolus, and reached and took Sardis without opposition ; all except the citidel, for Artaphernes with a strong garrison defended the citidel. The following accident prevented them, after they had taken the city, from plundering it. Most of the houses in Sardis were built with reeds ; and such of them as were built with brick, had roof of reeds. A soldier happened to set fire to one of these, and immediately the flame spread from house to house, and consumed the whole city. While the city was burning, the Lydians, and as many of the Persians as were in the city, being enclosed on every side, and having no means of escaping from the city, rushed together to the market-place, and to the river Pactolus, which, bringing down grains of gold from Mount Tmolus, flows through the middle of the market-place, and then discharges itself into the river Hermus, and that into the sea. The Lydians and Persians, being assembled on this Pactolus and at the market-place, were constrained to defend themselves : and the Ionians, seeing some of the enemy standing on their defence, and others coming up in great numbers, retired through fear to the mountain called Tmolus, and thence under favor of the night retreated to their ships. Thus Sardis was burnt, and in it the temple of the native goddess Cybebe ; the Persians, making a pretext of this, afterwards burnt in retaliation the temples of Greece. As soon as the Persians who had settlements on this side the river Halys were informed of these things, they drew together and marched to assist the Lydians ; the Ionians were no longer at Sardis ; but following on their track they overtook them at Ephesus, where the Ionians drew out in battle-array against them, and coming to an engagement, were sorely beaten ; and the Persians slew many of them, among other persons of distinction, Eualcis, general of the Eretrians, who had gained the prize in the contests for the crown, and had been much celebrated by Simonides the Cean. Those who escaped from the battle were dispersed throughout the cities.

Such was the result of the encounter. Afterward, the Athenians, totally abandoning the Ionians, though Aristagoras urgently solicited them by ambassadors, refused to send them any assistance. The Ionians, deprived of the alliance of the Athenians, (for they had conducted themselves in such a manner toward Darius from the first,) nevertheless prepared for war with the king. And sailing to the Hellespont, they reduced Byzantium and all the other cities in that quarter to their obedience. They then sailed out of the Hellespont, and gained over to their alliance the greater part of Caria ; for the city of Caunus, which before would not join their alliance, when they had burnt Sardis, came over to their side.

When it was told king Darius, that Sardis had been taken and burnt by the Athenians and Ionians, and that Aristagoras the Milesian was the chief of the confederacy and the contriver of that enterprise, it is related that he took no account of the Ionians, well knowing that they would not escape unpunished for their rebellion, but inquired where the Athenians were ; then having been informed, he called for a bow, put an arrow into it, let it fly toward heaven, and as he shot it into the air, exclaimed : " O Jupiter, grant that I may revenge myself on the Athenians ! " Then he commanded one of his attendants, every time dinner was set before him, to say thrice : " Sire, remember the Athenians." Summoning to his presence Histiæus the Milesian, whom he had already detained a long time, Darius said : " I am informed, Histiæus, that your lieutenant, to whom you intrusted Miletus, has attempted innovations against me ; for he has brought men from the other continent, and with them Ionians, who shall give me satisfaction for what they have done ; and has deprived me of Sardis. Now, can it appear to you that this is right ? Could such a thing have been done without your advice ? Beware lest hereafter you expose yourself to blame." To this Histiæus answered : " O king, what have you said ? That I should advise a thing from which any grief, great or little, should ensue to you ! With what object should I do so ? What am I in want of ? I, who have all things the same as you, and am deemed worthy to share all your counsels ? But if my lieutenant has done any such thing as you mention, be assured he has done it of his own contrivance. But I do not believe the account, that the Milesians and my lieutenant have attempted any innovations against your authority. Yet if you have heard the truth, consider, O king, what mischief you have done in withdrawing me from the coast. For the Ionians seem, when I was out of their sight, to have done what they long ago desired to do ; and had I been in Ionia not one city would have stirred. Suffer me therefore to go with all speed to Ionia, that I may restore all things there to their former condition, and deliver into your hands this lieutenant of Miletus, who has plotted the whole. When I have done this according to your mind, I swear by the royal gods, not to put off the garments which I shall wear when I go down to Ionia, before I have made the great island Sardinia tributary to you." His speaking thus deceived the king ; Darius was persuaded, and let him go, charging him to return to Susa, as soon as he should have accomplished what he had promised.

While the news concerning Sardis was going up to the king, tidings were brought to Onesilus the Salaminian, as he was besieging the Amathusians, that Artybius, a Persian, leading a large Persian force on shipboard, was to be expected in Cyprus. Onesilus accordingly sent heralds to the different parts of Ionia, inviting them to assist him ; and the Ionians, without any protracted deliberation, arrived at Cyprus with a large armament. The Persians crossed over in ships from Cilicia, and marched by land against Salamis.

Then the kings of the Cyprians drew up their forces in line, and stationed the best of the Salaminians and Solians against the Persians. Onesilus voluntarily took up his position directly against Artybius, the general of the Persians. Artybius used to ride on a horse, that had been taught to rear up against an armed enemy. Onesilus had a shield-bearer, a Carian, well skilled in matters of war, and otherwise full of courage, to whom he said : " I am informed that the horse of Artybius rears up, and with his feet and mouth attacks whomsoever he is made to engage with ; tell me which you will watch and strike, whether the horse or Artybius himself." His attendant answered : " I am ready to do both, or either of them, but a king and a general ought, I think, to engage with a king and a general. If you vanquish one who is a general, your glory is great ; while if he should vanquish you, which may the gods avert, to fall by a noble hand is but half the calamity. We servants should engage with other servants, and also against a horse, whose tricks you need not fear at all ; for I promise you he shall never again rear up against any man." Forthwith the forces joined battle by land and sea. Now, the Ionians fought valiantly on that day, when the armies met in close combat ; and when Artybius, seated on his horse, bore down upon Onesilus. Onesilus, as he had concerted with his shield-bearer, struck Artybius himself ; and as the horse was throwing his feet against the shield of

Onesilus, the Carian with a scythe cut off the horse's feet. So that Artybius, the general of the Persians, fell together with his horse on the spot. While the rest were fighting, Stesenor, of Curium, deserted with no inconsiderable body of men, and the chariots of war belonging to the Salaminians did the same as the Curians. Consequently the Persians became superior to the Cyprians. The army was put to flight, many fell, and amongst them Onesilus, and the king of the Solians, Aristocyprus, son of the Philocyprus whom Solon the Athenian, when he visited Cyprus, celebrated in his verses above all tyrants. The Amathusians cut off the head of Onesilus, because he had besieged them, took it to Amathus, and suspended it over the gates ; and when the head had become hollow, a swarm of bees entered it, and filled it with honey-comb. An answer was given to the Amathusians, who consulted the oracle respecting it, "that they should take down the head and bury it, and sacrifice annually to Onesilus, as to a hero, and that it would turn out better for them."

Afterward, the Persians crossed the Mæander and engaged the Carians on the banks of the river Marsyas. They fought an obstinate battle, and at last overpowered them. Of the Persians there fell about two thousand, and of the Carians ten thousand. The Carians, however, afterward recovered from this wound, and renewed the contest. For hearing that the Persians designed to invade their cities, they placed an ambuscade on the way to Pedasus, into which the Persians, falling by night, were cut in pieces, with their generals Daurises, Amorges, and Sisamaces.

Hymees, who was one of those who pursued the Ionians that had attacked Sardis, bending his march toward the Propontis, took Cius of Mysia. When he heard that Daurises had quitted the Hellespont, and was marching against Caria, he abandoned the Propontis, and led his army on the Hellespont. He subdued all the Æolians who inhabited the territory of Ilium, and subdued the Gergithæ, the remaining descendants of the ancient Teucrians. Just then, however, he died of disease in the Troad. But Artaphernes, governor of Sardis, and Otanes, who were appointed to

invade Ionia and the neighboring territory of Æolia, took Clazomenæ and Cyme.

Aristagoras the Milesian, for he was not, as it proved, a man
of strong courage, after he had thus thrown Ionia into confusion, and
raised great disturbances, thought of flight, when he saw these results. Besides, it appeared to him impossible to overcome King
Darius ; so calling his partisans together, he suggested " that it
would be better for them to have some sure place of refuge, in
case they should be expelled from Miletus." He asked, therefore,
whether he should lead them to Sardinia, to found a colony, or to
Myrcinus of the Edonians, which Histiæus had begun to fortify,
having received it as a gift from Darius. However, the opinion of
Hecatæus the historian, son of Hegesander, was, that they should
set out for neither of these places, but should build a fortress in the
island of Leros, and remain quiet, if they were compelled to quit
Miletus. But Aristagoras himself was decidedly in favor of proceeding to Myrcinus ; he therefore intrusted Miletus to Pythagoras,
a citizen of distinction, and, taking with him all who were willing,
sailed to Thrace, and took possession of the region to which he
was bound. But both Aristagoras himself and all his army perished while he was laying siege to a city in Thrace.

BOOK VI. ERATO.

CHAPTER I.

ARISTAGORAS thus induced the Ionians to revolt, and died ; and Histiæus, tyrant of Miletus, repaired to Sardis. When he arrived from Susa, Artaphernes, Governor of Sardis, asked him for what reason he supposed the Ionians had revolted. Histiæus said he did not know, and seemed surprised at what had happened, as if he knew nothing of the present state of affairs. But Artaphernes saw that he was dissembling, and being aware of the exact truth as to the revolt, said : " Histiæus, the state of the case is this : you made the shoe and Aristagoras has put it on." Histiæus in alarm fled to the coast as soon as night came on, and although he had promised to reduce the great island of Sardinia for Darius, he insinuated himself into the command of the Ionians in the war against him. At Chios he was taken and put in chains, being suspected by the Chians of planning some new design against them in favor of Darius. However, the Chians, being assured that he was an enemy to the king, released him, and conveyed him to Miletus, at his own request ; but the Milesians, delighted at being rid of Aristagoras, were by no means desirous to receive another tyrant into their country, as they had tasted of freedom. Thereupon Histiæus, going down to Miletus by night, endeavored to enter it by force, but was wounded in the thigh by one of the Milesians. When he was repulsed from his own country, he went back to Chios, and from there, since he could not persuade the Chians to help him, he crossed over to Mitylene, and prevailed with the Lesbians to furnish him with ships ; they manned eight triremes, and sailed with Histiæus to Byzantium. There taking up their station, they took all the ships that sailed out of the Pontus, except such of them as said they were ready to submit to Histiæus.

But a large naval and land-force was expected against Miletus itself. For the Persian generals had united their forces and formed one camp to march to Miletus, deeming the other cities of less consequence. The Ionians, hearing of this, sent their respective deputies to the Panionium, and determined not to assemble any land-forces to oppose the Persians ; but bade the Milesians themselves defend their walls, while they should man their navy, without leaving a single ship behind, and assemble as soon as possible at Lade, to fight in defence of Miletus. Lade is a small island lying off the city of the Milesians. Soon the Ionians came up with their ships manned, and formed their line, a fleet three hundred and fifty-three triremes strong. On the side of the barbarians the number of ships amounted to six hundred, and when they arrived on the Milesian coast, and all their land-forces had come up, the Persian generals began to fear they should not be strong enough to overcome them, and so should be also unable to take Miletus, since they were not masters at sea, and then might be in danger of receiving punishment at the hands of Darius. Taking these things into consideration, they summoned the tyrants of the Ionians, who had been deprived of their governments by Aristagoras, and had fled to the Medes, and who happened at that time to be serving in the army against Miletus. " Men of Ionia," they said, " let each of you now show his zeal for the king's house. For let each of you endeavor to detach his own countrymen from the rest of the confederacy, and proclaim this, that they shall suffer no hurt on account of their rebellion, nor shall their buildings, whether sacred or profane, be burnt, nor shall they be treated with more severity than they were before. But if they do not do this, and will at all events come to the hazard of a battle, threaten that, when conquered in battle, they shall all be enslaved." And the tyrants of the Ionians sent each by night to his own countrymen, to make known the warning. But the Ionians to whom these messages came, continued firm to their purpose and would not listen to treachery ; for each thought that the Persians had sent this message.

When the Ionians had assembled at Lade, a council was held, and the Phocæan general Dionysius spoke as follows : " Our affairs are in a critical[1] state, O Ionians ; we are to be freemen or slaves, and that too run-away slaves. But if you are willing to undergo hardships, for the present you will have to toil, but will be enabled, by overcoming your enemies, to be free ; on the other hand, if you abandon yourselves to ease and disorder, I have no hope that you will escape punishment at the hands of the king for your revolt. But be persuaded by me, and entrust yourselves to my guidance, and I promise you, that if the gods are impartial, either our enemies will not fight us at all, or if they do fight with us, they will be completely beaten." The Ionians intrusted themselves to the guidance of Dionysius without hesitation who daily led out the ships into a line, exercised the rowers, by practising the manœuvre of cutting through one another's line, put the marines under arms, and kept the ships at anchor for the rest of the day. For seven days they continued to obey, but on the eighth the Ionians, unaccustomed to such toil, and worn down by hardships and the heat of the sun, grumbled to each other in such terms as these : " What deity have we offended to fill up this measure of affliction ? we who were so beside ourselves, as to have intrusted ourselves to the guidance of a presumptuous Phocæan, who, all told, contributed only three ships, but having got us under his control, afflicts us with intolerable hardships. Many of us have already fallen into distempers, and many more must expect to meet with the same fate. Instead of these evils, it would be better for us to suffer any thing else, and to endure the impending servitude, be it what it may, than be oppressed by the present. Come, let us no longer obey him." And from that moment no one would obey ;

---

[1] The Greek words, literally translated, mean " on a razor's edge."

but, pitching their tents on the island, they continued under the shade, and would not go on board the ships, or perform their exercise. When the generals of the Samians observed what was passing among the Ionians, and saw great disorder among them, they accepted the proposal of Æaces, son of Syloson, which he had before sent them at the desire of the Persians, exhorting them to abandon the confederacy of the Ionians. Besides, it was clearly impossible for them to overcome the power of the king, because they were convinced, that if they should overcome Darius with his present fleet, another five times as large would come against them. So laying hold of this pretext, as soon as they saw the Ionians refusing to behave well, they deemed it for their advantage to preserve their own buildings, sacred and profane.

When therefore the Phœnicians sailed against them, the Ionians drew out their ships in line to oppose them; but when they came near and opposed each other, I am unable to affirm with certainty who of the Ionians proved themselves cowards, or brave men, in this sea-fight; for they mutually accuse each other. The Samians however are said at that moment to have hoisted sail, in pursuance of their agreement with Æaces, and steered out of the line to Samos, with the exception of eleven ships; the captains of which stayed and fought, refusing to obey their commanders; and for this action the commonwealth of the Samians conferred upon them the honor of having their names and ancestry engraved on a column, as those who had proved themselves valiant men; and this column now stands in the forum. The Lesbians also, seeing those stationed next them flee, did the same as the Samians; and most of the Ionians followed their example. Of those that persisted in the battle, the Chians were most roughly handled, as they displayed signal proofs of valor, and would not act as cowards. They had contributed one hundred ships, and on board each of them forty chosen citizens served as marines; and though they saw most of the confederates abandoning the common cause, they disdained to follow the example of their treachery; but choosing rather to remain with the few allies, they continued the fight, cutting through the enemies' line, until, after they had taken many of the enemies' ships, they lost most of their own. The Chians then fled to their own country with the remainder of their fleet. Those Chians whose ships were disabled in the fight, took refuge in Mycale, ran their ships aground, and left them there, and marched over-land across the continent. On their return they entered the territory of Ephesus, and arrived near the city by night, at a time when the women were celebrating the Thesmophoria; thereupon, the Ephesians, not having before heard how it had fared with the Chians, and seeing an army enter their territory, thinking they were certainly robbers, and had come to seize their women, rushed out in a body, and slew the Chians. When Dionysius the Phocæan perceived that the affairs of the Ionians were utterly ruined, he took three of the enemies' ships and sailed away, not indeed to Phocæa, well knowing that it would be enslaved with the rest of Ionia, but directly to Phœnicia; and there having disabled some merchantmen, and obtained great wealth, he sailed to Sicily, where he established himself as a pirate, attacking none of the Greeks, but only Carthaginians and Tyrrhenians.

When the Persians had conquered the Ionians in the sea-fight they besieged Miletus by land and sea, undermined the walls, and bringing up all kinds of military engines against it, took it completely, in the sixth year after the revolt of Aristagoras. They reduced the city to slavery, so that the event coincided with the oracle delivered concerning Miletus. For when the Argives consulted the oracle at Delphi respecting the preservation of their city, a double answer was given; part concerning themselves, and the addition concerning the Milesians. The part relating to the Argives I will mention when I come to that part of the history; the words the Pythian uttered relative to the Milesians, who were not present, were these: " Then Miletus, contriver of wicked deeds, thou shalt become a feast and a rich gift to many: thy wives shall wash the feet of many long-haired masters, and our temple at Didymi shall be tended by others." These things befell the Milesians at that time; for most of the men were killed by the

Persians, who wear long hair, their women and children were treated as slaves, and the sacred enclosure at Didymi, both the temple and the shrine, were pillaged and burnt. Of the riches in this temple I have frequently made mention in other parts of my history. Such of the Milesians as were taken alive were afterward conveyed to Susa; and King Darius did them no harm, but settled them on the Red Sea, in the city of Ampe, near by which the Tigris falls into the sea. Of the Milesian territory, the Persians themselves retained the parts round the city and the plain; the mountainous parts they gave to the Carians of Pedasus to occupy. When the Milesians suffered this at the hands of the Persians, the Sybarites, who inhabited Laos and Scydrus, did not show equal

AMPHITHEATRE AT POLA.

sympathy. But when Sybaris was taken by the Crotonians, all the Milesians of every age had shaved their heads and displayed marks of deep mourning: for these two cities had been more strictly united in friendship than any others we are acquainted with. The Athenians behaved in a very different manner; for the Athenians made it evident that they were excessively grieved at the capture of Miletus, both in many other ways, and more particularly when Phrynichus had composed a drama of the capture of Miletus, and represented it, the whole theatre burst into tears, and fined him a thousand drachmas [1] for renewing the memory of their domestic misfortunes; and they gave order that henceforth no one should act this drama.

---

[1] There is very good reason to believe that this fine was really imposed for the adoption of a modern theme by Phrynichus, when hitherto only the gods and heroes had been permissible subjects.

While Histiæus the Milesian was near Byzantium, intercepting the trading ships of the Ionians that sailed out of the Pontus, news was brought him of what had taken place at Miletus ; he therefore intrusted his affairs on the Hellespont to Bisaltes, son of Apollophanes, of Abydos, and with the Lesbians sailed to Chios, and engaged with a garrison of Chians, that would not admit him, at a place called Cœli in the Chian territory, and killed great numbers of them.   The deity is wont to give some previous warning when any great calamities are about to befall city or nation, and before these misfortunes great warnings happened to the Chians.   For in the first place, when they sent to Delphi a band of one hundred youths, two only of them returned home, for a pestilence seized and carried off the remaining ninety-eight.   In the next place, a little before the sea-fight, a house in the city fell in upon some boys, as they were learning to read, so that of one hundred and twenty boys one only escaped.   After this, the sea-fight following, threw the city prostrate ; and after the sea-fight Histiæus with the Lesbians came upon them ; and as the Chians had been much shattered, he easily reduced them to subjection.   From there Histiæus proceeded to attack Thasus with a large body of Ionians and Æolians ; and while he was besieging Thasus, Harpagus, the Persian, general of a considerable army, who, happening to be in those parts, engaged with him after his landing, took Histiæus himself prisoner, and destroyed the greater part of his army.

Now if, when Histiæus was taken prisoner, he had been conducted to king Darius, in my opinion, he would have suffered no punishment, and the king would have forgiven him his fault.   But for this very reason, lest by escaping he should again regain his influence with the king, Artaphernes, Governor of Sardis, and Harpagus, who received him as soon as he was conducted to Sardis, impaled his body on the spot, and embalmed the head and sent it to Darius at Susa.   Darius blamed those that had done it, because they had not brought him alive into his presence, and gave orders that they should wash and adorn the head of Histiæus, and inter it honorably, as the remains of a man who had been a great benefactor to himself and the Persians.

The naval force of the Persians wintered near Miletus. In the second year it set sail for the islands lying near the continent, Chios, Lesbos, and Tenedos, which it easily subdued. When they took any one of these islands, the barbarians netted the inhabitants in this manner : Taking one another by the hand, they would extend from the northern to the southern sea, and so march over the island, hunting out the inhabitants. They also took the Ionian cities on the continent with the same ease ; but did not net the inhabitants, for that was impossible. Thus the Ionians were for the third time reduced to slavery ; first by the Lydians, then twice successively by the Persians. The naval force, departing from Ionia, reduced all the places on the left of the Hellespont as one sails in ; and all the cities of the Chersonese, except Cardia, they subdued.

Till that time Miltiades, son of Cimon, was tyrant of these cities, Miltiades, son of Cypselus, having formally acquired this government in the following manner : The Thracian Dolonci possessed this Chersonese ; these Dolonci, being pressed in war by the Apsynthians, sent their kings to Delphi to consult the oracle concerning the war ; the Pythian answered them, "that they should take that man with them to their country to found a colony, who after their departure from the temple should first offer them hospitality." Accordingly the Dolonci, going by the sacred way, went through the territories of the Phocians and Bœotians, and when no one invited them, turned out of the road toward Athens. At that time Pisistratus had the supreme power at Athens ; but Miltiades, son of Cypselus, had considerable influence ; he was of a family that maintained horses for the chariot-races, and was originally descended from Æacus and Ægina, but in later times was an Athenian, Philæus, son of Ajax, having been the first Athenian of that family. This Miltiades, being seated in his own portico, and seeing the Dolonci passing by, wearing a dress not belonging to the country, and carrying javelins, called out to them ; and upon their coming to him, he offered them shelter and hospitality. They, grateful for their entertainment, made known to him the whole oracle, and entreated him to obey the deity. Their words persuaded Miltiades as soon as he heard them, for he was troubled with the government of Pisistratus, and desired to get out of his way. He therefore immediately set out to Delphi to ask the oracle whether he should do that which the Dolonci requested of him. The Pythian having bade him do so, Miltiades took with him all such Athenians as were willing to join in the expedition, and set sail with the Dolonci, and took possession of the country; and they who introduced him appointed him tyrant. He, first of all, built a wall on the isthmus of the Chersonese, from the city of Cardia to Pactya, in order that the Apsynthians might not be able to injure them by making incursions into their country. The width of this isthmus is thirty-six stades; and from this isthmus the whole Chersonese inward is four hundred and twenty stades in length. Miltiades next made war upon the Lampsacenians, who laid an ambush and took him prisoner. But Miltiades was well known to Crœsus, who, on hearing of this event, sent and commanded the Lampsacenians to release Miltiades; if not, he threatened that he would destroy them like a pine-tree. The Lampsacenians, uncertain as to what was the meaning of this saying, discovered, with some difficulty, from one of the elders, that the pine alone of all trees, when cut down, does not send forth any more shoots, but perishes entirely: whereupon the Lampsacenians, dreading the power of Crœsus, set Miltiades at liberty. He accordingly escaped by means of Crœsus, and afterward died childless, having bequeathed the government and his property to Stesagoras, his brother by the same mother. When he was dead the Chersonesians sacrificed to him, as is usual to a founder, and instituted equestrian and gymnastic exercises, in which no Lampsacenian is permitted to contend. The war with the Lampsacenians still continuing, it also befell Stesagoras to die childless; being struck on the head with an axe in the prytaneum, by a man who in pretence was a deserter, but was in fact an enemy, and a very vehement one.

Upon the death of Stesagoras, the Pisistratidæ sent Miltiades,

son of Cimon, and brother of Stesagoras who had died, with one
ship to the Chersonese, to assume the government; they had also
treated him with kindness at Athens, as if they had not been
parties to the death of his father Cimon.   Miltiades having arrived
in the Chersonese, kept himself at home under color of honoring the memory of his brother Stesagoras, and the principal persons of all the cities assembled together from every
quarter, and came in a body with the intention of condoling with
him, whereupon they were all thrown into chains by him.   Thus
Miltiades got possession of the Chersonese, maintaining five hundred auxiliaries, and married Hegesipyle, daughter of Olorus, King
of the Thracians.   This Miltiades, son of Cimon, had lately arrived
in the Chersonese, but having heard that the Phœnicians were at
Tenedos, he loaded five triremes with the property he had at hand,
and sailed away for Athens.   But when he had set out from the
city of Cardia, he sailed through the gulf of Melas, and as he was
passing by the Chersonese, the Phœnicians fell in with his ships.
Miltiades himself escaped with four of the ships to Imbrus, but the
fifth the Phœnicians pursued and took ; of this ship, Metiochus, the
eldest of the sons of Miltiades, happened to be commander, whom
the Phœnicians took together with the ship.   When they heard
that he was son of Miltiades, they took him up to the king,
thinking that they should obtain great favor for themselves, because Miltiades had given an opinion to the Ionians advising them
to comply with the Scythians, when the Scythians requested them
to loose the bridge and return to their own country.   But Darius
did the young man no injury, but many favors ; for he gave him a
house and an estate, and a Persian wife, by whom he had children,
who were reckoned among the Persians.   Meantime Miltiades
arrived safely at Athens.

CHAPTER II.

In the beginning of the spring, the other generals were dismissed by the king, but Mardonius, son of Gobryas, went down to the coast, taking with him a very large land-army, and a numerous naval force : he was young in years, and had lately married king Darius' daughter, Artazostra. When he arrived in Cilicia, and had gone in person on board ship, he proceeded with the rest of the fleet, while the other generals led the land-army to the Hellespont. When Mardonius reached Ionia, he did a thing, which, when I mention it, will be a matter of very great astonishment to those Greeks, who cannot believe that Otanes, one of the seven Persians, gave an opinion that it was right for the Persians to be governed by a democracy; for Mardonius deposed the tyrants of the Ionians, and established democracies in the cities.

After this, Darius made trial of what were the intentions of the Greeks, whether to make war with him or to deliver themselves up. He therefore despatched heralds, appointing different persons to go to different parts throughout Greece, with orders to ask earth and water for the king, the Persian method of demanding submission. These he sent to Greece, and despatched other heralds to the tributary cities on the coast, with orders to build ships of war and transports for horses. To the heralds who came to Greece many of the inhabitants of the continent gave what the Persian demanded, as did all the islanders also, and moreover the Æginetæ, whereupon the Athenians forthwith threatened them, thinking that the Æginetæ had given earth and water out of ill-will toward themselves, in order that they might make war on them in conjunction with the Persian. And the Athenians laying hold of the pretext, sent to Sparta to accuse the Æginetæ of what they had done as betraying Greece.

The Spartans say, that once upon a time there lived in Lacedæmon one Glaucus, son of Epicydes. This man attained to the first rank in all respects, and bore the highest character for justice of all who at that time dwelt at Lacedæmon. In the course of time a certain Milesian came to Sparta and wished to have a conference with him, and said: "I am a Milesian, and have come, Glaucus, with the desire of profiting by your justice, of which, throughout all the rest of Greece, and particularly in Ionia, there is great talk. Ionia is so continually exposed to great dangers, while with us one can never see the same persons retaining property. Having, therefore, reflected and deliberated on these things, I determined to change half of my whole substance into silver and deposit it with you, being well assured that with you, it would be safe. Do you, then, take this money, and preserve these tokens; and whosoever possessing these shall demand it back again, restore it to him." So spoke the stranger who came from Miletus, and Glaucus received the deposit, on the condition mentioned. After a long time had elapsed, the sons of this man who had deposited the money came to Sparta, and addressed themselves to Glaucus, showed the tokens, and demanded back the money. Glaucus repulsed them, answering as follows: "I don't remember the matter, nor any of the circumstances you mention; but if I can recall it to my mind, I am willing to do every thing that is just; if I really received it, I wish to restore it correctly; but if I have not received it at all, I shall have recourse to the laws of the Greeks against you. I therefore defer settling this matter with you for four months from the present time." The Milesians in disappointment departed, taking greatly to heart the loss of their money. But Glaucus went to Delphi to consult the oracle ; and, when he asked the oracle whether he should make a booty of the money by an oath, the Pythian assailed him in the following words: "Glaucus, son of Epicydes, thus to prevail by an oath, and to make a booty of the money, will be a present gain. But there is a nameless son of Perjury, who has neither hands nor feet; he pursues swiftly, until he has seized and destroyed the whole race, and all the house of him who has falsely sworn. But the race of a man who keeps his oath is afterward more blessed. Glaucus, hearing this, entreated the god to pardon the words he had spoken. But the Pythian said, that to tempt the god, and to commit the crime, were the same thing. So Glaucus sent for the Milesian strangers, and restored them the money. There is at present not a single descendant of Glaucus, nor any house which is supposed to have belonged to Glaucus; but he is utterly extirpated from Sparta. Thus it is right to have no other thought concerning a deposit, than to restore it when it is demanded.

The Æginetæ, offended at what they considered a great affront, prepared to revenge themselves on the Athenians : and as the Athenians happened to have a five-benched galley at Sunium, they formed an ambuscade and took the ship "Theoris," [1] filled with the principal Athenians, and put the men in chains. The Athenians, thus treated by the Æginetæ, no longer delayed to devise all sorts of plans against them. Now there was in Ægina an eminent man named Nicodromus, son of Cnœthus ; incensed against the Æginetæ on account of his former banishment from the island, and now hearing that the Athenians were preparing to do a mischief to the Æginetæ, he entered into an agreement with the Athenians for the betrayal of Ægina, mentioning on what day he would make the attempt, and on what it would be necessary for them to come to his assistance. Nicodromus, according to his agreement, on the appointed day seized that which is called the old town. The Athenians, however, did not arrive at the proper time, for they happened not to have a sufficient number of ships to engage with the Æginetæ ; and while they were entreating the Corinthians to furnish them with ships, their plan was ruined. The Corinthians, for they were then on very friendly terms with them, at their request supplied the Athenians with twenty ships, hiring

---

[1] The " Theoris " was a vessel which was sent every year to Delos to offer sacrifice to Apollo.

RUINS OF AN ANCIENT TEMPLE IN CORINTH.

them out at a nominal price of five drachmæ each; because by their laws they were forbidden to give them for nothing. The Athenians, taking these and their own, manned seventy ships in all, sailed to Ægina, and arrived one day after that agreed upon. When the Athenians did not arrive at the proper time, Nicodromus embarked on shipboard and made his escape from Ægina; and others of the Æginetæ accompanied him, to whom the Athenians gave Sunium for a habitation; and they, sallying from thence, plundered the Æginetæ in the island. This, however, happened subsequently. In the meantime the most wealthy of the Æginetæ overpowered the common people, who, together with Nicodromus, had revolted against them, and led them out to execution. On this occasion they incurred a guilt, which they were unable to expiate by any contrivance, as they were ejected out of the island before the goddess became propitious to them. For having taken seven hundred of the common people prisoners, they led them out to execution; and one of them, who escaped from his bonds, fled to the porch of Ceres the lawgiver, and seizing the doorhandle, held it fast; when they were unable by dragging to tear him away, they cut off his hands, and so took him away; and the hands were left sticking on the door-handles. So did the Æginetæ treat their own people. But when the Athenians arrived with their seventy ships, they came to an engagement, and being conquered in the sea-fight, they called upon the same persons as before for assistance, that is, on the Argives. They, however, would not any longer succor them, but complained that the ships of the Æginetæ, having been forcibly seized by Cleomenes, had touched on the territory of Argos, and the crews had disembarked with the Lacedæmonians. Some men had also disembarked from Sicyonian ships in the same invasion; and a penalty was imposed upon them by the Argives, to pay a thousand talents, five hundred each. The Sicyonians, acknowledging that they had acted unjustly, made an agreement to pay one hundred talents, and be free from the rest; but the Æginetæ would not own themselves in the wrong, and were very obstinate. On this account, therefore, none of the

Argives were sent by the commonwealth to assist them ; but, on their request, volunteers went to the number of a thousand ; a general, whose name was Eurybates, and who had practised for the pentathlon, led them. The greater number of these never returned home, but were slain by the Athenians in Ægina. The general, Eurybates, engaging in single combat, killed three several antagonists in that manner, but was slain by the fourth, Sophanes of Decelea. But the Æginetæ attacked the fleet of the Athenians when they were in disorder, and obtained a victory, and took four of their ships with the men on board.

CHAPTER III.

War was accordingly kindled between the Athenians and
Æginetæ. But the Persian pursued his own design, for the servant continually reminded him to remember the Athenians, and
the Pisistratidæ constantly importuned him and accused the Athenians ; and at the same time Darius was desirous of subduing those
people of Greece who had refused to give him earth and water. He
therefore dismissed Mardonius from his command, because he had
succeeded ill in his expedition ; and appointed other generals,
whom he sent against Eretria and Athens, namely, Datis, who was
a Mede by birth, and Artaphernes, son of Artaphernes, his own
nephew ; and he despatched them with strict orders to enslave
Athens and Eretria, and bring the bondsmen into his presence.
When these generals who were appointed left the king, and
reached the Aleian plain of Cilicia, bringing with them a numerous
and well-equipped army, they encamped there until the whole
naval force required from each people came up : the horse-trans-
ports were also present, which Darius in the preceding year had
commanded his tributaries to prepare. They put the horses on
board of these, and embarked the land-forces in the ships, and
sailed for Ionia with six hundred triremes. From there they did
not steer their ships along the continent direct to the Hellespont
and Thrace ; but parting from Samos they bent their course
across the Icarian sea, and through the islands, dreading the cir-
cumnavigation of Athos, because in the preceding year, in attempt-
ing a passage that way, they had sustained great loss.
While they were doing this, the Delians also, abandoning

Delos, fled to Tenos; but as the fleet was sailing down toward it, Datis would not permit the ships to anchor near the island, but further on, off Rhenea; and he, having ascertained where the Delians were, sent a herald and addressed them as follows: " Sacred men, why have you fled, forming an unfavorable opinion of me? For both I myself have so much wisdom, and am so ordered by the king, that in the region where the two deities[1] were born, no harm should be done either to the country itself or its inhabitants. Return, therefore, to your houses, and resume possession of the island." This message he sent to the Delians by means of a herald; and afterward heaped up three hundred talents of frankincense upon the altar, and burnt it. Then Datis sailed with the army first against Eretria, taking with him both Ionians and Æolians. But after he had put out to sea from there, Delos was shaken by an earthquake, as the Delians say, the first and last time that it was ever so affected. And the deity assuredly by this portent intimated to men the evils that were about to befall them. For during the three successive reigns of Darius, son of Hystaspes, of Xerxes, son of Darius, and of Artaxerxes, son of Xerxes, more disasters befell Greece than during the twenty generations that preceded the time of Darius, partly brought upon it by the Persians, and partly by the chief men amongst them contending for power. So that it is not at all improbable that Delos should be moved at that time, though until then unmoved; and in an oracle respecting it, it had been thus written: " I will move even Delos, although hitherto unmoved." And in the Greek language these names mean: Darius, " one who restrains "; Xerxes, " a warrior "; and Artaxerxes, " a mighty warrior."

After the barbarians had parted from Delos, and touched at the islands, they took with them men to serve in the army, and carried away the sons of the islanders for hostages. Having subdued Eretria, and rested a few days, they sailed to Attica, pressing the inhabitants very close, and expecting to treat them in the same way as they had the Eretrians. Now as Marathon was the spot

---

[1] Apollo and Diana.

in Attica best adapted for cavalry, and nearest to Eretria, they gathered their forces there. When the Athenians heard of this, they also sent their forces to Marathon: and ten generals led them, of whom the tenth was Miltiades, whose father, Cimon, had been banished from Athens by Pisistratus. During his exile, it was his good fortune to obtain the Olympic prize in the four-horse chariot race, the honor of which victory he transferred to Miltiades, his brother by the same mother; afterward, in the next Olympiad, being victorious with the same mares, he permitted Pisistratus to be proclaimed victor, and returned home under terms. But after he had gained a third Olympic prize with the same mares, it happened that he died by the hands of the sons of Pisistratus, when Pisistratus himself was no longer alive; they slew him near the Prytaneum, having placed men to waylay him by night. Cimon was buried in front of the city, beyond that which is called the road to Cœla, and opposite him these same mares were buried, which won the three Olympic prizes. Stesagoras, the elder son of Cimon, was at that time being educated by his uncle in the Chersonese, but the younger by Cimon himself at Athens, and he had the name of Miltiades, from Miltiades, the founder of the Chersonese. At that time, then, this Miltiades, coming from the Chersonese, and having escaped a twofold death, became general of the Athenians; for in the first place, the Phœnicians pursued him as far as Imbros, exceedingly desirous of seizing him and carrying him up to the king; and in the next, when he had escaped them, and had returned to his own country, and thought himself in safety, his enemies attacked him, and brought him before a court of justice, to prosecute him for tyranny in the Chersonese. These also he escaped, and was at length appointed general of the Athenians by the choice of the people.

And first, while the generals were yet in the city, they despatched a herald to Sparta, one Phidippides, an Athenian, a courier by profession, who arrived in Sparta on the following day after his departure from the city of the Athenians, and on coming in presence of the magistrates, said: "Lacedæmonians, the Athenian entreat you to assist them, and not to suffer the most ancient city among the Greeks to fall into bondage to barbarians ; for Eretria is already reduced to slavery, and Greece has become weaker by the loss of a renowned city." He delivered the message according to his instructions, and they resolved to assist the Athenians ; but it was out of their power to do so immediately, as they were unwilling to violate the law ; for it was the ninth day of the current month ; and they said they could not march out until the moon's circle should be full.

Meanwhile the traitor Hippias, son of Pisistratus, had guided the barbarians to Marathon. He first of all landed the slaves from Eretria on the island of the Styreans, called Ægilia ; and next he moored the ships as they came to Marathon, and drew up the barbarians as they disembarked on land. But as he was busied in doing this, it happened that he sneezed and coughed more violently than he was accustomed ; and as he was far advanced in years, several of his teeth were loose, so that through the violence of his cough he threw out one of these teeth. It fell on the sand, and he used every endeavor to find it ; but when the tooth could nowhere be found, he drew a deep sigh, and said to the bystanders : "This country is not ours, nor shall we be able to subdue it ; whatever share belongeth to me, my tooth possesses."

When the Athenians were drawn up in a place sacred to Hercules, the Platæans came to their assistance with all their forces. For the Platæans had given themselves up to the Athenians, as the Athenians had already undergone many toils on their account.

The opinions of the Athenian generals were divided : one party not consenting to engage, "because they were too few to engage with the army of the Medes"; and the others, among whom was Miltiades, urging them to give battle. There was an eleventh voter who was appointed minister of war among the Athenians, who had an equal vote with the generals, and at that time Callimachus of Aphidnæ was minister of war. To him Miltiades came and spoke as follows : "It now depends on you, Callimachus, either to enslave Athens, or, by preserving its liberty, to leave a memorial of yourself to every age, such as not even Harmodius and Aristogeiton have left. For the Athenians were never in so great danger from the time they were first a people. If they succumb to the Medes, it has been determined what they are to suffer when delivered up to Hippias; but if the city survives, it will become the first of the Greek cities. How, then, this can be brought to pass, and how the power of deciding the matter depends on you, I will now proceed to explain. The opinions of us generals, who are ten, are equally divided; the one party urging that we should engage, the other that we should not. Now, if we do not engage, I expect that some great dissension arising amongst us will shake the minds of the Athenians so as to induce them to a compliance with the Medes. But if we engage before any dastardly thought arises in the minds of some of the Athenians, if the gods are impartial, we shall be able to get the better in the engagement. All these things now entirely depend on you. For if you will support my opinion, your country will be free, and the city the first in Greece; but if you join with those who would dissuade us from an engagement, the contrary of the advantages I have enumerated will fall to your lot." Miltiades, by these words, gained over Callimachus, and it was determined to engage. Afterward the generals whose opinions had been given to engage, as the command for the day devolved upon each of them, gave it up to Miltiades; but though he accepted it, he would not come to an engagement before his own turn to command came.

The war-minister, Callimachus, commanded the right wing, for the law at that time was so settled among the Athenians; the Platæans were drawn out last of all, occupying the left wing. Now, ever since that battle, when the Athenians offer sacrifices and celebrate the public festivals which take place every five years, the Athenian herald prays, saying: "May blessings attend both the Athenians and the Platæans." Their line was equal in extent to the Medic line, but the middle of it was but few deep, and there the line was weakest, while each wing was strong in numbers. When they were drawn up, and the victims were favorable, the

Athenians, at the order to charge, advanced against the barbarians
in double-quick time; and the space between them was not less
than eight stades. The Persians, seeing them charging at full
speed, prepared to receive them, laughing at their madness when
they saw that they were so few in number, and that they rushed on
at full speed without cavalry or archers. The Athenians, however,
when they engaged in close ranks with the barbarians, fought in a
manner worthy of record. For they, the first of all the Greeks
whom we know of, charged the enemy at full speed, and first en-
dured the sight of the Medic garb and the men that wore it; for
until that time the very name of the Medes was a terror to the
Greeks. The battle at Marathon lasted a long time: and in the
middle of the line, where the Persians themselves and the Sacæ
were arrayed, the barbarians were victorious, and having broken
the line, pursued to the interior; but in both wings the Athenians
and the Platæans were victorious. Here they allowed the defeated
portion of the barbarians to flee; and having united both wings,
they fought with those who had broken their centre until at last
the Athenians were victorious. They followed the Persians in
their flight, cutting them to pieces, till, reaching the shore, they
called for fire and attacked the ships.

In this battle the brave war-minister, Callimachus, was killed,
and among the generals, Stesilaus, son of Thrasylas, perished;
Cynægeirus, son of Euphorion, laid hold of a ship's stern and had
his hand severed by an axe and fell; and besides, many other
distinguished Athenians were slain. In this manner the Athenians
made themselves masters of seven ships: but with the rest the
barbarians rowed rapidly back, and after taking off the Eretrian
slaves from the island in which they had left them, sailed round
Sunium, wishing to anticipate the Athenians in reaching the
city. But the Athenians marched with all speed to the assistance
of the city, and reached it before the barbarians arrived; and
as they had come from the precinct of Hercules at Marathon, they
took up their station in another precinct of Hercules at Cynos-
arges. The barbarians, having laid to with their fleet off Phale-

rum for a time, soon sailed away for Asia. In this battle at Maráthon there died of the barbarians about six thousand four hundred men ; and of the Athenians, one hundred and ninety-two. An Athenian, Epizelus, son of Cuphagoras, while fighting in the medley, and behaving valiantly, was deprived of sight, though wounded in no part of his body, nor struck from a distance ; and he continued to be blind from that time for the remainder of his life. I have heard that he used to give the following account of his loss. He thought that a large heavy-armed man stood before him, whose beard shaded the whole of his shield ; that this spectre passed by him, and killed the man that stood by his side, smiting him with this loss as it passed.

King Darius, before the Eretrians were made captive, harbored a deep resentment against them, as the Eretrians had been the first to begin acts of injustice : but when he saw them brought into his presence, and subject to his power, he did them no other harm, but settled them in the Cissian territory at a station of his own, the name of which is Ardericca ; it is two hundred and ten stades distant from Susa, and forty from the well which produces three different substances ; for asphalt, salt, and oil are drawn up from it, in the following manner. It is pumped up by means of a swipe, and, instead of a bucket, half of a wine-skin is attached to it ; having dipped down with this, a man draws it up and then pours the contents into a receiver ; and being poured from this into another, it assumes three different forms : the asphalt and the salt immediately become solid, but the oil they collect, and the Persians call it rhadinace ; it is black and emits a strong odor. Here king D...ius settled the Eretrians ; who, even to my time, occupied this territory, retaining their ancient language. Two thousand of the Lacedæmonians came to Athens after the full moon, making such haste to be in time, that they arrived in Attica on the third day after leaving Sparta. Too late for the battle, they, nevertheless, proceeded to Marathon, saw the slain, commended the Athenians and their achievement, and returned home.

After the defeat of the Persians at Marathon, Miltiades, asked of the Athenians seventy ships, and troops, and money, without telling them what country he purposed to invade, but saying that he would make them rich if they would follow him, for he would take them to a country, from which they would easily bring an abundance of gold, and the Athenians, elated by these hopes, granted the ships. Miltiades, accordingly took the troops and sailed against Paros, alleging as a pretext, that the Parians had first begun hostilities by sending a trireme with the Persians to Marathon. But his real reason was that he had a grudge against the Parians on account of Lysagoras, son of Tisias, who was a Parian by birth and who had calumniated him to Hydarnes the Persian. Miltiades arrived with his forces and besieged the Parians, who were driven within their walls; and sent a herald to them to demand a hundred talents, saying, that if they did not furnish him that sum, he would not draw off his army until he had destroyed them. The Parians never entertained the thought of giving Miltiades any money; but devised means by which they might defend the city; and in several parts where the wall was most exposed to attack, they raised it, during the night, to double its former height. Up to this point of the story all the Greeks agree; but after this the Parians themselves say that it happened as follows. That when Miltiades was in a state of perplexity, a captive woman, by birth a Parian, and named Timo, conferred with him; she was an inferior priestess of the infernal goddesses. When she came into the presence of Miltiades, she advised him, if he deemed it of great consequence to take Paros, to act as she should suggest. Following out her suggestions he came to the mound before the city and leaped over the fence of Ceres Thesmophora, as he was unable to open the door; and went to the temple, for the purpose either to move some of the things that may not be moved, or to do something or other, I know not what. He was just at the door, when suddenly a thrill of horror came over him, and he went back by the same way; and in leaping over the fence his thigh was dislocated, or his knee was hurt. Miltiades, in a bad plight, sailed back home, neither bringing money to the Athenians, nor having reduced Paros, but having besieged it for six and twenty days, and ravaged the island. When the Parians were informed that Timo, the priestess of the goddesses, had directed Miltiades, they desired to punish her, and sent deputies to the oracle at Delphi, as soon as they were relieved from the siege, to inquire whether they should put to death the priestess of the goddesses, for having made known to the enemy the means of capturing the country, and for having discovered to Miltiades sacred things, which ought not to be revealed to the male sex. But the Pythian did not allow them, but said, " that Timo was not to blame for this, but that it was fated Miltiades should come to a miserable end, and she had appeared to him as a guide to misfortune." When Miltiades returned from Paros, the Athenians were loud in their complaints against him, especially Xanthippus, son of Ariphron, who brought a capital charge against Miltiades before the people, and prosecuted him for deception. Miltiades, though present in person, made no defence, through inability, as his thigh had begun to mortify But while he lay on a couch his friends made a defence for him, dwelling much on the battle that had been fought at Marathon, and on the capture of Lemnos; since he had taken Lemnos, and inflicted vengeance on the Pelasgians, and had given it up to the Athenians. The people so far favored him as to acquit him of the capital offence, but fined him fifty talents for the injury he had done. Miltiades soon after ended his life by the mortification of his thigh, and his son Cimon paid the fifty talents.

BOOK VII. POLYMNIA.

CHAPTER I.

DEATH OF DARIUS AND REIGN OF XERXES.

WHEN the news of the battle fought at Marathon reached Darius, who was before much exasperated with the Athenians on account of the attack upon Sardis, he grew still more eager to prosecute the war against Greece. He therefore immediately sent messengers to the several cities, and bade them prepare an army much greater than they had furnished before, and ships, horses, corn, and transports. Asia was thrown into agitation during the space of three years, the bravest men being enrolled and prepared for the purpose of invading Greece. In the fourth year the Egyptians, who had been subdued by Cambyses, revolted from the Persians; whereupon Darius only became the more eager to march against both. Just then a violent dissension arose between the sons of Darius concerning the sovereignty; for by the customs of the Persians he was obliged to nominate his successor before he marched out on any expedition. Before Darius became king, he had three sons born to him by his former wife, the daughter of Gobryas; and after his accession to the throne, four others by Atossa, daughter of Cyrus. Of the former, Artabazanes was the eldest; of those born after, Xerxes: and these two, not being of the same mother, were at variance. Artabazanes urged that he was the eldest of all the sons, and that it was the established usage among all men that the eldest son should succeed to the sovereignty: on the other hand, Xerxes alleged that he was son of Atossa, daughter of Cyrus, and that it was Cyrus who had acquired freedom for the Persians. At this very juncture, when Darius had not yet declared his opinion, Demaratus, son of Ariston, happened to come up to Susa, deprived of his kingly office at Sparta, and having imposed on himself a voluntary exile from Lacedæmon. This man went to Xerxes, as report has it, and advised him to say in addition to what he had already said, that " he was born after his father Darius had become king, and was possessed of the empire of the Persians ; whereas Artabazanes was born while he was yet a private person ; wherefore it was not reasonable or just that any other should possess that dignity in preference to himself. "Since in Sparta also," Demaratus continued to suggest, " this custom prevailed, that if some children were born before their father became king, and one was born subsequently, when he had come to the throne, this last-born son should succeed to the kingdom." Darius acknowledged this point, and declared Xerxes king. But it appears to me that even without this suggestion Xerxes would have been made king, for Atossa had unbounded influence. So Darius appointed Xerxes to be king over the Persians, and prepared to march. But just at this juncture, and in the year after the revolt of Egypt, Darius himself, while making preparations, died, having reigned thirty-six years in all ; nor was he able to avenge himself either on the Egyptians, who had revolted, or on the Athenians ; and when Darius was dead, the kingdom devolved on his son Xerxes.

Xerxes was at first by no means inclined to make war against Greece, but he levied forces for the reduction of Egypt. Mardonius, son of Gobryas, who was cousin to Xerxes, and son of Darius' sister, and who had the greatest influence with him of all the Persians, constantly held the following language : " Sire, it is not right that the Athenians, who have already done so much mischief to the Persians, should go unpunished ? However, for the present, finish the enterprise you have in hand ; and when you have quelled the insolence of Egypt, lead your army against Athens ; that you may acquire a good reputation among men, and any one for the future may be cautious of marching against your territory."

This language was used by him for the purpose of revenge, but he frequently made the following addition to it, that " Europe was a very beautiful country, and produced all kinds of cultivated trees,— and was very fertile, and worthy to be possessed by the king alone of all mortals." Mardonius was desirous of new enterprises, and wished to be himself governor of Greece, and in time he persuaded Xerxes to do as he advised. Xerxes, in the second year after the death of Darius, reduced all Egypt to a worse state of servitude than ever under Darius, and committed the government to Achæmenes, his brother.

He then convoked an assembly of the principal Persians, that he might hear their opinions, and make known his intentions to them all. " Men of Persia," said Xerxes, " I learn from older men that we have never remained inactive since we wrested the sovereign power from the Medes, and Cyrus overthrew Astyages ; but the deity has led the way, and we have followed his guidance to our advantage. What deeds Cyrus and Cambyses and my father Darius have achieved, and what nations they have added to our empire, no one need mention to you who know them well. But since I have succeeded to the throne, I have carefully considered how I may not fall short of my predecessors in honor, nor acquire less additional power to the Persians."

" I have now called you together, that I may communicate to you what I purpose to do. I intend to throw a bridge over the Hellespont, and to march an army through Europe against Greece, that I may punish the Athenians for the injuries they have done to the Persians and to my father. You have already seen Darius preparing to make war against those people ; but he died, and had it not in his power to avenge himself. But I, in his cause and that of the other Persians, will not rest till I have taken and burnt Athens ; for they began by doing acts of injustice against my father and me. First they came to Sardis, with Aristagoras the Milesian, our servant, and burnt down the groves and the temples. You all know well enough how they treated us on our making a descent on their territory, when Datis and Artaphernes led our forces.   For these reasons, therefore, I have resolved to make war upon them.   And I am sure that if we subdue them, and their neighbors, who inhabit the country of Pelops the Phrygian, we shall make the Persian territory co-extensive with the air of heaven, for the sun will not look down upon any land that borders on ours.   When I shall have informed you of the time, it will be the duty of each of you to come promptly.   And whosoever shall appear with the best-appointed troops, to him I will give such presents as are accounted most honorable in our country."

After this, when Xerxes had resolved to undertake the expedition, a vision appeared to him in his sleep, which the magi interpreted to signify that all mankind should serve him.   Xerxes imagined that he was crowned with the sprig of an olive tree, whose branches covered the whole earth ; and that afterward the crown that was placed on his head disappeared.   After the magi had given this interpretation, all the Persians who were assembled departed immediately to their own governments, and used all diligence to execute what had been ordered, every man hoping to obtain the proposed reward ; Xerxes thus levied his army, searching out every region of the continent.   He was employed four whole years in assembling his forces and providing things necessary for the expedition.   In the fifth he began his march with a vast multitude of men.   For this was by far the greatest of all the expeditions with which we are acquainted.   What nation did not Xerxes lead out of Asia against Greece ? what stream, except that of great rivers, did not his army drink dry ?   Some supplied ships ; others were ordered to furnish men for the infantry, others cavalry, some transports for horses, together with men to serve in the army ; others had to furnish long ships for the bridges, and others provisions and vessels.

And first of all, as those who had first attempted to double Mount Athos had met with disaster, preparations were made for nearly three years to cut Athos off by a canal.   Triremes were stationed at Eleus in the Chersonese, and from there men of every nation from the army dug under the lash.   They went in succession ; and the people who dwelt round Athos dug also. Bubares, son of Megabazus, and Artachæus, son of Artæus, both Persians, presided over the work. Athos is a vast and celebrated mountain, stretching into the sea, and inhabited by men. Where the mountain terminates toward the continent, it is in the form of a peninsula connected with the continent by an isthmus of about twelve stades ; this is a plain with hills of no great height from the sea of the Acanthians to the sea which is opposite Torone. On this isthmus stands Sana, a Grecian city ; and on Athos itself are the cities of Dion, Olophyxus, Acrothoon, Thyssus, and Cleonæ. To make the excavation the barbarians divided the ground among the several nations, having drawn a straight line near the city of Sana. When the trench was deep, some stood at the bottom and continued to dig, and others handed the soil that was dug out to men who stood above on ladders ; they again in turn handed it to others, until they reached those that were at the top ; the last carried it off and threw it away. In the case of all, except the Phœnicians, the brink of the excavation fell in and gave double labor, for as they made the upper and the lower opening of equal dimensions, this must necessarily happen. But the Phœnicians, who show their skill in other works, did so especially in this ; for they dug the portion that fell to their share, making the upper opening of the trench twice as large as it was necessary for the trench itself to be ; and as the work proceeded they contracted it gradually, so that when they came to the bottom the work was equal in width to the rest ; near adjoining is a meadow, where they had a market and bazaar, and great abundance of meal was brought to them from Asia. According to my deliberate opinion, Xerxes ordered this excavation to be made from motives of ostentation, wishing to display his power, and to leave a memorial of himself. For though it was possible, without any great labor, to have drawn the ships over the isthmus, he commanded them to dig a channel for the sea of such a width that two triremes might pass through rowed abreast. And the same persons, to whom the excavation was committed, were ordered also to throw a bridge over the river Strymon. He also caused cables of papyrus and of white flax to be prepared for the bridges, and ordered the Phœnicians and Egyptians to lay up provisions for the army, that neither the men nor the beasts of burden might suffer from famine on their march toward Greece, conveying them to various quarters in merchant-ships and transports from all parts of Asia.

While these men were employed in their appointed task, the whole land-forces marched with Xerxes to Sardis, setting out from Critalla in Cappadocia, where it had been ordered that all the troops throughout the continent should assemble. They crossed the river Halys, entered Phrygia, and arrived at Celænæ, where rise the springs of the Mæander, and of another river not less than the Mæander, which is called the Catarractes, which, springing up in the very forum of the Celænians, discharges itself into the Mæander; in this city the skin of Silenus Marsyas is suspended, which, as the Phrygians report, was stripped off and suspended by Apollo. In this city Pythius, son of Atys, a Lydian, being in waiting, entertained the whole army of the king, and Xerxes himself, with most sumptuous feasts; and he offered to contribute money toward the expense of the war. Xerxes asked the Persians near him who this Pythius was, and what riches he possessed, that he made such an offer. They answered: "O king, this is the person who presented your father Darius with the golden plane-tree and the vine; and he is now the richest man we know of in the world, next to yourself." Xerxes in surprise next asked Pythius what was the amount of his wealth. He said: "O king, as soon as I heard you were coming down to the Grecian sea, wishing to present you with money for the war, I made inquiry, and found by computation that I had two thousand talents of silver, and of gold four millions of Doric staters, lacking seven thousand. These I freely give you; for myself I have sufficient subsistence from my slaves and lands." Xerxes, delighted with his offer, replied: "My Lydian friend, since I left the Persian country I have met with no man to the present moment who was willing to

TRIPOLITZA.

entertain my army, or who, having come into my presence, has voluntarily offered to contribute money toward the war. But you have entertained my army magnificently, and have offered me vast sums; in return for this, I make you my friend. Keep what you have acquired, and I will myself make up to you the seven thousand staters which you lack of four millions. Be careful always to continue such as you are, and you shall never repent hereafter."

From Phrygia he entered Lydia, crossed the river Mæander, and passed by the city of Callatebus, in which confectioners make honey with tamarisk and wheat. Xerxes, by the way, met with a plane-tree, which, on account of its beauty, he presented with golden ornaments, and having committed it to the care of one of the Immortals,[1] on the next day he arrived at Sardis, the capital of the Lydians.

In the meanwhile those who were appointed had joined the Hellespont from Asia to Europe. There is in the Chersonese on the Hellespont, between the city of Sestos and Madytus, a craggy shore extending into the sea, directly opposite Abydos. From this shore to Abydos, they had constructed two bridges, the Phœnicians one with white flax, and the Egyptians the other with papyrus. The distance is seven stades. When the strait was thus united, a violent storm arose and broke in pieces and scattered the whole work. When Xerxes heard of this, exceedingly indignant, he commanded that the Hellespont should be stricken with three hundred lashes with a scourge, and that a pair of fetters should be let down into the sea. I have moreover heard that with them he likewise sent branding instruments to brand the Hellespont. He certainly charged those who flogged the waters to utter these barbarous and impious words : " Thou bitter water! thy master inflicts this punishment upon thee, because thou hast injured him, although thou hadst not suffered any harm from him. And king Xerxes will cross over thee, whether thou wilt or not ; it is with justice that no man sacrifices

[1] One of the ten thousand chosen men called Immortals, of whom we shall hear more hereafter.

to thee, because thou art both a deceitful and briny river!" He accordingly commanded them to chastise the sea in this manner, and to cut off the heads of those who had to superintend the joining of the Hellespont. They on whom this thankless office was imposed, carried it into execution ; and other engineers constructed bridges in the following manner. They connected together penteconters and triremes, under the bridge toward the Euxine sea, three hundred and sixty ; and under the other, three hundred and fourteen, obliquely to the Pontus, but in the direction of the current of the Hellespont, that it might keep up the tension of the cables. They then let down very long anchors, some on the bridge toward the Pontus, on account of the winds that blew from it within ; others on the other bridge toward the west and the Ægean, on account of the south and southeast winds. They left an opening as a passage through between the penteconters, in three places, that any one who wished might be able to sail into the Pontus in light vessels, and from the Pontus outward. Having done this, they stretched the cables from the shore, twisting them with wooden capstans, not as before using the two kinds separately, but assigning to each two of white flax and four of papyrus. The thickness and quality was the same, but those of flax were stronger in proportion, every cubit weighing a full talent. When the passage was bridged over, they sawed up trunks of trees, equal in length to the width of the bridge, and laid them upon the extended cables in regular order, fastening them securely together. They put brush-wood on the top, and earth over the whole ; and having pressed down the earth, they drew a fence on each side, that the beasts of burden and horses might not be frightened by looking down upon the sea.

At last the works at the bridges and Mount Athos were completed, as well as the mounds at the mouths of the canal which had been made on account of the tide in order that the mouths of the trench might not be choked up. News was brought that all was ready, and the army, fresh from their winter at Sardis, set out fully

prepared at the beginning of the spring toward Abydos. But just
as they were on the point of starting, the sun quit his seat in the
heavens and disappeared, though there were no clouds, and the
air was perfectly serene, and night ensued in the place of day.
This occasioned Xerxes much uneasiness ; but the magi said
" The deity foreshows to the Greeks the extinction of their cities ;
the sun is the portender of the future to the Greeks, and the moon
to the Persians."   Xerxes, at this, was much delighted, and set
out upon his march.   As he was leading his army away, Pythius
the Lydian, terrified by the prodigy in the heavens, and emboldened by the gifts of Xerxes, went to the king and spoke thus :
" Sire, would you indulge me by granting a boon I wish to obtain,
which is easy for you to grant, and of much importance to me."
Xerxes, expecting that he would wish for anything rather than
what he did ask, said that he would grant his request, and bade
him declare what he wanted.   " Sire," said he, " I have five sons ;
and it happens that they are all attending you in the expedition
against Greece.   But pity me, O king, who am advanced in years,
and release one of my sons from the service, that he may take
care of me and my property.   Take the other four with you, accomplish your designs, and return home."   Xerxes was highly incensed, and answered : " Base man ! hast thou dared, when I am
marching in person against Greece, and taking with me my
children, and brothers, and kinsmen, and friends to make mention
of thy son ? thou who art my slave, and who wert bound in duty to
follow me with all thy family, even with thy wife.   But I promise
to grant your request; I will leave your dearest son."   When he
had given this answer, he immediately commanded to find out the
eldest of the sons of Pythius, and to cut his body into two halves,
and to stand one on the right of the road, and the other on the
left, while the army should pass between them.

This done the army passed between.   The baggage-bearers
and beasts of burden first led the way ; after them came a host of
all nations.   When more than one half of the army had passed, an
interval was left that they might not mix with the king's troops.

Before him a thousand horsemen led the van, chosen from among all the Persians; and next to them a thousand spearmen, these also chosen from among all, carrying their lances turned downwards to the earth. After these, ten immense sacred horses, gorgeously caparisoned, called Nisæan, from the plain in the Medic territory, which produces them; then came the sacred chariot of Jupiter, drawn by eight white horses, followed by a charioteer on foot, holding the reins; for no mortal ever ascends this seat. Behind this came Xerxes himself on a chariot drawn by Nisæan horses; and a charioteer walked at his side, whose name was Patiramphes. In this manner Xerxes marched out of Sardis, and whenever he thought right, he used to pass from the chariot to a covered carriage. Behind him marched a thousand spearmen, the bravest and noblest of the Persians, carrying their spears in the usual manner; and after them another body of a thousand horse, chosen from among the Persians; then ten thousand chosen Persian infantry. Of these, one thousand had golden pomegranates on their spears instead of ferrules, and they enclosed the others all round; the nine thousand within had silver pomegranates. Those also that carried their spears turned to the earth had golden pomegranates, and those that followed nearest to Xerxes had golden apples. Behind the ten thousand foot were placed ten thousand Persian cavalry; and after the cavalry was left an interval of two stades; then the rest of the throng followed promiscuously.

Once when the army halted during the night under Mount Ida, thunder and lightning fell upon them, and destroyed a considerable number of the troops on the spot. At the Scamander, the first river on their march from Sardis, the stream failed and did not afford sufficient drink for the army and beasts of burden. Here Xerxes went up to the Pergamus or citadel of Priam, and sacrificed a thousand oxen to the Ilian Minerva, and the magi poured out libations in honor of the heroes of the Trojan War. At Abydos, Xerxes wished to behold the whole army. And there had been previously erected on a hill at this place, for his use, a lofty throne of white marble; the people of Abydos had made it, in obedience to an order of the king. Seated there, he beheld both the land army and the fleet; he desired also to see a contest take place between the ships, in which the Sidonian Phœnicians were victorious. Exceedingly gratified he was, both with the contest and the army. But while he was viewing the whole Hellespont covered by the ships, and all the shores and the plains of Abydos full of men, he suddenly burst into tears. Artabanus, his paternal uncle, observed him, and exclaimed: "O king, a moment ago you pronounced yourself happy, but now you weep." "Alas," he answered: "Commiseration seized me, when I considered how brief all human life is, since of these, numerous as they are, not one will be alive in a hundred years!"

That day they made preparations for the passage over; and on the following they waited for the sun, as they wished to see it rising, in the mean time burning all sorts of perfumes on the bridges, and strewing the road with myrtle branches. When the sun rose, Xerxes poured a libation into the sea out of a golden cup, and offered up a prayer to the sun, that no such accident might befall him as would prevent him from subduing Europe, until he had reached its utmost limits. After the prayer, he threw the cup into the Hellespont, and a golden bowl, and a Persian sword, which they call acinace. But I cannot determine with certainty, whether he dropped these things into the sea as an offering to the sun, or whether he repented of having scourged the Hellespont, and presented these gifts to the sea as a compensation. These ceremonies finished, the infantry and all the cavalry crossed over by that bridge which was toward the Pontus; and the beasts of burden and the attendants by that toward the Ægean. I have heard that Xerxes crossed over last of all. In seven days and seven nights without a halt his army crossed. On this occasion it is related, that when Xerxes had crossed over the Hellespont, a certain Hellespontine said: "O Jupiter, why, assuming the form of a Persian, and taking the name of Xerxes, do you wish to subvert Greece, bringing all mankind with you? since without them it was in your power to do this."

THE TOMB OF JONAH, KONYUNJIK, AND THE RUINS OPPOSITE MOSUL.

Doriscus is a shore and extensive plain of Thrace. Through it flows a large river, the Hebrus. A royal fort had been built, and a Persian garrison had been established in it by Darius, from the time that he marched against the Scythians. At Doriscus Xerxes numbered his army. The whole land forces were found to be seventeen hundred thousand. They were computed in this manner: having drawn together ten thousand men in one place, and crowded them as close together as it was possible, they traced a circle on the outside; removed the ten thousand, threw up a stone fence on the circle, a yard high, and made others enter within the enclosed space, until they had in this manner computed all.

The Persians were equipped as follows: On their heads they wore loose coverings, called tiaras; on the body various-colored sleeved breastplates, with iron scales like those of fish; and on their legs, loose trousers; instead of shields they had bucklers made of osiers; and under them their quivers were hung. They had short spears, long bows, and arrows made of cane, besides daggers suspended from the girdle on the right thigh. They had for their general, Otanes, father of Amestris, wife of Xerxes. They were formerly called Cephenes by the Grecians, but by themselves and neighbors, Artæans. But when Perseus, son of Danae and Jupiter, came to Cepheus, son of Belus, and married his daughter Andromeda, he had a son to whom he gave the name of Perses; and from him they derived their appellation. The Medes marched equipped in the same manner as the Persians; for the above is a Medic and not a Persian costume. The Medes had for their general, Tigranes, of the family of the Achæmenidæ: they were formerly called Arians by all nations; but when Medea of Colchis came from Athens to these Arians, they also changed their names. The Assyrians who served in the army had helmets of bronze, twisted in a barbarous fashion, not easy to describe; and shields and spears, with daggers similar to those of the Egyptians, besides wooden clubs knotted with iron, and linen cuirasses. By the Greeks they were called Syrians, but by the barbarians,

Assyrians. Among them were the Chaldeans; and Otaspes, son of Artachæus commanded them. The Bactrians had turbans on their heads, very much like those of the Medes, and bows made of cane peculiar to their country, and short spears. The Sacæ, who are Scythians, had on their heads caps, which came to a point and stood erect: they also wore loose trousers, and carried bows peculiar to their country, and daggers, and also battle-axes, called sagares. The Indians, clad with garments made of cotton, had bows of cane, and arrows of cane tipped with iron.

The Arabians wore cloaks fastened by a girdle; and carried on their right sides long bows which bent backward. The Ethiopians were clothed in panthers' and lions' skins, and carried long bows, not less than four cubits in length, made from branches of the palm-tree; and on them they placed short arrows made of cane, instead of iron, tipped with a stone, which was made sharp, and of the sort on which they engrave seals. Besides, they had javelins, and at the tip was an antelope's horn, made sharp, like a lance; they had also knotted clubs. When they were going to battle, they smeared one half of their body with chalk, and the other half with red ochre. The Arabians and Ethiopians who dwell above Egypt were commanded by Arsames, son of Darius and Artystone, daughter of Cyrus, whom Darius loved more than all his wives, and whose image he had made of beaten gold. The Ethiopians from the sun-rise (for two kinds served in the expedition) were marshalled with the Indians, and did not at all differ from the others in appearance, except in their language and their hair. For the eastern Ethiopians are straight-haired; but those of Libya have hair more curly than that of any other people. These Ethiopians from Asia were accoutred almost the same as the Indians; but they wore on their heads skins of horses' heads, as masks, stripped off with the ears and mane; and the mane served instead of a crest, and the horses' ears were fixed erect; and as defensive armor they used the skins of cranes instead of shields. The Libyans marched, clad in leathern garments, and made use of javelins hardened by fire. They had for their general, Massages, son of

Oarizus. The Paphlagonians joined the expedition, wearing on their heads plated helmets, and carried small shields, and not large spears, besides javelins and daggers : and on their feet they wore boots, peculiar to their country, reaching up to the middle of the leg. The Thracians wore fox-skins on their heads, and tunics around their bodies, and over them they were clothed with various-colored cloaks, and on their feet and legs they had buskins of fawn-skin, and carried javelins, light bucklers, and small daggers. These people having crossed over into Asia, were called Bithynians ; but formerly, as they themselves say, were called Strymonians, as they dwelt on the river Strymon.

These, with very many others, were the nations that marched on the continent and composed the infantry. Over these and the whole infantry was appointed as general, Mardonius, son of Gobryas. But of the ten thousand chosen Persians, Hydarnes was general. These Persians were called Immortal, for the following reason : If any one of them made a deficiency in the number, compelled either by death or disease, another was ready chosen to supply his place ; so that they were never either more or less than ten thousand. The Persians displayed the greatest splendor of all, and were also the bravest ; their equipment was such as has been described ; but besides this, they were conspicuous from having a great profusion of gold. They also brought with them covered chariots and a numerous and well-equipped train of attendants. Camels and other beasts of burden conveyed their provisions, apart from that of the rest of the soldiers.

All these nations have cavalry ; they did not, however, all furnish horse, but only the following. First, the Persians, equipped in the same manner as their infantry, except that on their heads some of them wore bronze and wrought-steel ornaments. There is a certain nomadic race, called Sagartians, of Persian extraction and language, who wear a dress fashioned between the Persian and the Pactyan fashion ; they furnished eight thousand horse, but they are not accustomed to carry arms either of bronze or iron, except daggers : they use lassos made of twisted thongs. The

mode of fighting of these men is as follows : When they engage
with the enemy they throw out the ropes, which have nooses at
the end, and whatever any one catches, whether horse or man, he
drags toward himself; and they that are entangled in the coils are

BRIDGE OVER THE GORTYNIUS.

put to death. The Arabians had the same dress as their infantry,
but all rode camels not inferior to horses in speed. The number
of the horse amounted to eighty thousand, besides the camels and
chariots. All the rest of the cavalry were marshalled in troops;

but the Arabians were stationed in the rear, as horses cannot endure camels. Armamithres and Tithæus, sons of Datis, were generals of the cavalry. Their third colleague in command, Pharnuches, had been left at Sardis sick. For as they were setting out from Sardis he met with a sad accident. When he was mounted, a dog ran under the legs of his horse, and the horse, frightened, reared and threw Pharnuches, who vomited blood, and the disease turned to a consumption. With respect to the horse, his servants immediately led him to the place where he had thrown his master, and cut off his legs at the knees.

The number of the triremes amounted to twelve hundred and seven.

Persians, Medes, and Sacæ served as marines on board all the ships. Of these the Phœnicians furnished the best sailing ships, and of the Phœnicians the Sidonians. The admirals of the navy were: Ariabignes, son of Darius; Prexaspes, son of Aspathines; Megabazus son of Megabates; and Achæmenes, son of Darius. Of the other captains I make no mention, as I deem it unnecessary, except of Artemisia, whom I most admire, as having, though a woman, joined this expedition against Greece. Her husband was dead, but, holding the sovereignty while her son was under age, she joined the expedition from a feeling of courage and manly spirit, though there was no necessity for her doing so. Her name was Artemisia, and she was the daughter of Lygdamis, by birth of Halicarnassus on her father's side, and on her mother's a Cretan. She commanded the Halicarnassians, the Coans, the Nisyrians, and the Calyndians, having contributed five ships: and of the whole fleet, next to the Sidonians, she furnished the most renowned ships, and of all the allies, gave the best advice to the king. The cities which I have mentioned as being under her command, I pronounce to be all of Doric origin; the Halicarnassians being Trœzenians, and the rest Epidaurians.

When Xerxes had numbered his forces, and the army was drawn up he desired to pass through and inspect them in person. Accordingly he drove through in a chariot, by each separate nation, made inquiries, and his secretaries wrote down the answers; until he had gone from one extremity to the other, both of the horse and foot. When he had finished this, and the ships had been launched into the sea. Xerxes, in a Sidonian ship, under a gilded canopy, sailed by the prows of the ships, asking questions of each, as he had done with the land-forces, and having the answers written down.

When Xerxes arrived at Therma, he ordered his army to halt. And seeing from Therma the Thessalonian mountains, Olympus and Ossa, which are of vast size, and having learnt that there was a narrow pass between them, through which the river Peneus runs, and hearing that at that spot there was a road leading to Thessaly, very much wished to sail and see the mouth of the Peneus. When Xerxes arrived, and beheld its mouth, he was struck with great astonishment. For several rivers, five of them greatly noted, the Peneus, the Apidanus, the Onochonus, the Enipeus, and the Pamisus, meeting together in this plain from the mountains that enclose Thessaly, discharge themselves into the sea through one channel, and that a narrow one; but as soon as they have mingled together, from that spot the names of the other rivers merge in that of the Peneus.¹ The Thessalians say, that Neptune made the pass through which the Peneus flows; and their story is probable. For whoever thinks that Neptune shakes the earth, and that rents occasioned by earthquakes are the works of this god, on seeing this, would say that Neptune formed it. For it appears evident to me, that the separation of these mountains is the effect of an earthquake.

---

¹ Literally, "the river Peneus gaining the victory as to the name, causes the others to be nameless."

CHAPTER II.

When the Greeks arrived at the Isthmus they consulted in what way and in what places they should prosecute the war. The opinion which prevailed was that they should defend the pass at Thermopylæ; for it appeared to be narrower than that into Thessaly, and at the same time nearer to their own territories. On the western side of Thermopylæ is an inaccessible and precipitous mountain, stretching to Mount Œta; and on the eastern side of the way is the sea and a morass. In this passage there are hot baths, which the inhabitants call Chytri, and above these is an altar to Hercules. A wall had been built in this pass, and formerly there were gates in it. The Phocians built it through fear, when the Thessalians came from Thesprotia to settle in the Æolian territory which they now possess, apprehending that the Thessalians would attempt to subdue them; at the same time they diverted the hot water into the entrance, that the place might be broken into clefts; having recourse to every contrivance to prevent the Thessalians from making inroads into their country. Now this old wall had been built a long time, and the greater part of it had already fallen through age; but they determined to rebuild it, and in that place to repel the barbarian from Greece. Very near this road there is a village called Alpeni, from which they expected to obtain provisions.

The naval forces of Xerxes, setting out from the city of Therma, advanced with ten of the fastest sailing ships straight to Scyathus, where were three Greek ships keeping a look-out, a Trœzenian an Æginetan, and an Athenian. These, seeing the ships of the barbarians at a distance, betook themselves to flight. The

Trœzenian ship, which Praxinus commanded, the barbarians pursued and soon captured ; and then, having led the handsomest of the marines to the prow of the ship, they slew him, deeming it a good omen that the first Greek they had taken was also very handsome. The name of the man that was slain was Leon, and perhaps he in some measure reaped the fruits of his name. The Æginetan ship, which Asonides commanded, gave them some trouble, Pytheas, son of Ischenous, being a marine on board, a man who on this day displayed the most consummate valor ; who,

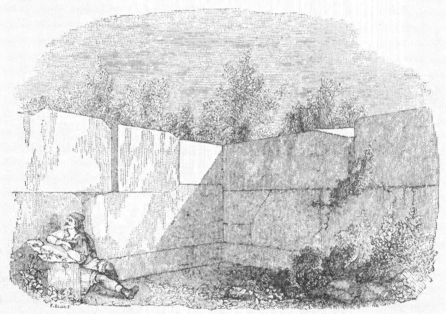

CYCLOPEAN WALLS AT CEPHALLOMA.

when the ship was taken, continued fighting until he was almost cut to pieces. But when they found that he was not dead, but still breathed, the Persians who served on board the ships were very anxious to save him alive, on account of his valor, healing his wounds with myrrh, and binding them with bandages of flaxen cloth. And when they returned to their own camp, they showed him with admiration to the whole army, and treated him well ; but the others, whom they took in this ship, they treated as slaves.

Thus, two of the ships were taken ; but the third, which Phormus, an Athenian, commanded, in its flight ran ashore at the mouth of the Peneus ; and the barbarians got possession of the ship, but not of the men : for as soon as the Athenians had run the ship aground, they leaped out, and, proceeding through Thessaly, reached Athens. The Greeks who were stationed at Artemisium were informed of this event by signal-fires from Scyathus.

As far as Thermopylæ, the army of Xerxes had suffered no loss, and the numbers were at that time, as I find by calculation of those in ships from Asia, a total of five hundred and seventeen thousand six hundred and ten. Of infantry there were seventeen hundred thousand, and of cavalry eighty thousand ; to these I add the Arabians who rode camels, and the Libyans who drove chariots, reckoning the number of twenty thousand men. Accordingly, the numbers on board the ships and on the land added together, make up two millions three hundred and seventeen thousand six hundred and ten, exclusive of the servants that followed, and the provision ships, and the men that were on board them. But the force brought from Europe must still be added to this whole number, of which I suppose that there were three hundred thousand men. So that these myriads added to those from Asia, make a total of two millions six hundred and forty one thousand six hundred and ten fighting men. I think that the servants who followed them, together with those on board the provision ships and other vessels that sailed with the fleet, were not fewer than the fighting men, probably more numerous ; but supposing them to be equal in number with the fighting men, Xerxes, son of Darius, led five millions two hundred and eighty-three thousand two hundred and twenty men to Thermopylæ. This, then, was the number of the whole force of Xerxes. But the number of women who made bread, wives of officers, and servants, no one could mention with accuracy ; nor of draught-cattle and other beasts of burden ; nor of Indian dogs that followed. I am not astonished that the streams of some rivers failed ; rather is it a wonder to me how the provisions held out for so many myriads. For I find by calculation, if each man had a chœnix of wheat

ISLAND AND CASTLE OF CORFU.

daily, and no more, one hundred and ten thousand three hundred
and forty medimni must have been consumed every day ; and I
have not reckoned the food for the women, beasts of burden, and
dogs. But, of so many myriads of men, not one of them, for beauty
and stature, was more entitled than Xerxes himself to possess this
power.

The Greeks who awaited the Persian at Thermopylæ were : of
Spartans three hundred heavy-armed men ; of Tegeans and Man-
tineans one thousand, half of each ; from Orchomenus in Arcadia
one hundred and twenty ; and from the rest of Arcadia one thousand ; from Corinth four hundred ; from Phlius two hundred men,
and from Mycenæ eighty. These came from Peloponnesus. From
Bœotia, of Thespians seven hundred, and of Thebans four hundred. In addition to these, the Opuntian Locrians, being invited,
came with all their forces, and a thousand Phocians. These nations had separate generals for their several cities ; but the one
most admired, and who commanded the whole army, was a Lacedæmonian, Leonidas, son of Anaxandrides, and a descendant of
Hercules, who had unexpectedly succeeded to the throne of Sparta.
For as he had two elder brothers, Cleomenes and Dorieus, he was
far from any thought of the kingdom. However, Cleomenes and
Dorieus both died, and the kingdom thus devolved upon Leonidas.
He had chosen the three hundred men allowed by law, and
marched to Thermopylæ.

When the Persian came near the pass, the Greeks, alarmed,
consulted about a retreat, and it seemed best to the other Peloponnesians to retire to Peloponnesus, and guard the Isthmus ; but
Leonidas, perceiving the Phocians and Locrians very indignant at
this proposition, determined to stay there, and to despatch messengers to the cities, desiring them to come to their assistance, as
being too few to repel the army of the Medes. Meantime Xerxes
sent a scout on horseback, to see how many they were, and what
they were doing. For while he was still in Thessaly, he had heard
that a small army had been assembled at that spot, whose leader
was Leonidas, of the race of Hercules. When the horseman rode

up to the camp, he reconnoitred, and saw not indeed the whole camp, for it was not possible that they should be seen who were posted within the wall, but he had a clear view of those on the outside, whose arms were piled in front of the wall. At this some of the Lacedæmonians were performing gymnastic exercises, and others combing their hair. On beholding this he was astonished, but having ascertained their number, he rode back at his leisure, for no one pursued him, and he met with general contempt. On his return he gave an account to Xerxes of all that he had seen, who could not comprehend the truth, that the Greeks were preparing to be slain and to slay to the utmost of their power.

Xerxes let five days pass, constantly expecting that they would betake themselves to flight. But on the fifth day, as they had not retreated, but appeared to him to stay through arrogance and rashness, in rage he sent the Medes and Cissians against them, with orders to take them alive, and bring them into his presence. When the Medes bore down impetuously upon the Greeks, many of them fell; others followed to the charge, and were not repulsed, though they suffered greatly. But they made it evident to every one, and not least of all to the king himself, that they were indeed many men, but few soldiers. The engagement lasted through the day. The Medes, roughly handled, retired; and the Persians whom the king called "Immortal," and whom Hydarnes commanded, took their place and advanced to the attack, thinking that they indeed should easily settle the business. But they succeeded no better than the Medic troops, but just the same, as they fought in a narrow space, and used shorter spears than the Greeks, and were unable to avail themselves of their numbers. The Lacedæmonians fought memorably, showing that they knew how to fight with men who knew not, and whenever they turned their backs, they retreated in close order; but the barbarians seeing them retreat, followed with a shout and clamor; then they, being overtaken, wheeled round so as to front the barbarians and overthrew an inconceivable number of the Persians; and then some few of the Spartans themselves fell. So that when the Persians were unable to gain any thing in their attempt on the pass, by attacking in troops and in every possible manner, they retired. It is said that during these onsets of the battle, the king, who witnessed them, thrice sprang from his throne, being alarmed for his army. On the following day the barbarians fought with no better success ; for considering that the Greeks were few in number, and expecting that they were covered with wounds, and would not be able to raise their heads against them any more, they renewed the contest. But the Greeks were marshalled in companies and according to their several nations, and each fought in turn, except the Phocians, who were stationed at the mountain to guard the pathway. Again the Persians failed and retired.

While the king was in doubt what course to take, Ephialtes, son of Eurydemus, a Malian, obtained an audience of him, expecting that he should receive a great reward from the king, and informed him of the path which leads over the mountain to Thermopylæ ; and by that means caused the destruction of those Greeks who were stationed there. Afterwards, fearing the Lacedæmonians, he fled to Thessaly, and a price was set on his head by the Pylagori, when the Amphictyons were assembled at Pylæ. But some time after, he went down to Anticyra, and was killed by Athenades, a Trachinian. This Athenades killed kim for another reason, which I shall mention in a subsequent part of my history ;[1] he was however rewarded none the less by the Lacedæmonians. Xerxes, exceedingly delighted with what Ephialtes promised to perform, immediately despatched Hydarnes with his troops from the camp about the hour of lamp-lighting.

All night long the Persians marched, and at dawn reached the summit of the mountain. Here, as I have already mentioned, a thousand heavy-armed Phocians kept guard, to defend their own country, and to secure the pathway. The whole mountain was covered with oaks ; there was a perfect calm, and as a considerable rustling took place from the leaves strewn under foot, the Phocians sprang up and put on their arms, just as the barbarians

---

[1] The promised account is no where given in any extant writings of the historian.

made their appearance. Hit by many thick-falling arrows, the
Phocians fled to the summit of the mountain, prepared to perish.
But the Persians took no further notice of the Phocians, but
marched down the mountain with all speed.

To the Greeks at Thermopylæ, the augur Megistias, having
inspected the sacrifices, first made known the death that would

BRIDGE AT CORFU.

befall them in the morning ; certain deserters afterwards came and
brought intelligence of the circuit the Persians were taking while
it was yet night ; and, thirdly, the scouts running down from the
heights, as soon as day dawned, brought the same intelligence.
It had been announced to the Spartans, by the oracle of Apollo,

when they went to consult concerning this war, "that either Lacedæmon must be overthrown by the barbarians, or their king perish." This answer the prophetess gave in hexameter verses to this effect :

> " Hear me, ye men of spacious Lacedæmon !
> Either your glorious town must be destroyed,
> By the fell hand of warriors sprung from Perseus,
> Or else the confines of fair Lacedæmon
> Must mourn a king of Heracleidan race,
> For all the strength of lions or of bulls
> Is nought to him who has the strength of Zeus ;
> And never shall that monarch be restrained
> Until he takes your city or your king."

Xerxes poured out libations at sun-rise, waited a short time, and began his attack about the time of full market, as he had been instructed by Ephialtes. The Greeks with Leonidas, marching out as if for certain death, now advanced much farther than before into the wide part of the defile. For the fortification of the wall had protected them, on the preceding day, in the narrow part. But now engaging outside the narrows, great numbers of the barbarians fell. The officers of the companies from behind, with scourges, flogged every man, constantly urging them forward, so that many of them falling into the sea, perished, and many more were trampled alive under foot by one another ; and no regard was paid to any that perished. The Greeks, knowing that death awaited them at the hands of those who were going round the mountain, were desperate, and regardless of their own lives, displayed the utmost possible valor against the barbarians. Already were most of their javelins broken, and they had begun to despatch the Persians with their swords. In this part of the struggle fell Leonidas, fighting valiantly, and with him other eminent Spartans, whose names, seeing they were deserving men, I have ascertained ; indeed I have ascertained the names of the whole three hundred. On the side of the Persians, also, many other eminent men fell on this occasion, amongst them two sons of Darius, Abrocomes and Hyperanthes, fighting for the body of Leonidas ; and there was a violent struggle between the Persians

PLAINS OF ARGOS.

and Lacedæmonians, until at last the Greeks rescued it by their
valor, and four times repulsed the enemy. Thus the contest continued until the Greeks heard that those with Ephialtes were
approaching. Then they retreated to the narrow part of the way,
and, passing beyond the wall, came and took up their position on
the rising ground, all in a compact body, with the exception of the
Thebans : the rising ground is at the entrance where the stone
lion now stands to the memory of Leonidas. On this spot they
defended themselves, first with their swords, then with their hands
and teeth, until the barbarians overwhelmed them with missiles in
front, and from above, and on every side.

Dieneces, a Spartan, is said to have been the bravest man.
They relate that before the engagement with the Medes, having
heard a Trachinian say, that when the barbarians let fly their
arrows, they would obscure the sun by the multitude of their
shafts, so great were their numbers, he replied, not at all alarmed :
" That 's good ; we shall have the pleasure, then, of fighting in
the shade." In honor of the slain, who were buried on the spot
where they fell, and of those who died before, these inscriptions
have been engraved upon stones above them ; the first :

> " From Peloponnesus came four thousand men ;
> And on this spot fought with three hundred myriads."

The second was in honor of the three hundred Spartans :

> " Go, stranger ! tell the Lacedæmonians, here
> We lie, obedient to their stern commands ! "

An engraved monument was also erected to Megistias the
augur, by his friend Simonides, and was as follows :

> " The monument of famed Megistias,—
> Slain by the Medes what time they passed the Sperchius ;
> A seer, who though he knew impending fate,
> Would not desert the gallant chiefs of Sparta."

Two of these three hundred, Eurytus and Aristodemus, had
been dismissed from the camp by Leonidas, and were lying
at Alpeni desperately afflicted with a disease of the eyes. But
when Eurytus heard of the circuit made by the Persians, 'e called

for his arms and ordered his helot to lead him to the combatants; and, while the slave in terror ran away, his brave half-blind master rushed into the midst of the throng and perished; but Aristodemus, failing in courage, was left behind. Now if it had happened that Aristodemus had returned sick to Sparta, or if both had gone home together, in my opinion the Spartans would not have shown any anger against them. But since one of them perished, and the other, who had only the same excuse, refused to die, they must needs get exceedingly angry with Aristodemus. On his return to Lacedæmon he was met with insults and infamy. Not one of the Spartans would either give him fire or converse with him; and he was jeered and hooted at by the boys who called him "Aristodemus the coward." However, in the battle of Platæa he removed all the disgrace that attached to him, for he earned the title of the bravest of the Spartans, and recklessly lost his life. Xerxes after the massacre passed through among the dead; and having heard that Leonidas was king and general of the Lacedæmonians, he commanded them to cut off his head, and fix it upon a pole. It is clear to me from many other proofs, and not least of all from this, that king Xerxes was more highly incensed against Leonidas during his life, than against any other man; for otherwise he would never have violated the respect due to his dead body; since the Persians, most of all men with whom I am acquainted, are wont to honor men who are brave in war.

BOOK VIII. URANIA.

CHAPTER I.

THE INVASION OF ATTICA AND THE BATTLE OF SALAMIS.

The Greek fleet from Artemisium put in at Salamis at the request of the Athenians, who wished to remove their children and wives out of Attica, and consult what measures were to be taken. The Athenians caused proclamation to be made, " that every one should save his children and family by the best means he could." Thereupon the greatest part sent away their families to Trœzen, some to Ægina, and others to Salamis. They used all diligence to remove them to a place of safety, from a desire to obey the oracle, but more particularly for the following reason. The Athenians say that a large serpent used to live in the temple as a guard to the Acropolis ; they used to do it honor by placing before it its monthly food, consisting of a honey-cake : this honey-cake in former time had always been consumed, but now it remained untouched. When the priestess made this known, the Athenians, with more readiness, abandoned the city, since even the goddess had forsaken the Acropolis. As soon as every thing had been deposited in a place of safety, they sailed to the encampment. Many more ships were assembled together than had fought at Artemisium, and from a greater number of cities. The same admiral commanded them as at Artemisium, Eurybiades, son of Euryclides, a Spartan, though he was not of the royal family : The Athenians, however, furnished by far the most and the best sailing ships. The whole number of ships besides the penteconters, amounted to three hundred and seventy-eight.

When the leaders from the various cities met together at Salamis, they held a council, in which Eurybiades proposed that any one who chose should deliver his opinion, where he thought it would be most advantageous to come to an engagement by sea, of all the places of which they were still in possession : for Attica was already given up. Most of the opinions of those who spoke coincided, that they should sail to the Isthmus, and fight before Peloponnesus ; alleging this reason, that if they should be conquered by sea while they were at Salamis, they would be besieged in the island, where no succor could reach them ; but if at the Isthmus, they might escape to their own cities.

ANCIENT GREEK WALLS RESTORED.

While the commanders from Peloponnesus were debating these matters, an Athenian arrived with intelligence, that the barbarian had entered Attica, and was devastating the whole of it by fire. The army with Xerxes were thus three months en route from the passage over the Hellespont, till they arrived at Athens. They took the city, deserted of inhabitants, but found a few of the Athenians in the temple, with the treasurers of the temple and some poor people ; who, having fortified the Acropolis with planks and stakes, tried to keep off the invaders : they had not withdrawn to Salamis, partly through want of means, and

moreover they thought they had found out the meaning
of the oracle which the Pythian delivered to them, that the
wooden wall "should be impregnable"; imagining, that this
was the refuge according to the oracle, and not the ships. The
Persians, posting themselves on the hill opposite the Acropolis,
which the Athenians call the Areopagus, wrapped tow round their
arrows, and setting fire to it, shot them at the fence. But those
Athenians who were besieged, still defended themselves, though
driven to the last extremity, and the fence had failed them; nor,
when the Pisistratidæ proposed them, would they listen to terms of
capitulation; but still defending themselves, they contrived other
means of defence, and when the barbarians approached the gates,
they hurled down large round stones; so that Xerxes was for a
long time kept in perplexity, not being able to capture them. At
length, in the midst of these difficulties, an entrance was discovered
by the barbarians; for it was necessary, according to the oracle,
that all Attica, on the continent, should be subdued by the Persians. In front of the Acropolis, but behind the gates and where
no one kept guard, nor would ever have expected that any man
would ascend, there some of them ascended near the temple of
Cecrops' daughter Aglauros. When the Athenians saw that the
enemy were in the Acropolis, some threw themselves down from
the wall and perished, and others took refuge in the recess of the
temple. But the Persians who had ascended first turned to the
gates, opened them, and put the suppliants to death : and when all
were thrown prostrate, they pillaged the temple and set fire to the
whole Acropolis.

The Greeks at Salamis, when intelligence was brought them
how matters stood in Athens, were thrown into such consternation,
that some of the generals would not wait until the subject before
them was decided on, but rushed to their ships and hoisted sail, as
about to hurry away; by such of them as remained it was determined to come to an engagement before the Isthmus. Night came
on, and they, being dismissed from the council, went on board their
ships. Thereupon Mnesiphilus, an Athenian, inquired of Themis-

tocles, on his return to his ship, what had been determined on by them. And being informed by him that it was resolved to conduct the ships to the Isthmus, and to come to an engagement before the Peloponnesus, he said, " If they remove the ships from Salamis, you will no longer fight for any country ; for they will each betake themselves to their cities ; and neither will Eurybiades nor any one else be able to detain them, so that the fleet should not be dispersed ; and Greece will perish through want of counsel. But, if there is any possible contrivance, go and endeavor to annul the decree, if by any means you can induce Eurybiades to alter his determination, so as to remain here." The suggestion pleased Themistocles exceedingly ; and without answer he went to the ship of Eurybiades, and said that he wished to confer with him on public business. He desired him to come on board his ship, and say what he wished. Thereupon Themistocles, seating himself by him, repeated all that he had heard from Mnesiphilus, making it his own, and adding much more, until he prevailed on him, by entreaty, to leave his ship, and assemble the commanders in council. The upshot of the matter was that Themistocles persuaded the generals in council to remain and fight at Salamis. Day came, and at sunrise an earthquake took place on land and at sea. They determined to pray to the gods, and to invoke the Æacidæ as allies. For having prayed to all the gods, they forthwith, from Salamis, invoked Ajax and Telamon; and sent a ship to Ægina for Æacus, and the Æacidæ. In the mean time, all the admirals and captains of Xerxes' fleet advised engaging in a sea-fight, except Artemisia, who spoke as follows: " Tell the king from me, Mardonius, that I say this. It is right that I, sire, who proved myself by no means a coward in the sea-fight off Eubœa, and performed achievements not inferior to others, should declare my real opinion, and state what I think best for your interest. Therefore I say this, abstain from using your ships, nor risk a sea-fight; for these men are as much superior to your men by sea, as men are to women. And why must you run a risk by a naval engagement? Have you not possession of Athens, for the sake of which you undertook this expedition, and have you not the rest of Greece? They will not be able to hold out long against you ; but will soon disperse, and fly to their cities."

Xerxes was very much pleased with the opinion of Artemisia ; he had before thought her an admirable woman, but now he praised her much more. However, he gave orders to follow the advice of the majority in this matter, thinking that they had behaved ill at Euboea on purpose, because he was not present. He now prepared in person to behold them engaging by sea.[1]

Meanwhile, those at Salamis were growing alarmed, and wondered at the imprudence of Eurybiades ; till at last their discontent broke out openly, and a council was called, and much was said on the subject. Some said that they ought to sail for the Peloponnesus, and hazard a battle for that, and not stay and fight for a place already taken by the enemy ; but the Athenians, Æginetæ, and Megareans, declared that they should stay there and defend themselves. Thereupon, Themistocles, when he saw his opinion was overruled by the Peloponnesians, went secretly out of the council, and despatched a man in a boat to the encampment of the Medes instructing him what to say : his name was Sicinnus, and he was a domestic, and preceptor to the children of Themistocles. After these events, Themistocles got him made a Thespian, when the Thespians augmented the number of their citizens, and gave him a competent fortune. He, arriving in the boat, spoke as follows to the generals of the barbarians : "The general of the Athenians has sent me, unknown to the rest of the Greeks, (for he is in the interest of the king, and wishes that your affairs may prosper, rather than those of the Greeks,) to inform you that the Greeks, in great consternation, are deliberating on flight ; and you have now an opportunity of achieving the most glorious of all enterprises, if you do not suffer them to escape. For they do not agree among themselves, nor will they oppose you ; but you will see those who are in your interest, and those who are not, fighting with one another." Having delivered this

---

[1] Seated on the mountain side upon a magnificent throne of ivory and gold, as others relate.

message to them, he immediately departed. As these tidings appeared to them worthy of credit, they immediately landed a considerable number of Persians on the little island of Psyttalea, lying between Salamis and the continent ; and, when it was midnight, they got their western wing under way, drawing it in a circle toward Salamis, and those who were stationed about Ceos and Cynosura got under way and occupied the whole passage as far as Munychia with their ships, so that the Greeks might have no way to escape, but, being shut up in Salamis, might suffer punishment for the conflicts at Artemisium ; and they landed the Persians at the little island of Psyttalea for this reason : that, when an engagement should take place, as they expected the greater part of the men and wrecks would be driven there, they might save the one and destroy the other. These things they did in silence, that the enemy might not know what was going on.

I am unable to speak against the truth of oracles, when I think of the remarkable oracle of Bacis : " When they shall bridge with ships the sacred shore of " Diana with the golden sword," and sea-girt Cynosura, having with mad hope destroyed beautiful Athens, then divine Vengeance shall quench strong Presumption, son of Insolence, when thinking to subvert all things. For bronze shall engage with bronze, and Mars shall redden the sea with blood. Then the far-thundering son of Saturn and benign victory shall bring a day of freedom to Greece." After such a prediction and its fulfilment, I neither dare myself say any thing in contradiction to oracles, nor allow others to do so.

All this night there was a great altercation between the generals at Salamis. They did not yet know that the barbarians had surrounded them with their ships. They supposed that they were in the same place where they had seen them stationed during the day. While the generals were disputing, Aristides, son of Lysimachus, crossed over from the Ægina. He was an Athenian, but had been banished by ostracism. From what I have heard of his manner of life, I consider him to have been the best and most upright man in Athens. He, standing at the entrance of the council,

called Themistocles out, who was not indeed his friend, but his
most bitter enemy ; yet from the greatness of the impending
danger, he forgot that, and called him, for he had aleady heard
that those from Peloponnesus were anxious to get the ships under
way for the Isthmus.   When Themistocles came out, Aristides
spoke as follows : " It is right that we should strive, both on other
occasions, and particularly on this, which of us shall do the greatest
service to our country.   I assure you, that to say little or much to
the Peloponnesians about sailing from here is a waste of breath ;
for I, an eye-witness, tell you, now, even if they would, neither
the Corinthians, nor Eurybiades himself, will be able to sail away ;
for we are on all sides enclosed by the enemy.   Go in, and acquaint them with this."   But Themistocles bade Aristides go in
himself and convey the tidings.   This he did, but the generals
would not even then give credence to his report until there arrived
a trireme of Tenians that had deserted, which Panætius, son of
Socimenes, commanded, and which brought an account of the
whole truth.   For that action the name of the Tenians was engraved on the tripod at Delphi, among those who had defeated
the barbarian.   With this ship that came over at Salamis, and
with the Lemnian before, off Artemisium, the Grecian fleet was
made up to the full number of three hundred and eighty ships; for
before it wanted two of that number.

Day dawned, and when they had mustered the marines,
Themistocles, above all the others, haranged them most eloquently.
His speech was entirely taken up in contrasting better things with
worse, exhorting them to choose the best of all those things which
depended on the nature and condition of man.   As soon as the
trireme from Ægina, which had gone to fetch the Æacidæ returned the Greeks got all their ships under way.   The barbarians
immediately fell upon them.   Now all the other Greeks began to
back water and make for the shore ; but Aminias of Pallene, an
Athenian, being carried onward, attacked a ship ; and his ship becoming entangled with the other, and the crew not being able to
clear, the rest thereupon came to the assistance of Aminias and

engaged. Thus the Athenians say the battle commenced ; but the Æginetæ affirm that the ship which went to Ægina to fetch the Æacidæ, was the first to begin. It is also said, that a phantom of a woman appeared to them, that she cheered them on, so that the whole fleet of Greeks heard her, after she had first reproached them in these words : " Dastards, how long will you back water ? " Opposite the Athenians the Phœnicians were drawn up, for they occupied the wing toward Eleusis and westward ; opposite the Lacedæmonians, the Ionians occupied the wing toward the east and the Piræus. Of these some few behaved ill on purpose, in compliance with the injunctions of Themistocles. The greater part of the ships were run down at Salamis ; some being destroyed by the Athenians, others by the Æginetæ. For the Greeks fought in good order, in line, but the barbarians were neither properly formed nor did any thing with judgment. However they proved themselves to be far braver on this day than off Eubœa, every one exerting himself vigorously, and dreading Xerxes ; for each thought that he himself was observed by the king.

I am unable to say with certainty how each of the barbarians or Greeks fought ; but with respect to Artemisia, the following incident occurred, by which she obtained still greater credit with the king. For when the king's forces were in great confusion, the ship of Artemisia was chased by an Attic ship, and not being able to escape, she resolved upon a strategem. For being pursued by the Athenian, she bore down upon a friendly ship, manned by Calyndians, and with Damasithymus himself, king of the Calyndians, on board ; whether she had any quarrel with him while they were at the Hellespont, I am unable to say, or whether she did it on purpose, or whether the ship of the Calyndians happened by chance to be in her way ; however, she ran it down, and sunk it, and by good fortune gained a double advantage to herself. For when the captain of the Attic ship saw her bearing down on a ship of the barbarians, he concluded Artemisia's ship to be either a Greek or one that had deserted from the enemy and was assisting them, and so turned aside and attacked others. Thus she escaped, and in consequence of it became still more in favor with Xerxes. For it is said that Xerxes, looking on, observed her ship making the attack, and that some near him said : " Sire, do you see how well Artemisia fights ; she has sunk one of the enemy's ships ? " Whereupon he asked if it was in truth the exploit of Artemisia ; they answered " that they knew the ensign of her ship perfectly well." But they thought that it was an enemy that was sunk ; for no one of the crew of the Calyndian ship lived to tell the tale and accuse her. And it is related that Xerxes exclaimed : " My men have become women, and my women men."

In this battle perished the admiral, Ariabignes, son of Darius, and brother of Xerxes, and many other illustrious men of the Persians and Medes, and the other allies ; but only a very few of the Greeks : for as they knew how to swim, they whose ships were destroyed, and who did not perish in actual conflict, swam safe to Salamis ; whereas, many of the barbarians, not knowing how to swim, perished in the sea. When the foremost ships were put to flight, then the greatest number were destroyed ; for those who were stationed behind, endeavoring to pass on with their ships to the front, that they, too, might give the king some proof of their courage, fell foul of their own flying ships. The following event also occurred in this confusion. Some Phœnicians, whose ships were destroyed, went to the king and accused the Ionians of destroying their ships and betraying him. It, however, turned out that the Ionian captains were not put to death, but that those Phœnicians who accused them, received the following reward. For while they were yet speaking, a Samothracian ship bore down on an Athenian ship and sunk it. Just then an Æginetan ship, coming up, sunk the ship of the Samothracians. But the Samothracians being javelin-men, by hurling their javelins, drove the marines from the ship that had sunk them, and boarded and got possession of it. This action saved the Ionians : for when Xerxes saw them perform so great an exploit, he turned round upon the Phœnicians, and ordered their heads to be struck off, that they who had proved themselves cowards, might no more accuse those who were braver.

The barbarians turned to flight, and sailing away towards Phalerus, the Æginetæ waylaid them in the strait, and performed actions worthy of record. For the Athenians in the rout ran down both those ships that resisted and those that fled ; and the Æginetæ, those that sailed away from the battle : so that when any escaped the Athenians they fell into the hands of the Æginetæ.

In this engagement the Æginetæ obtained the greatest renown ; and next, the Athenians. Aristides, of whom I made mention a little before as a most upright man, in this confusion that took place about Salamis, took with him a considerable number of heavy-armed men, who were stationed along the shore of the Salaminian territory and were Athenians by race, landed them on the island of Psyttalea, and put to the sword all the Persians who were on that little island.

CHAPTER II.

WHEN the sea-fight was ended, the Greeks hauled on shore at Salamis all the wrecks that still happened to be there and held themselves ready for another battle, expecting the king would still make use of the ships that survived. But a west wind carrying away many of the wrecks, drove them on the shore of Attica, which is called Colias, so as to fulfil both all the other oracles delivered by Bacis and Musæus concerning this battle, and also that relating to the wrecks which were drifted on this shore, which many years before had been delivered by Lysistratus, an Athenian augur, but had not been understood by any of the Greeks: "The Colian women shall broil their meat with oars."

When Xerxes saw the defeat he had sustained he was afraid that some of the Ionians might suggest to the Greeks, or might themselves resolve to sail to the Hellespont, for the purpose of breaking up the bridges, and shut him up in Europe. So he planned immediate flight. But wishing that his intention should not be known either to the Greeks or his own people, he pretended to throw a mound across to Salamis. He fastened together Phœnician merchantmen, that they might serve instead of a raft and a wall, and made preparation for war, as if about to fight another battle at sea. Every body who saw him thus occupied, was firmly convinced that he had seriously determined to stay and continue the war, except Mardonius, who was well acquainted with his design. At the same time Xerxes despatched a messenger to the Persians, to inform them of the misfortune that had befallen him. There is nothing mortal that reaches its destination more rapidly than these couriers of the Persians. They say that as many days as are occupied in the whole journey, so many horses and men are posted at regular intervals; neither snow nor rain, nor heat, nor night, prevents them from performing their appointed stage as quickly as possible. The first courier delivers his orders to the second, the second to the third, and so it passes throughout, being delivered from one to the other, just like the torch-bearing among the Greeks, which they perform in honor of Vulcan. The first message that reached Susa, with the news that Xerxes was in possession of Athens, caused so great joy among the Persians who had been left behind, that they strewed all the roads with myrtle, burnt perfumes, and gave themselves up to sacrifices and festivity. But the arrival of the second messenger threw them into such consternation, that they all rent their garments, and uttered unbounded shouts and lamentations, laying the blame on Mardonius, not so much grieved for the ships as anxious for Xerxes himself. And this the Persians continued to do until Xerxes himself arrived home.

CELES RIDDEN BY A CUPID.

Mardonius, seeing Xerxes much afflicted by the defeat at Salamis, and suspecting he was meditating a retreat, thus addressed the king: "Sire, do not think you have suffered any great loss in consequence of what has happened; for the contest with us does not depend on wood alone, but on men and horses. Be not discouraged; for the Greeks have no means of escape from rendering an account of what they have done now and formerly, and from becoming your slaves. If you have resolved not to stay here, return to Susa, and take with you the greatest part of the army; but give me three hundred thousand picked men and I will deliver Greece to you reduced to slavery." Xerxes, delighted and relieved, granted Mardonius his request. As to Xerxes himself, if all the men and women of the world had advised him to stay, in my opinion, he would not have yielded, so great was his terror. Leaving Mardonius in Thessaly, he marched in all haste to the Hellespont; and arrived at the place of crossing in forty-five days, bringing back no part of his army, so to speak. Wherever, and among whatever nation, they happened to be marching, they seized and consumed their corn ; but if they found no fruit, overcome by hunger, they ate up the herbage as it sprung from the ground, and from sheer hunger stripped off the bark of trees, and gathered leaves, both of wild and cultivated plants. But a pestilence and dysentery falling on the army, destroyed them on their march.   Such of them as were sick, Xerxes left behind, ordering the cities through which he happened to be passing, to take care of and feed them : some in Thessaly, others at Siris of Pæonia, and in Macedonia.   It was here he had left the sacred chariot of Jupiter, when he marched against Greece, but he did not receive it back, as he returned ; for the Pæonians had given it to the Thracians, and when Xerxes demanded it back, said that the mares had been stolen, as they were feeding, by the upper Thracians, who dwell round the sources of the Strymon.   There the king of the Bisaltæ and of the Crestonian territory, a Thracian, perpetrated a most unnatural deed ; he declared that he would not willingly be a slave to Xerxes, but he went up to the top of Mount Rhodope, and enjoined his sons not to join the expedition against Greece.   They, however, disregarded his prohibition, from a desire to see the war, and served in the army with the Persian : but when they all returned safe, six in number, their father had their eyes put out for this disobedience.

The Persians, in great haste crossed over the Hellespont to Abydos in their ships ; for they found the rafts no longer stretched across, but broken up by a storm.   While detained there, they got more food than on their march, and having filled themselves immoderately, and drunk of different water, a great part of the army that survived, died ; the rest with Xerxes reached Sardis.   Another account is also given, that when Xerxes in his retreat from Athens arrived at Eïon on the Strymon, from there he no longer continued his journey by land, but committed the army to Hydarnes to conduct to the Hellespont, and he himself went on board a Phœnician ship to pass over to Asia.   During his voyage a violent and tempestuous wind from the Strymon overtook him ; the storm increased in violence, and the ship was overloaded, many of the Persians having accompanied Xerxes. Then the king, becoming alarmed, calling aloud, and asked the pilot if there was any hope of safety for them ; and he said : "There is none, sire, unless we get rid of some of this crowd of passengers." Xerxes, hearing this answer, said : "O Persians, now let some among you show his regard for the king, for on you my safety seems to depend." Many having done homage, leapt into the sea, and the ship, being lighted, thus got safe to Asia. It is added, that Xerxes, immediately after he landed, presented the pilot with a golden crown, because he had saved the king's life ; but ordered his head to be struck off, because he had occasioned the loss of many Persians. This story appears to me not at all deserving of credit, for if such a speech had been made by the pilot to Xerxes, I should not find one opinion in ten thousand to deny that the king would have sent down into the hold of the ship those who were on deck, since they were Persians, and Persians of high rank, and would have thrown into the sea a number of Phœnicians, equal to that of the Persians.

When the division of the booty, after the battle of Salamis was completed, the Greeks sailed to the Isthmus, for the purpose of conferring the palm of valor upon him among the Greeks who had proved himself most deserving throughout the war. The generals distributed the ballots at the altar of Neptune, selecting the first and second out of all ; thereupon every one gave his vote for himself, each thinking himself the most valiant ; but with respect to the second place, the majority concurred in selecting Themistocles. So each had but one vote, for first place, but Themistocles had a great majority for the second honor. Though the Greeks, out of envy, would not determine this matter, but returned to their several countries without coming to a decision, yet Themistocles was applauded and extolled throughout all Greece, as being by far the wisest man of the Greeks. Because he was not honored by those who fought at Salamis, although victorious, he immediately afterward went to Lacedæmon, hoping to be honored there. The

Lacedæmonians received him nobly, and paid him the greatest honors. They gave the prize of valor to Eurybiades, a crown of olive ; and of wisdom and dexterity to Themistocles, also a crown of olive. And they presented him with the most magnificent chariot in Sparta ; praising him highly, and on his departure, three hundred chosen Spartans, called knights, escorted him as far as the Tegean boundaries. He is the only man that we know of whom the Spartans ever escorted on his journey.

Mardonius' first movement was to send Alexander, son of Amyntas, a Macedonian, as an ambassador to Athens ; as well because the Persians were related to him as because he had been informed that Alexander was a friend and benefactor of the Athenians. For in this way he thought he should best be able to gain over the Athenians, having heard that they were a numerous and valiant people ; and besides, he knew that the Athenians had been the principal cause of the late disaster of the Persians at sea. If these were won over, he hoped that he should easily become master at sea, which indeed would have been the case ; and on land he imagined that he was much superior : thus he calculated that his power would get the upper hand of the Greeks. But the Athenians gave the following answer to Alexander : " We ourselves are aware that the power of the Medes is far greater than ours ; so that there is no need to insult us with that. But do not you attempt to persuade us to come to terms with the barbarian, for we will not. Go, and tell Mardonius that the Athenians say : ' So long as the sun shall continue in the same course as now, we will never make terms with Xerxes ; but we will go out to oppose him, trusting in the gods, who fight for us, and in the heroes, whose temples and images he has burned. Know, therefore, if you did not know it before, that so long as one Athenian is left alive, the fight shall be continued.' "

BOOK IX. CALLIOPE.

CHAPTER I.

THE WAR CONTINUED ; BATTLE OF PLATÆA AND SIEGE OF THEBES.

WHEN Alexander returned and made known to Mardonius the answer of the Athenians, he set out from Thessaly, and led his army in haste against Athens ; and wherever he arrived from time to time, he joined the people to his own forces. So far were the leaders of Thessaly from repenting of what had been before done, that they urged on the Persian much more : and Thorax of La-rissa, who had assisted in escorting Xerxes in his flight, now openly gave Mardonius a passage into Greece. When the army on its march arrived among the Bœotians, the Thebans endeavored to restrain Mardonius from advancing farther, assuring him that to take up his station there would be equivalent to subduing the whole of Greece without a battle. For if the Greeks should continue firmly united, as they had done before, it would be difficult even for all mankind to overcome them. " But," they continued, " if you do what we advise, you will without difficulty frustrate all their plans. Send money to the most powerful men in the cities ; split Greece into parties, and then, with the assistance of those who side with you, you may easily subdue those who are not in your interest." But he was infatuated with a vehement desire to taking Athens a second time, and fondly hoped, by signal-fires across the islands, to make known to the king while he was at Sardis, that he was in possession of Athens. When he arrived in Attica, he did not find the Athenians there ; but was informed that most of them were at Salamis on board their ships. So he took the deserted city ten months after its capture by the king.

But Mardonius was by no means desirous to stay longer in Attica. He lingered awhile there to see what the Athenians would do, but neither ravaged nor injured the Attic territory, being in expectation all along that they would come to terms. But when he could not persuade them he withdrew, before the Spartans, under Pausanias, could reach the Isthmus, having first set fire to Athens, and if any part of the walls, or houses, or temples happened to be standing, these he threw down and laid all in ruins. He marched out for the reason that the Attic country was not adapted for cavalry ; and if he should be conquered in an engagement, there was no way to escape except through a narrow pass, so that a very small number of men could intercept them. He determined therefore to retire to Thebes, and to fight near a friendly city, and in a country adapted for cavalry.

The Lacedæmonians arrived at the Isthmus and went into camp. When the rest of the Peloponnesians, who favored the better cause, saw the Spartans marching out, they thought it would be a disgrace to absent themselves from the expedition of the Lacedæmonians. Accordingly, when the victims proved favorable, they all marched out from the Isthmus and advanced to Eleusis. The Athenians crossed over from Salamis, and joined them there. At Erythræ in Bœotia, they learnt that the barbarians were encamped on the Asopus, at which they consulted together, and formed opposite, at the foot of Mount Cithæron. When the Greeks did not come down to the plain, Mardonius sent against them all his cavalry, under command of Masistius, a man highly esteemed among the Persians. He was mounted on a Nisæan horse, that had a golden bit, and was otherwise gorgeously caparisoned. When the cavalry rode up to the Greeks, they charged them in squadrons, and called them women. By chance the Megarians happened to be stationed in that part which was most exposed, and there the cavalry chiefly made their attack. The Megarians, being hard pressed, sent a herald to the Greek generals with this message : "The Megarians say, We, O confederates, are not able alone to sustain the Persian cavalry. So far we have held out against them by our constancy and courage, though hard pressed; but now, unless you will send some others to relieve us, we must abandon our post." Pausanias immediately called for

BŒOTIA.

volunteers to go to that position, and relieve the Megarians. When all the others refused, three hundred chosen men of the Athenians undertook to do it, whom Olympiodorus, son of Lam-

pon, commanded.   After a short but spirited battle, as the cavalry
were charging, the horse of Masistius, being in advance of the
others, was wounded in the flank by an arrow, and in pain, reared
and threw Masistius.   As he fell, the Athenians immediately
seized his horse and attacked him.   At first they were unable to
kill Masistius, he was so thoroughly armed.   Underneath he had
a golden cuirass covered with scales, and over the cuirass a purple
cloak.   By striking against the cuirass they did nothing ; until one
of them, perceiving what was the matter, pierced him in the eye.
So he fell and died.   The whole Persian army, and Mardonius
most of all, mourned the loss of Masistius.   They cut off their own
hair and that of their horses and beasts of burden, and gave themselves up to unbounded lamentations.   The sound reached over
all Bœotia, of mourning for the loss of a man who, next to Mardonius, was most esteemed by the Persians and the king.

The Greeks placed the body on a carriage, and carried it along
the line—an object worthy of admiration, on account of its stature
and beauty—and the men, leaving their ranks, came out to view
Masistius.   After this, they determined to go down toward Platæa,
for the Platæan territory appeared to be much more convenient
for them to encamp in than the Erythræan, as it was better
supplied with water.   Over the foot of Mount Cithæron, near Hy-
siæ, into the Platæan territory they marched, and formed in line,
nation by nation, near the fountain of Gargaphia, and the precinct
of the hero Androcrates, on slight elevations and the level plain.
The whole Grecian army assembled at Platæa, reckoning heavy-
armed and light-armed fighting men, amounted to one hundred
and ten thousand.

When the barbarians, with Mardonius, had ceased to mourn for
Masistius, they also marched to the Asopus, which flows by
Platæa, and on their arrival were drawn up by Mardonius.   Of
barbarians there were three hundred thousand, as has been already shown ; but of Greeks who were allies of Mardonius no one
knows the number, for they were not reckoned up ; but, to make
a guess, I conjecture that they were assembled to the number of

fifty thousand. These were infantry; the cavalry were marshalled apart.

On the second day, both sides offered sacrifices. For the Greeks, Tisamenus, son of Antiochus, was the person who sacrificed, for he accompanied this army as diviner. The sacrifices were favorable to the Greeks, if they stood on the defensive ; but if they crossed the Asopus, and began the battle, not so.

To Mardonius, who was very desirous to begin the battle, the sacrifices were not propitious ; but to him also, if he stood on the defensive, they were favorable : for he too adopted the Greek sacrifices, having for his diviner Hegesistratus, an Elean, and the most renowned of the Telliadæ. This man, before these events, the Spartans had taken and bound for death, because they had suffered many atrocious things from him. In this sad condition, as being in peril for his life, and having to suffer many tortures before death, he performed a deed beyond belief. For as he was confined in stocks bound with iron, he got possession of a knife, which had by some means been carried in, and immediately cut off the broad part of

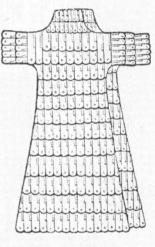

COAT OF MAIL.

his foot—the most resolute deed I ever heard of. Then, as he was guarded by sentinels, he dug a hole through the wall and escaped to Tegea, travelling by night, and by day hiding himself in the woods and tarrying there. Thus, though the Lacedæmonians searched for him with their whole population, on the third night he arrived at Tegea ; but they were struck with great amazement at his daring, when they saw half his foot lying on the ground, and were not able to find him. In time, cured of his wounds, he procured a wooden foot, and became an avowed enemy to the Lacedæmonians. However, at last his hatred conceived against the Lacedæmonians did not benefit him ; for he was taken by them when acting as diviner at Zacynthus, and put to death. The death of Hegesistratus took place after the battle of Platæa : but at that time, on the Asopus, he was hired by Mardonius for no small sum to sacrifice, and was very zealous, both from hatred to the Lacedæmonians and from a love of gain.

Meantime, Timagenides, a Theban, advised Mardonius to guard the passes of Mount Cithæron ; saying, that the Greeks were continually pouring in every day, and that he would intercept great numbers. Eight days had already elapsed since they had been posted opposite each other : but Mardonius thought the suggestion good, and as soon as it was night, sent some cavalry to the passes of Cithæron, that lead to Platæa, which the Bœotians call The Three Heads ; but the Athenians, The Heads of Oak. The horsemen that were sent did not arrive in vain ; for issuing on the plain, they took five hundred beasts carrying provisions from Peloponnesus to the army, with the men who attended the beasts of burden. The Persians not only took the booty, but killed without mercy, sparing neither beast nor man. Two more days passed, neither being willing to begin the battle ; but when the eleventh day after the two armies had been encamped opposite each other in Platæa was almost gone, and the night was far advanced, and silence appeared to prevail throughout the camps, Alexander, son of Amyntas, who was general and king of the Macedonians, rode up on horseback to the sentries of the Athenians, and desired to confer with their generals. Most of the sentries remained at their posts, while some ran to the generals, and told them, " that a man had come on horseback from the camp of the Medes, who uttered not a word more, but, naming the generals, said he wished to confer with them." They immediately repaired to the out-posts, and Alexander addressed them as follows : " O Athenians, I leave these words with you as a deposit, entreating you to keep them secret, and not tell them to any other than Pausanias, lest you should ruin me. I should not utter them, were I not extremely concerned for the safety of all Greece ; for I am myself a Greek by origin, and would by no means wish to see Greece enslaved instead of free. I tell you, then, that the victims have not been favorable to Mardonius and his army, or else you would have fought long ago ; but now, he has determined to dismiss the victims, and to come to an engagement at dawn of day ; fearing, as I conjecture, that you may assemble in greater numbers. Therefore be ready. But if Mardonius should defer the engagement, and not undertake it, persevere remaining where you are, for in a few days provisions will fail him. And if this war should terminate according to your wishes, it is right that you should bear it in mind to effect my freedom, who on behalf of the Greeks have undertaken so hazardous a task, as to acquaint you with the intention of Mardonius, in order that the barbarians may not fall upon you unexpectedly. I am Alexander the Macedonian." Thus having spoken, he rode back to the camp and his own station.

THE FISHERMAN.

The generals of the Athenians went to the right wing, and told Pausanias what they had heard from Alexander ; but as the army was deprived of water and harassed by the cavalry of Mardonius, they remained to deliberate on these and other matters. They had no longer any provisions, and their attendants, who had been despatched to the Peloponnesus to get provisions, were shut out by the cavalry, and unable to reach the camp.

On consultation the generals of the allies resolved, if the Persians should defer making the attack on that day, to remove to the island of Oëroë, ten stades distant from the Asopus, on which they were then encamped. This is an island in the midst of the continent. For the river, dividing higher up, flows down to the plain from Mount Cithæron, having its streams about three stades separate from each other, and united together below. To this place they determined to remove, that they might have an abundant supply of water, and the cavalry might not harass them, as when they were directly opposite. So, in the night, at the hour agreed upon, they fled from the cavalry toward the city of the Platæans until they arrived at the temple of Juno, which stands before the city of the Platæans, twenty stades distant from the fountain of Gargaphia. They then encamped round the Heræum and stood to their arms before the sacred precinct.

When Mardonius was informed that the Greeks had withdrawn under cover of night, and saw the place deserted, he summoned Thorax, of Larissa, and said : " O son of Aleuas, what will you say now, when you see this ground deserted ? For you, their neighbor, said that the Lacedæmonians never fled from battle, but were the first of men in matters of war ; but now we all see that they have fled away during the past night, in terror of us, who are truly the most valiant in the world." Then without more ado he led the Persians at full speed, crossing the Asopus in the track of the Greeks, as if they had betaken themselves to flight. He directed his course only against the Lacedæmonians and Tegeans ; for on account of the hills he did not espy the Athenians, who had turned into the plain. The rest of the commanders of the barbarians' brigades, seeing the Persians advancing to pursue the Greeks, all immediately took up their standards, and pursued, each as quick as he could, without observing either rank or order ; thus they advanced with a shout and in a throng, as if they were about to overwhelm the Greeks.

The Persians made a fence with their osier-shields, and let fly their arrows so incessantly that the Spartans being hard pressed, and the victims continuing unfavorable, Pausanias looked toward the temple of Juno of the Platæans, and invoked the goddess, praying that they might not be disappointed of their hopes.

While he was yet making this invocation, the Tegeans, starting first, advanced against the barbarians ; and immediately after the prayer of Pausanias, the victims became favorable to the Lacedæmonians. Then they advanced against the Persians, who withstood them, laying aside their bows. First of all a battle took place about the fence of bucklers ; and when that was thrown down, a long, obstinate fight ensued near the temple of Ceres, till at last they came to close conflict, when the barbarians laid hold of the Spartan spears and broke them. Indeed, in courage and strength, the Persians were not inferior, but were lightly armed,

JUNO.

ignorant of military discipline, and not equal to their adversaries in skill. They rushed forward upon the Spartans, only to perish.

In that part where Mardonius happened to be, fighting upon a white horse, at the head of a thousand chosen men, the best of the Persians, there they pressed their adversaries most vigorously. For as long as Mardonius survived, they held out, defended themselves, and overthrew many of the Lacedæmonians; but when Mardonius had died, and the troops stationed round him, which were the strongest, had fallen, then the rest turned to flight, and gave way to the Lacedæmonians. Their dress, too, was particularly disadvantageous to them, being destitute of defensive armor. Here satisfaction for the death of Leonidas, according to the oracle, was paid to the Spartans by Mardonius; and Pausanias obtained the most signal victory we have ever heard of. Mardonius died by the hand of Aïmnestus, a man of distinction at Sparta, who, some time after the Medic affairs, at the head of three hundred men, engaged at Stenyclerus with all the Messenians, and he himself perished and his three hundred. When the Persians at Platæa were put to flight by the Lacedæmonians, they fled in disorder to their own camp, and to the wooden fortification which they had made in the Theban territory. It is a wonder to me that, when they fought near the grove of Ceres, not one of the barbarians was seen to enter into the sacred enclosure, or to die in it, but most fell round the precinct in unconsecrated ground. I am of opinion, if it is allowable to form an opinion concerning divine things, that the goddess would not receive them because they had burnt her royal temple at Eleusis.

When the Persians and the rest of the throng arrived in their flight at the wooden wall, they mounted the towers before the Lacedæmonians came up, and defended the wall in the best way they could; so that when the Lacedæmonians arrived, a vigorous battle took place before the walls. So long as the Athenians were absent, the barbarians defended themselves, and had much the advantage over the Lacedæmonians, as they were not skilled in attacking fortifications; but when the Athenians came, then a vehement fight at the walls took place, and continued for a long time. But at length the Athenians, by their valor and pluck, surmounted the wall, and made a breach ; there at length the Greeks poured in. The Tegeans entered first, and plundered the tent of Mardonius, and among other things took away the manger for his horse, all of bronze, and well worth seeing. This manger of Mardonius the Tegeans placed in the temple of the Alean Minerva ; but all the other things they took they carried to the same place as the rest of the Greeks. The barbarians no longer kept in close

ELEGANT VASES AND AMPHORÆ.

order, nor did any one think of valor ; but they were in a state of consternation, as so many myriads of men were enclosed within so small a space ; and the Greeks had such an easy opportunity of slaughtering them, that of an army of three hundred thousand men, except forty thousand with whom Artabazus fled, not three thousand survived. Of Lacedæmonians from Sparta, all that died in the engagement were ninety-one; of Tegeans, sixteen; and of Athenians, fifty-two.

Pausanias made proclamation that no one should touch the booty, and commanded the helots to bring together all the treasures. Dispersing themselves through the camp, they found tents decked with gold and silver, and couches gilt and plated, and golden bowls, and cups, and other drinking vessels; they also found sacks on the waggons, in which were discovered gold and silver cauldrons: and from the bodies that lay dead they stripped bracelets, necklaces, and scimetars of gold; but no account at all was taken of the variegated apparel. Of this the helots stole a great deal and sold it to the Æginetæ, so that the great wealth of the Æginetæ here had its beginning, for they purchased gold from the helots as if it had been bronze. They collected the treasures together, and took from them a tithe for the god at Delphi, from which the golden tripod was dedicated, which stands on the three-headed bronze serpent, close to the altar; they also took a tithe for the god at Olympia, from which they dedicated the bronze Jupiter, ten cubits high; and a tithe to the god at the Isthmus, from which was made the bronze Neptune, seven cubits high. They divided the rest, and each took the share he was entitled to, of the gold, silver, and other treasures, and beasts of burden. Now what choice treasures were given those others who most distinguished themselves at Platæa, is mentioned by no one. But for Pausanias, ten of every thing was selected and given him—slaves, horses, talents, camels, and all other treasures in like manner. It is said also that when Xerxes fled from Greece, he left all his own equipage to Mardonius; Pausanias, therefore, seeing Mardonius' equipage furnished with gold, silver, and various-colored hangings, ordered the bakers and cooks to prepare a supper in the same manner as for Mardonius: and, astonished at the profusion set before him of gold and silver couches handsomely carved, and gold and silver tables, and magnificent preparations for the supper, he in derision ordered his own attendants to prepare a Laconian supper by the

side of it, and when the repast was spread, the difference was so
ridiculous that he laughed, and sent for the generals of the Greeks
and said : " Men of Greece, I have called you together to show
you the folly of the leader of the Medes, who left such sumptuous
fare as this, to come to us, who have such poor fare, to take it
from us." A considerable time after these events, many of the
Platæans found chests of gold and silver, and other precious
things. And still later was discovered a skull without any seam,
consisting of one bone, and an upper jaw which had teeth growing
in a piece, all in one bone, both the front teeth and the grinders ;
and there was likewise discovered the skeleton of a man five cubits
high.

When the Greeks had buried their dead in Platæa, they immediately determined, on consultation, to march against Thebes,
and to demand the surrender of those who had sided with the
Medes, amongst the first of them Timegenides and Attaginus,
who were the chief leaders ; and, if they should not give them up,
they resolved not to depart from the city before they had taken it.
On the eleventh day after the engagement, they arrived and besieged the Thebans, requiring them to give up the men ; and, receiving " No " for an answer, they ravaged the country, and
attacked the walls. As they did not cease damaging them, on the
twentieth day Timegenides spoke thus to the Thebans : " Men of
Thebes, since the Greeks have so resolved that they will not give
over besieging us until either they have taken Thebes, or you
have delivered us up to them, let not the Bœotian territory suffer
any more on our account. But if, being desirous of money, they
demand us as a pretence, let us give them money from the public
treasury ; for we sided with the Mede by general consent, and not
of ourselves alone. If, however, they carry on the siege really because they want us, we will present ourselves before them to plead
our cause." He appeared to speak well and to the purpose ; and
the Thebans immediately sent a herald to Pausanias, expressing
their willingness to surrender the men. When they had agreed
on these terms, Attaginus escaped from the city, and his sons, who

were brought before him, Pausanias acquitted from the charge, saying that boys could have no part in the guilt of siding with the Mede. As to the others whom the Thebans delivered up, they thought that they should be admitted to plead their cause, and moreover trusted to repel the charge by bribery; but he, as soon as he had them in his power, suspecting this very thing, dismissed the whole army of the allies, and, conducting the men to Corinth, put them to death.

CHAPTER II.

THE BATTLE OF MYCALE.

ON the same day on which the defeat at Platæa occurred, another happened to take place at Mycale in Ionia. For while the Greeks were stationed at Delos, there came to them as ambassadors from Samos, Lampon, Athenagoras, and Hegesistratus, being sent by the Samians, unknown to the Persians. When they came to the generals, Hegesistratus urged that " if only the Ionians should see them, they would revolt from the Persians, and that the barbarians would not withstand them ; or, if they should withstand them, the Greeks would not find any other such booty." Invoking, too, their common gods, he besought them to deliver Grecian men from servitude, and to repel the barbarian ; and he said, " that this would be easy for them to do, for their ships sailed badly, and were not fit to fight with them ; and, if they suspected at all that they were leading them on deceitfully, they were themselves ready to go on board their ships as hostages." The Samian stranger was so earnest in his entreaties, that Leotychides asked : " O Samian friend, what is your name ? " " Hegesistratus," he answered ; upon which, interrupting the rest of his discourse, Leotychides exclaimed : " I accept the " Hegesistratus," [1] my Samian friend ; only do you take care that before you sail away both you yourself and those who are with you, pledge your faith that the Samians will be zealous allies to us." The Samians immediately pledged their faith and made oath of confederacy with the Greeks. The others sailed home, but he ordered Hegesistratus to sail with the fleet, regarding his name as an omen. The Greeks tarried that day, and on the next sacrificed auspiciously,

[1] Hegesistratus means " leader of an army."

Deiphonus, son of Evenius, of Apollonia in the Ionian gulf, acting as diviner.

The following incident befel his father, Evenius. There are in this Apollonia sheep sacred to the sun, which by day feed near the river that flows from Mount Lacmon through the Apollonian territory into the sea, near the port of Oricus ; but by night, chosen men, the most eminent of the citizens for wealth and birth, keep watch over them, each for a year : for the Apollonians set a high value upon these sheep, in consequence of some oracle. They are folded in a cavern at a distance from the city. There, once on a time, Evenius, being chosen, kept watch, and one night when he had fallen asleep during his watch, wolves entered the cave, and destroyed about sixty of the sheep. When he discovered what had happened, he mentioned it to no one, purposing to buy others, and put them in their place. This occurrence, however, did not escape the notice of the Apollonians ; and as soon as they discovered it, they brought him to trial, and gave sentence that, for having fallen asleep during his watch, he should be deprived of sight. But after they had blinded Evenius, from that time forward neither did their sheep multiply, nor did the land yield its usual fruit. An admonition was given them at Dodona and Delphi, when they inquired of the prophets the cause of the present calamities " that they had unjustly deprived Evenius, the keeper of the sacred sheep, of his sight ; for they themselves had sent the wolves, and would not cease avenging him, until the people should give such satisfaction for what they had done, as he himself should choose, and think sufficient : then, the gods themselves would give such a present to Evenius, that most men would pronounce him happy, from possessing it." The Apollonians, keeping this answer secret, deputed some of their citizens to negociate the matter with Evenius. One day when he was seated on a bench, they went and sat down by him, and conversed on different subjects, till at length they began to commiserate his misfortune, and leading him artfully on, they asked, " what reparation he would choose, if the Apollonians were willing to give him satisfaction for what they had done." Not having heard of the oracle he made this choice, "if any one would give him the lands of certain citizens," naming those who he knew had the two best estates in Apollonia, "and besides these a house," which he knew was the handsomest in the city, he said, "he would thenceforth forego his anger, and this reparation would content him." Immediately taking him up they said, "the Apollonians make you this reparation for the loss of your eyes, in obedience to an oracle they have received." He thereupon was very indignant, on hearing the whole truth, for he had been deceived; but the Apollonians bought the property from the owners, and gave him what he had chosen, and immediately the gift of divination was implanted in him, so that he became very celebrated.

Deiphonus, the son of this Evenius, was brought by the Corinthians to officiate as diviner to the army.

The Greeks at length determined to sail to the continent: having therefore prepared boarding-ladders, and all other things that were necessary for a sea-fight, they sailed to Mycale. No one was seen near the camp, ready to meet them, but they beheld the ships drawn up within the fortification, and a numerous land-force disposed along the beach, thereupon Leotychides, advancing first in a ship, and nearing the beach as closely as possible, made proclamation by a herald to the Ionians, saying: "Men of Ionia, as many of you as hear me, attend to what I say; for the Persians will understand nothing of the advice I give you. When we engage, it behooves every one first of all to remember Liberty; and next the watch-word, Hebe; and let him who does not hear this, learn it from those who do hear." The meaning of this proceeding was the same as that of Themistocles at Artemisium; for either these words, being concealed from the barbarians, would induce the Ionians to revolt, or, if they should be reported to the barbarians, would make them distrustful of the Greeks. Then the Greeks put their ships to shore, landed on the beach, and drew up in order of battle. But when the Persians saw them preparing for action, and knew that they had admonished the Ionians, they suspected that the Samians favored the Greeks, and took away their arms.

Then the Greeks advanced toward the barbarians ; and a rumor flew through the whole army that a herald's staff was seen lying on the beach and that the Greeks had fought and conquered the army of Mardonius in Bœotia. Thus the interposition of heaven is manifest by many plain signs ; since on this same day on which the defeat at Platæa took place, and when that at Mycale was just about to happen, a rumor reached the Greeks in this latter place ; so that the army was inspired with much greater courage, and was more eager to meet danger.

The Athenians, and those who were drawn up next to them, forming about half the army, had to advance along the shore over level ground ; but the Lacedæmonians and their associates, along a ravine and some hills. So that whilst the Lacedæmonians were making a circuit, those in the other wing were already engaged. Now, so long as the bucklers of the Persians remained standing, they defended themselves strenuously, and had not the worst of the battle ; but when the Athenians and their comrades mutually encouraged one another, in order that the victory might belong to them, and not to the Lacedæmonians, they flew with such vigor into the battle, that the face of affairs was immediately changed. They broke through the bucklers and fell in a body upon the Persians. They sustained the attack and defended themselves for a time but at last fled to the fortification. The Athenians, Corinthians, Sicyonians, and Trœzenians, drawn up in order together, following close upon them, rushed into the fortification at the same time. When the fortification was taken, the barbarians no longer thought of resisting, but all except the Persians betook themselves to flight ; they, in small detachments, fought with the Greeks who were continually rushing within the fortification. And of the Persian generals, two made their escape, and two died. Artayntes and Ithramitres, commanders of the naval forces escaped ; but Mardontes, and Tigranes, generals of the land army, died fighting. While the Persians were still fighting, the Lacedæmonians came up, and assisted in accomplishing the rest. Of the Greeks themselves many fell on this occasion, especially the Sicyonians, and their general Perilaus. The Samians, who were in the camp of the Medes and had been deprived of their arms, as soon as they saw the battle turning, did all they could, wishing to help the Greeks; and the rest of the Ionians, as the Samians led the way, fled from the Persians and attacked the barbarians. The Milesians had been appointed to guard the passes for the Persians so that in the event of failure they might have guides to conduct them to the heights of Mycale. They, however, did every thing contrary to what was ordered; guiding them in their

BAS-RELIEF OF THE MUSES.

flight by other ways which led to the enemy, and at last themselves assisted in slaying them. Thus Ionia revolted a second time from the Persians. In this battle of the Greeks, the Athenians most distinguished themselves. When they had killed most of the barbarians, some fighting and others flying, they brought out all the booty on the beach, including several chests of money, and burnt the ships and the whole fortification. Then they took into their alliance the Samians, Chians, Lesbians, and other islanders, who were then serving with the Greeks, bound them by pledges and oaths that they would remain firm and not revolt; then sailed to the Hellespont, and home.

SYNCHRONISTICAL TABLE OF

GREEKS.

Attica, Bœotia, Phocis, Ætolia, etc.

	B. C.
Deucalion	1570
Cecrops	1550
Erectheus	1510
Ion, son of Xuthus	1427
Rape of Medea by the Argonauts	1349
Theseus defeated Eurystheus	1311
Decaleans give up Helen to the Tyndaridæ	1296
Pelasgians expelled from Attica, conquer Lemnos	1162
Codrus	1153
Rape of Ath. women from Brauron	1152
Alcmæon, the last Archon	683
Conspiracy of Ceylon	612
Legislation of Solon	594
Megacles mar. Clisthenes' daughter	570
Pisistratus, tyrant	561
Expelled	559
Re-established	555
Re-expelled	553
Regains it	542
Dies	528
Hipparchus succeeds	528
Assassina. of Cimon	527
Hipparchus assassinated	514
Hippias succeeds	514
Expelled	510
Factions of Clisthenes and Isagoras	509
Clisthenes expelled	508
Inv. of Cleomenes	507
Athenians defeat the Bœotians, invade Eubœa, and conquer the Chalcidians	506
Miltiades gains the battle of Marathon	490
Dies	489
Xerxes takes Athens	480
Battle of Salamis	480
Mardonius retakes Athens	479

Peloponnesus.

	B. C.
Rape of Io from Argos	1687
Pelops conq. the Pelopon.	1362
Eurystheus conquered	1311
Rape of Helen	1290
Aristodemus conq. the Pelo.	1190

Lacedæmon.

Procles and Eurysthenes kings	1178
Theras col. Callista (Thera)	1150
Lycurgus	884
Battus migrates from Cal. and founds Cyrene	632
First war with Tegea	620
Ariston and Anaxandrides, kings of Lacedæmon	574
Ally with Crœsus	554
Tegea taken	546
War with Argives about Thyrea	545
Send troops ag't. Polycrates	525
Demaratus	520
Cleomenes	515
Dorieus migrates to Libya	515
Cleo. violates the Argive grove	514
Cleomenes expels Clisthenes from Athens	508
Invades Attica	507
Demaratus exiled	492
Leotychides king	492
Cleomenes kills himself	490
Leonidas slain at Thermopylæ	480
Pausanias wins at Platæa	479
Leotychides at Mycale	479

Corinth.

Oligarchy of Bacchiadæ.	
Cypselus born	700
Seizes the trannny	663
Periander	633
Banishes Lycophron	575
Sends 300 Corcyræan boys to Alyattes	565
Dies	563
Miltiades, son of Cypselus, founds Chersonesus	560
Stesagoras succeeds	531
Miltiades, son of Cimon, succeeds	515
Takes Lemnos	510
Retires before the Scythians	507
Escapes from the Persians to Imbros	497
At the battle of Salamis	480

Greeks in Asia and the Islands.

	B. C.
Ion goes to Asia	1391
Æolian migrations under Orestes, Penthilus, and Echelatus	1210-1174
Ionian migrations (driven from the Pelop. by the Achæans)	1130
Dorian migration.	
Samians reach Tartessus	640
Thrasybulus	625
Conquered by Crœsus	
Conquered by Harpagus	542
Phocæans defeat Carthaginians, etc.	
Found Hyela	535
Polycrates tyrant at Samos	532-523
Samians found Cydonia	524
Syloson obtains Samos	512
Ionians commence disturbances	504
Burn Sardis	503
Joined by the Cyprians	502
Miletus taken	498
Aristagoras slain	498
Samians take Zancle	497
Chios, Tenedos, etc., taken by the Persians	497
Phocians defeat Thessalians	482
Ionians join the allies at Mycale	479

BARBARIANS.

Phœnicians.	Egyptians.	Assyrians and Babylonians.		Lydians.	Scythians and Cimmerians.
			B.C.		
Migrated	God-kings,	Empire . . 1221—711		Atyadæ to	Cimmerians
from the	17570	Semiramis . 747—733		1221.	invade
Erythræan	to	Medic revolt . . 711		Heraclidæ,	Asia,
to	15570.			1221—716.	but
Phœnicia,	Menes	*Babylonia.*	*Media, etc.*	Gyges, 716.	expelled
about	to			Ardys, 678.	by the
2267.	Mœris,	Nitocris,	Deioces, 700.	Cimmerians	Scythians
	2235	604 to 561.	Div. the Medes.	take Sardis,	about
	to	Turns the	Phraortes, 647.	634.	624.
Colonized	1416.	Euphrates	Invades Assyria	Sadyattes,	
Thasos,	Sesostris	and im-	Perished before	629.	
1550.	to	proves	Nineveh.	Milesian war,	
	Sethon,	Babylon.	Cyaxares, 625.	622—610.	Scythians
	1416		Conq. Assyria.	Alyattes, 617.	rule
Founded	to	Labynetus	Besieges	Drove out	Upper
Carthage,	671.	(Belshazzar),	Nineveh, 603.	Cimmerians,	Asia,
819.	Twelve kings	son of	Scythian inva-	613.	624
	to	Nitocris,	sion, 624—596.	War with	to
	Amasis	succeeds.	Astyages, 585.	Cyaxares, 602.	596.
Circumnavi-	671	Arbitrates	CYRUS born,	Cœsus, 560.	
gate Libya,	to	between	571.		
600.	525.	Cyaxares	King in sport,	Conquers	
		and	561.	Greeks.	
		Alyattes.	*Persian Empire*	Visited by	Invaded
				Solon.	by
			CYRUS, king.		Darius,
			550.		508.

Attacked by Crœsus. Conquers
Lydia, and takes Sadis. Ma-
zares punishes Lydian rebels.
Harpagus takes Phocæa, con-
quers Ionia and Æolis.
Babylon taken by Cyrus, 536.
Massagetan expedition. Cyrus slain, 530.
CAMBYSES, 530—523. Conquers Egypt, 525.
Unsuccessful expedition against the Ethiopians and Ammonians. Wounds
Apis. Goes mad. Slays his brother Smerdis. Marries and kills his sister.
Magian revolt. Dies, 523.
SMERDIS MAGUS, 523. Conspiracy of the Seven. Death of the Magi.
DARIUS, 522—485. Sends Democydes to spy Greece. Babylonian revolt. Baby-
lon taken by Zopyrus, 516. Restores Syloson to Samos, 512. Barca conquered,
512. Invades Scythia, 508. Megabazus subdues Thrace. Otanes subdues
Lemnos and Imbros. Disturbances in Ionia. Burning of Sardis, 503. Cy-
prians join the revolt, 502; conquered, 501. Miletus taken, 498. Pacifica-
tion of Ionia, 497. Mardonius marches against Greece, 495. Wrecked at
Athos. Darius sends to Greece for earth and water, 493. Expedition of
Datis and Artaphernes, 492; enslave Naxos and Eretria, 490. Marathon, 490.
Preparations for another invasion, 489. Egyptian revolt, 486.
XERXES, 485—479. Subdues Egypt, 484. Prepares for a Greek expedition.
Leaves Susa, April, 481. Winters at Sardis. Battle of Thermopylæ, 480.
Takes Athens, 480. Battle of Salamis, Sept., 480. Retires to Asia. Mar-
donius defeated at Platæa, and the Persian fleet at Mycale, the same day, Sept.
22, 479.

Scythians and Cimmerians column (bottom): Invade the Cherso-
nesus; Miltiades retires, 507.

HERODOTEAN WEIGHTS AND MONEY, DRY AND LIQUID MEASURES, AND MEASUREMENTS OF LENGTH.

Eubœic or Attic Silver Weights and Money.

			WEIGHT (Avoirdupois).			VALUE.
			lbs.	oz.	grs.	
1 Obol	. . . . . .		—	—	11.08	$.033
6 Obols .	. . .	1 Drachma	—	—	66.5	.198
100 Drachmæ	. . .	1 Mina	—	15	33.75	19.784
60 Minæ .	. . .	1 Talent . .	56	15¼	100.32	1187.00

Æginetan Silver Weights and Money.

			lbs.	oz.	grs.	
1 Obol	. . . . . .		—	—	16	$.04½
6 Obols .	. .	1 Drachma	—	—	96	27.00
100 Drachmæ	. .	1 Mina	1	5¾	78.96	—
60 Minæ .	. .	1 Talent . . .	82	3¾	30.46	1620.00

The gold Stater of Crœsus and the gold Daric are each supposed to be worth about 20 Attic silver drachmæ, or about $4.00 in our money.

Herodotus makes the Babylonian Talent equal to 70 Eubœic Minæ, but Hussey calculates its weight at 71*lbs*. 1½*oz*. 69.45*grs*. If, however, these are reckoned by comparison with our gold money, they are worth much more.

Attic Dry Measures.

			Gallons.	Quarts.
1 Chœnix	. . . . . .	.	—	1
48 Chœnices	. .	1 Medimnus . . .	12	—
1 Medimnus and 3 Chœnices .	. .	1 Persian Artaba . .	12	3

Liquid Measures.

			Gallons.	Pints.
1 Chœnix	. . . . . .	.	—	1½
48 Chœnices	. . .	1 Amphora . . .	9	

Hesychius considers the Aryster to be the same as the Cotyla, which Hussey calculates to hold half a pint.

Measures of Length.

			Miles.	Yards.	Feet.	Inches.
1 Digit (finger's breadth)	.		—	—	—	.7584
4 Digits .	. . .	1 Palm (hand-breadth) .	—	—	—	3.0336
3 Palms	. . .	1 Span . . .	—	—	—	9.1008
4 Palms .	. . .	1 Foot . . .	—	—	1	0.135
2 Spans or 6 Palms	. .	1 Cubit . . .	—	—	1	6.2016
1 Cubit and 6 Digits	.	1 Royal Cubit . .	—	—	1	8.4768
4 Cubits	. .	1 Fathom (Orgya) .	—	—	6	0.81
100 Feet or 16⅔ Orgyæ	.	1 Plethrum . . .	—	33	2	1.5
6 Plethra	. .	1 Stadium . .	—	202	0	9
30 Stadia .	. . .	1 Persian Parasang	3	787	1	6
2 Parasangs .	. .	1 Schœnus . .	6½	494	3	0

The Egyptian Cubit contained nearly 17¾ inches.

The Arura contained 21,904 square English feet, or a fraction over half an acre.

A Selection from the
Catalogue of

G. P. PUTNAM'S SONS

Complete Catalogues sent
on application

CPSIA information can be obtained
at www.ICGtesting.com
Printed in the USA
BVHW030501040720
582952BV00001B/66

Tales of the Heroic Ages.

By ZENAÏDE A. RAGOZIN, author of "Chaldea," "Vedic India, etc.

No. I.—Siegfried the Hero of the North, and Beowulf, the Hero of the Anglo-Saxons. Illustrated. 12° . . $1.50

No. II.—Frithjof, the Viking of Norway, and Roland, the Paladin of France. Illustrated. 12° $1.50

No. III.—Salammbô, the Maid of Carthage. Illustrated. 12°. $1.50

"The author is one who knows her subject as a scholar, and has the skill and imagination to construct her stories admirably. Her style is terse and vivid, well adapted to interest the young in these dignified and thrilling tales."—*Dial.*

Plutarch for Boys and Girls.

Selected and Edited by JOHN S. WHITE. Illustrated. 8°. $1.75

Library edition. 2 vols. 16° $2.50

"It is a pleasure to see in so beautiful and elegant a form one of the great books of the world. The best Plutarch for young readers."—*Literary World.*

"Shows admirable scholarship and judgment."—*Critic.*

Pliny for Boys and Girls.

The Natural History of Pliny the Elder. Edited by JOHN S. WHITE. With 52 illustrations. 4° $2.00

"Mr. White's selections are admirably made. He has gleaned in all directions for his notes, and the result is one which reflects on him great credit, and adds another to the number of juvenile books which may be commended without reservation."—*Independent.*

"For the libraries of the young—and every boy and girl in the land should collect a library of their own—these superb books have a special adaptation ; they open the classics to them."—*Boston Journal of Education.*

Herodotus for Boys and Girls.

Edited by JOHN S. WHITE. With 50 illustrations. 8° . $1.75

Library edition. 2 vols. 16° $2.50

"The book really contains those parts of Herodotus which a judicious parent would most likely have his boys and girls acquainted with, and Mr. White has succeeded in condensing these by omitting multitudes of phrases inserted in the Greek text. The print is so large and clear that no one need fear that it will foster a tendency to near-sightedness on the part of boy or girl."—*Nation.*

The Travels of Marco Polo.

Edited for Boys and Girls, with explanatory notes and comments, by THOMAS W. KNOX. With over 200 illustrations. 8°. $1.75

"To the student of geography Marco Polo needs no introduction. He is revered as the greatest of all travellers in the Middle Ages, and by more than one careful geographer his work is believed to have led to the discovery of the New World by the Hardy Mariner of Genoa. . . . The story of his travels was received with incredulity, and he died while Europe was gravely doubting its truth. It has remained for later generations to establish the correctness of his narrative and accord him the praise he so richly deserves."

G. P. PUTNAM'S SONS, NEW YORK AND LONDON

By ELBRIDGE S. BROOKS

Historic Boys. Their Endeavors, Their Achievements and Their Times. With 29 full-page illustrations. 8°, pp. viii + 259 . . . . $1.25

"Told with a spirit that makes them capital reading for boys. Mr. Brooks writes in a clear and vivacious English, and has caught the art of throwing into high relief the salient point of his stories."—*Christian Union.*

Historic Girls. Stories of Girls Who Have Influenced the History of Their Times. 8°, illustrated, pp. viii + 225. $1.25

"The stories are worth telling on their own account, and will serve at once to give their young readers some knowledge, and to quicken the historical imagination."—*N. Y. Evening Post.*

Chivalric Days and Youthful Deeds. Stirring Stories, presenting faithful pictures of historic times. Illustrated, 8°. $1.25

"The historic episodes upon which these stories are based are well chosen, and handled with considerable skill and picturesqueness." — *Mail and Express.*

Heroic Happenings, Told in Verse and Story. Illustrated. 8° $1.25

"Told in a manner to elicit and hold the attention of both younger and older readers. . . . The book possesses the fascination of fiction, while imparting the facts of history."—*Chautauquan.*

Great Men's Sons. Stories of the Sons of Great Men from Socrates to Napoleon. Fully illustrated, 8° . $1.25

Including the Sons of Socrates, Alexander, Cicero, Marcus Aurelius, Mahomet, Charlemagne, Alfred, William the Conqueror, Saladin, Dante, Tamerlane, Columbus, Luther, Shakespeare, Cromwell, Peter the Great, Napoleon.

"Mr. Brooks has performed his task faithfully, and made a book which every thoughtful man ought to read. It is very charming."—*N. Y. Herald.*

The Long Walls. An American Boy's Adventures in Greece. A Story of Digging and Discovery, Temples and Treasures. By E. S. Brooks and John Alden. Illustrated by George Foster Barnes. 8° $1.25

"The characters in the book are clearly drawn . . . the picturesque and exciting adventures are told with vivacity."—*Philadelphia Press.*

New York—G. P. PUTNAM'S SONS—London